UNIV

THE PHILOSOPHY OF
SOCIAL PRACTICES

This is the first systematic philosophical and conceptual study of the notion of a social practice. Raimo Tuomela explains social practices in terms of the interlocking mental states of the agents; he shows how social practices (for example customs and traditions) are "building blocks of society"; and he offers a clear and powerful account of the way in which social institutions are constructed from these building blocks as established, interconnected sets of social practices with a special new social status. His analysis is based on the novel concept of shared "we-attitudes," which represent a weak form of collective intentionality, and he makes instructive connections to major topics and figures in philosophy and the social sciences. His book will be of interest to a wide range of readers in philosophy of mind, philosophy of social science, psychology and sociology, and artificial intelligence.

RAIMO TUOMELA is Professor of Philosophy at the University of Helsinki. His recent publications include *The Importance of Us: A Philosophical Study of Basic Social Notions* (1995), and *Cooperation: A Philosophical Study* (2000).

THE PHILOSOPHY OF
SOCIAL PRACTICES

A Collective Acceptance View

BY

RAIMO TUOMELA

CAMBRIDGE
UNIVERSITY PRESS

PUBLISHED BY THE PRESS SYNDICATE OF THE UNIVERSITY OF CAMBRIDGE
The Pitt Building, Trumpington Street, Cambridge, United Kingdom

CAMBRIDGE UNIVERSITY PRESS
The Edinburgh Building, Cambridge CB2 2RU, UK
40 West 20th Street, New York, NY 10011-4211, USA
477 Williamstown Road, Port Melbourne, VIC 3207, Australia
Ruiz de Alarcón 13, 28014 Madrid, Spain
Dock House, The Waterfront, Cape Town 8001, South Africa

http://www.cambridge.org

First published 2002

Printed in the United Kingdom at the University Press, Cambridge

Typeface Baskerville Monotype 11/12.5 pt   *System* LaTeX 2ε   [TB]

A catalogue record for this book is available from the British Library

Library of Congress Cataloguing in Publication data
Tuomela, Raimo.
The philosophy of social practices : a collective acceptance view / by Raimo Tuomela.
p.   cm.
Includes bibliographical references and index.
ISBN 0 521 81860 5
1. Collective behavior.   2. Social psychology.   3. Manners and customs.
4. Social institutions.   I. Title.
HM866 .T86   2002
302.3′5 – dc21   2002023790

ISBN 0 521 81860 5 hardback

To my friend, Wolfgang Balzer

Contents

Figures

ix

Acknowledgments

I have worked on philosophical and, more broadly, theoretical problems related to joint attitudes, joint action, cooperation, and related topics for a couple of decades. Therefore it is somewhat difficult to say when and where the basic ideas presented in the present book were conceived. Nevertheless, the Collective Acceptance model, which is central to the account of social practices and institutions, was mainly developed only a few years ago; the more technical parts of it were conceived in Munich in relation to my joint work with Professor Wolfgang Balzer of the University of Munich.

Some of the chapters of this book make use of my earlier papers. More precisely, I use revised versions of some passages of the following articles of mine with appropriate permission from the publisher: "Collective Acceptance and Collective Social Notions" (authored jointly with Wolfgang Balzer), *Synthese* 117 (1999), 175–205; "Collective Intentionality and Social Institutions," in G. Grewendorf and G. Meggle (eds.), *Speech Acts, Mind, and Social Reality* (Kluwer Academic Publishers, Dordrecht, forthcoming); "Collective Intentions and the Maintenance of Social Practices" (authored jointly with Wolfgang Balzer), forthcoming in *Autonomous Agents and Multi-Agent Systems*; "Social Institutions, Norms, and Practices" (authored jointly with Wolfgang Balzer), in R. Conte and C. Dellarocas (eds.), *Social Order in Multiagent Systems* (Kluwer Academic Publishers, Dordrecht and Norwell, Mass., forthcoming); "From Social Imitation to Teamwork" (authored jointly with Maj Bonnevier-Tuomela), in G. Holmström-Hintikka and R. Tuomela (eds.), *Contemporary Action Theory* 2 (Kluwer Academic Publishers, Dordrecht and Boston, 1997), pp. 1–47.

I am grateful to several persons for discussions related to the themes of this book. First and foremost, I would like to thank Professor Wolfgang Balzer, who has been my collaborator for several years and has also been a marvelous host during my lengthy stays in Munich. The last chapter of this book uses passages from our two joint papers and it is closely based on our joint research. I am grateful to Wolfgang for permission to use this material in the present book.

I am grateful to Frank Hindriks for reading through a version of the book manuscript and for making excellent comments concerning both the content and the exposition of the text. I also want to thank members of the research group related to my research professorship at the Academy of Finland during 1995–2000. They include Kaarlo Miller, Pekka Mäkelä, Petri Ylikoski, and Maj Tuomela. Their criticisms have been important for the views and results in some chapters of this book. My thanks also go to Professor Ausonio Marras for comments on chapter 3 and to Raul Hakli for comments on the early chapters of the book. I wish to thank my wife Maj, not only for support but for incisive comments on a great many topics discussed in this book. Two anonymous referees made comments that I found very good. Professor Henry Fullenwider skillfully checked the language of much of the book.

I also want to thank the Academy of Finland for supporting the research on which this book is based. Much important groundwork was done while I was an academy professor during the latter half of the last decade. Some of the earlier research included in this book was supported by a research award (*Forschungspreis*) from the Alexander von Humboldt Foundation. I prepared the final version of the book in the fall of 2001, while working as a researcher at the Helsinki Collegium for Advanced Studies. My thanks are accordingly extended to the collegium as well.

Introduction

It is acknowledged in philosophical and theoretical writings concerning the basic nature of the social world that social practices are central elements of "forms of life" and, consequently, of social life. Nevertheless, very little serious analytical work concerning social practices and, for that matter, social institutions exists in philosophy or elsewhere. The present work aims at remedying this situation. The novel approach taken in this book is called the "Collective Acceptance" account, and it is heavily based on "*shared we-attitudes*," which represent a weak form of collective intentionality (or "social representations," in social psychology terminology). As a slogan, "we-attitudes drive human life."

There are several good reasons for embarking on a conceptual and philosophical study of social practices. The deepest sense is that they form the conceptual basis of thinking and other conceptual activities, viz., thinking and acting on the basis of concepts. They can be regarded as conceptually crucial in that they – or rather some fundamental kinds of them – can in themselves be meaningful, "rock-bottom" activities. Furthermore, it can be argued that the concept of correctness of such activities as rule following and in general rational conceptual activities crucially depend on the social practices of the community in question and that basic social practices are a kind of irreducible and noncircular conceptual *fundamentum* of conceptual activities. If this is right – a mild version of this view will indeed be adopted in this work – the notion of a social practice is central not only for social science and the philosophy of social science, but for systematic philosophy in general. Secondly, social life centrally contains recurrent social activities – social practices such as business practices, educational, religious, and political practices – as everyone knows from one's own experience. Social practices thus are part of the domain of investigation of social studies and therefore are also a philosopher's concern. Included here is also the study of multiagent systems in artificial intelligence, insofar as it attempts to capture – even approximately – the important aspects of the social world. Thirdly, as many sociologists have argued, social practices are de facto central for the creation, maintenance, and renewal of social systems and structures.

All the above-mentioned themes will be taken up in the present systematic philosophical work, which in a self-contained way constructs the central notions needed for its topic. The most central – and novel – claim of this book is that collective intentionality in the form of shared we-attitudes is constitutive of standard social practices and social institutions. Underlying this central theme, and closely related to it, is the thesis that collective intentionality is also central for the ontology of the social world in that a central part of the social realm is collectively constructed in terms of collective acceptance, understanding collective acceptance in terms of coming to hold and holding a we-attitude. This I call the *wide program of social constructivism* in this book and is, of course, to be understood strictly in terms of the theory created rather than in terms of any preconceived views on social construction. Philosophically, the most central chapters of the book are 4–6, which develop the main theory of collective sociality and defend the wide program of constructivism. The book also, and most importantly, defends the *narrow program of constructivism*, according to which collective intentionality in terms of shared we-attitudes in part constitute social practices in the core sense, which in turn are central for the conceptual construction and factual maintenance of social institutions.

The Collective Acceptance account of this book is based on three central features, the third of which has not been made use of in the literature. The first feature is that many social entities and their characteristics are performatively constructed by the group members. For example, they may collectively bring it about that certain pieces of paper qualify as money. Secondly, institution concepts have been regarded as self-referring (reflexive) – thus greenbacks are not money unless collectively accepted to be money. Although the features of performativity and reflexivity have been considered earlier, precise analyses of them seem not to exist. I will try to improve the situation in this book. My account adds another aspect of sociality, the "we-mode" aspect, which relates to the idea of thinking and acting as a group member. We may distinguish between attitudes and actions in the "I-mode" and those in the we-mode (thinking and acting as a group member with proper "collective" commitment). Thus a we-mode attitude involves thinking and acting from the group's perspective, and such activities are meant for the use of members. The members are collectively committed to the content of the attitude, whereas the I-mode lacks the mentioned two features of we-modeness and concerns basically the agent's self-directed (but possibly altruistic) benefit (or "utility") and action. There can be social practices in either mode, but we-mode practices are anyhow central especially for institutional practices.

The kind of collective acceptance that is needed for the conceptual construction of such central notions as social institutions can then be explicated basically as holding, and acting on, either a collective intention (viz., we-intention) or a collective belief (viz., we-belief) in the we-mode. This entails that collective intentionality in the form of shared we-attitudes has a central place in the theoretical analysis of social life. We-attitudes of these kinds are the underlying building blocks of social practices, and they are also causally relevant to the initiation and maintenance of both social practices and social institutions. Social practices include a variety of cases, for example organic farming, wearing blue jeans, eating with the fork in one's right hand, or various teaching practices in schools. A social practice in its core sense is taken to consist of recurrent collective social actions performed for a shared social reason, expressed in the collective attitude (viz., shared we-attitude) underlying the social practice. A shared we-attitude represents the (or at least *a*) standard kind of collective intentionality. The idealized, "pure" notion is this: a person has a we-attitude A (say a goal, intention, or belief) if he has A, believes that the others in his collective (group) have A and believes in addition that there is a mutual belief in the collective that the members have A.

Basically, the notion of a social institution (in a general sense) is a reflexive notion concerning a core social practice or practices governed by a system of norms based on collective acceptance for the group's benefit and use. The collective acceptance in question confers a new conceptual and social status on the practices or on some items that they involve (cf. the case of money). It is argued in detail in this book that social institutions must involve we-mode activities and not only I-mode activities. Social institutions in the sense of organizations are treated in precise mathematical terms in the final chapter.

The "big picture" that emerges from the account given in this book is this: "jointness" notions involving collective intentionality, especially shared we-attitudes (of which joint intentions and mutual beliefs represent special cases), together with collective and joint action form an "interrelationistic" basis for the conceptual and ontological construction of the social world, or at least its artificial parts. The account makes use of some presumably irreducible social notions. Especially the notion of we-mode attitude (and action) is to some extent a holistic notion, although its primary area of application is the "jointness" level. In current social science jointness factors tend not to be taken seriously into account. Thus, accounts of institutions tend to ignore joint intentions, wants, beliefs, and actions. To account for jointness, nevertheless, no social macronotions (e.g., social structures) need to be postulated in an ontologically committing sense, even if in a sense holistic concepts (basically we-mode concepts) are needed. The account of human and social agency on which the account ultimately relies is a mental-causationist and realist one. The kind of constructivism involved in collective acceptance does not extend to the physical world in an ontological sense.

Over and above their intrinsic importance, the detailed analyses of the key notions of social life given here are relevant and important both for normative work, for example in ethics and political philosophy, and for theory-building and empirical research in the social sciences. The theoretical framework created in this book should be of interest also to researchers in the field of distributed artificial intelligence (DAI). Both researchers and graduate students in philosophy and in neighboring fields of study should accordingly find the book to be of interest, as it contains a new theory of social practices and institutions based on a well-developed account of collective intentionality.

CHAPTER I

Collective intentionality and the construction of the social world

1.1 WIDE AND NARROW SOCIAL CONSTRUCTIVISM

The central claim of this book is that collective intentionality in the form of "shared we-attitudes" is crucial for the proper understanding of social practices and social institutions as well as sociality in general. The systematic elaboration of this grand thesis will occupy most of what follows. Underlying this central theme, and closely related to it, is that collective intentionality is also central for the ontology of the social world in that a central part of the social realm is collectively constructed in terms of "collective acceptance." I will start by a brief discussion of this grand thesis, which can also be called the *social constructivist program in the wide sense.*

It may sound like a platitude to say that the social world is made and maintained by people by means of their social practices. Today the various views that fall under the label "social constructivism" emphasize the constructed nature of the social world. The construction can be performed on purpose or it can take place in part in terms of the unintended consequences of intentional action.[1] As to modern literature related to social constructivism, I will not attempt to survey it here, nor will I take a stand on its various versions. I wish to emphasize that the physical world on my account, contrary to some other forms of constructivism, is not a social construct and that, furthermore, only some parts of the social world are intentionally collectively constructed. Thus, my wide program is compatible with (scientific) realism in general and especially with realism concerning the physical part of the world.

The theory that is created in this book has points of connection to some recent accounts, all of which emphasize two features of sociality in collective contexts (cf. Barnes, 1983; Bloor, 1997; Kusch, 1997; Searle, 1995). The first feature is that many social entities and their characteristics are performatively created by "us" (group members). For example, we

5

may collectively bring it about that certain pieces of metal qualify as money. Secondly, some central collective and social concepts have been regarded as reflexive in roughly the sense indicated by saying that money is not money unless it is collectively accepted to be money. Although the features of performativity and reflexivity have been discussed earlier (especially outside philosophy), little effort has been made to give a precise analysis of them. I will try to improve the situation in this book (cf. especially chapters 5 and 6). The present account, furthermore, adds a third feature of sociality, namely the distinction between "I-mode" and "we-mode" attitudes and actions. There can be social practices in either mode. The we-mode aspect will entail the collective availability or "forgroupness" of collective social items and the participants' (group members') collective commitment to them.

The wide constructivist program advocated in this book investigates in what sense the social world is man-made, viz., an artifact. Thus, it is shown what kinds of conceptual and ontological building blocks the social world is made of and how these building blocks are to be fitted together in order to arrive at a conceptually and normatively right or acceptable result. Among the central notions are collective social actions, social practices, and social institutions, and they will accordingly be discussed in detail. Underlying them are such notions as collective intentions and mutual beliefs, as well as other notions expressing collective intentionality. These notions are needed for an analysis of the notion of social practice, and they are also argued to be causally relevant to the initiation and maintenance of social practices and, more importantly, of social institutions, too. Furthermore, these kinds of deeper, detailed analyses of the key notions of social life are also important both for normative work, for example in ethics and political philosophy, and for theory-building and empirical research in the social sciences. The authors mentioned above and some other authors, like Bourdieu (1977), Pettit (1993), and Brandom (1994), have worked on some of the topics dealt with in this book. However, contrary to the account in this book, none of these authors has developed (or used) a detailed theory of collective intentionality or of social practices in their work. In this book, collective intentionality will be characterized by shared we-attitudes.

Part of the wide constructivist program of this book is formed by the subprogram that constructs social practices and social institutions from collective acceptance, viz. from holding relevant we-attitudes. This program, which will be argued for in detail, will be called the *narrow program of social constructivism*.

As this is a philosophical book, its research method consists of an analytic study of relevant concepts and their interconnections, and in the course of developing the theory I will consider some metaphysical questions as well as certain factual questions that are also studied by the social sciences. My starting point is the common-sense framework of agency, viz. the conceptual framework concerned with human agents as thinking, intending, feeling, and norm-obeying agents capable of intentional action (action performed on purpose and presumed to express free will). As we have learned to use this framework as children, we all carry an enormous amount of information related to agents, including especially agents acting in the social world. Such information, and examples related to it, form an important part of the "data basis" of the present study. This basis not only helps to generate philosophical and (general) factual hypotheses, but is also central for testing the hypotheses so generated. It should be noted that the preanalytic framework of agency is not a precisely formulated framework and it is often argued to be incoherent (think of the free will debate, for instance). Therefore, making this framework a coherent and detailed theory-like system involves much philosophical and theoretical work. Furthermore, the resulting account does not really compete with what social scientists are doing as it rather is meant in part to critically analyze the presuppositions of current scientific research and, especially in the present book, to provide a new conceptual system for theory-building.

After these remarks on the methodology used in the book, let me formulate the *wide program of social constructivism* in terms of the following broad theses to be defended in the book.

(1) Social practices are central for full-blown conceptuality, viz., conceptual thinking and acting.

(2) Social practices in their core sense are repeated collective social actions based on collective intentionality in the sense of shared we-attitudes.

(3) Social institutions conceptually depend on collective acceptance, viz., on the group members' holding a relevant we-attitude, and on the social practices satisfying and maintaining those we-attitudes.

(4) Central aspects of sociality (and, as a consequence, of social reality), including social norms and social institutions, are created and maintained by collective acceptance and the social practices that the maintenance of collective acceptance requires. In particular, the maintenance of social structures and institutions involves causally induced effects (including unintended and unforeseen ones)

generated by collective acceptance and feeding back to collective attitudes and acceptance.

What I above call the *narrow program of social constructivism* consists of theses (2) and (3). While the development and defense of the narrow program will occupy most of this book, the wide program will also be defended.

Here is a preliminary comment on the theses, which will be enriched later in the chapter. In thesis (1) centrality is in part conceptually constitutive and in part causal. The conceptual aspect that has been focused on in the literature is the claim that there are conceptual activities which criterially require suitable underlying social practices. The causal aspect which will be of most interest has to do with the kind of causal grounding that the *collective* "pattern-governed behaviors," to be discussed in chapter 3 provide. Thesis (2) makes the point that the most central notion of social practice will rely on collective intentionality in the sense of shared we-attitudes. This thesis will be argued for in detail in chapter 4, on the basis of conceptual tools developed earlier in the book, in chapters 2 and 3. Thesis (3) is defended primarily in chapter 6, but the groundwork, viz., the "Collective Acceptance" account of collective sociality, needed for it is developed in chapter 5. Thesis (4) is a broad one, the various aspects of which will be discussed in chapters 4–7, which anyhow are the central ones for the theory developed in the book. Note concerning thesis (4) that even if collective acceptance is central for social institutions, this does not entail that they are intentionally constructed and maintained by people in the "conduct" sense based on collective intentions (cf. chapter 3): collective acceptance can be at least collectively *nonintentional* in the conduct sense, and, what is more, social institutions need not even be *collectively* initiated. However, collectively accepted items (e.g. social institutions) nevertheless express collective intentionality in the "aboutness" sense of intentionality.

As indicated, the focus of this book is on detailed analyses of its central notions. Given such analyses, it is much easier to discuss in which sense the four theses are true. Thus, while an important part of the general philosophical message of the book lies in these theses, many related minor topics will be discussed.

The main argument for the wide thesis of social constructivism proceeds as follows. First, chapter 2 presents the required underlying concepts related to collective intentionality, especially the required we-attitude concepts. The argument is started in chapter 3 by claiming that social practices are central for conceptuality and defends what will be called the "weak" communitarian view. Next, chapter 4 presents a new theory of social practices relying heavily on collective intentionality in the form of shared we-attitudes and also on the notion of collective pattern-governed behavior. Chapter 5 relies both on collective intentionality and social practices and develops the "Collective Acceptance" account of sociality, which gives the central argument for the wide constructivism in this book. Collective acceptance is argued to amount to holding shared we-attitudes of relevant kinds. Chapter 6 applies the Collective Acceptance model to social institutions (in the synchronic case) and chapter 7 shows how the account can be mathematically analyzed and applied to the diachronic (viz., dynamic) case, where such features as unintended and unforeseen consequences of social practices (including institutional ones) also find a place. The key issues in the narrow program will be the treatment of we-attitudes in chapter 2, the theory of social practices in chapter 4, and the basic account of social institutions in chapter 6.

1.2 THE CONTENTS OF THIS BOOK

Chapter 2 is a background chapter in that it develops an account of shared we-attitudes, with special reference to the notions of collective intention and mutual belief applicable to several agents collectively. In principle the account also covers attitudes attributable to groups (collectives). Thus a group's belief that the earth is flat or a group's goal to merge with another group are dependent on the group's decision makers' ("operative members'") relevant shared we-attitudes (e.g., joint acceptances, joint intentions) that normatively bind the whole group.

Chapter 3 discusses conceptual activity and rule following. The centrality of the notion of "pattern-governed behavior" (in the sense of Wilfrid Sellars) for a viable account of rule following is emphasized. (Pattern-governed activities form a subclass of Ludwig Wittgenstein's "blind actions" and "bedrock practices.") The most central contribution of this chapter is probably an account of the notion of *collective* pattern-governed behavior (the collective version is not available in Sellars' work). Thesis (1) above expresses the philosophically deep sense in which social practices are central, for they are taken to form the conceptual core of our lives as social human agents. This chapter also discusses and defends the view that the notion of a social practice is central for giving an account of conceptual activity and, hence, for rule following (cf. thesis (1)). The account is given in terms of the broadly understood "negotiation" model of collective acceptance. This account bears resemblance to Sellars' games of "giving and asking" reasons and their further development by Robert Brandom (1994, 2000). It also resembles the "holistic" and "communitarian" accounts of rule following and concept use that have been defended in the context of the extensive literature on rule following related to Wittgenstein's late work. However, my account also accepts "solitary," nonsocial language and thinking, while emphasizing that full-blown conceptual activities (e.g., typically those requiring speech acts) are essentially social.

Chapter 4 investigates social practices in detail, starting from the idea that they are meaningful recurrent patterns of collective behavior. While their meaningfulness may in part depend on their being based on meaningful, intentionally performed, individual component actions, the main source of their meaningfulness nevertheless comes from the underlying productive collective attitudes serving to coordinate and "assemble" those component actions. In other words, a social practice consists of recurrent collective social actions performed for a shared social reason, expressed in the collective attitude underlying the social practice. Social practices include a variety of cases, for example teaching practices in schools, driving on the right-hand side of the road, standing in line, eating ham at Christmas dinner, cleaning the house together every Saturday.

Many kinds of social practices are discussed in chapter 4. The central ones, however, are connected and unified by the notion of a collective attitude, analytically explicated as a shared we-attitude. The content of the we-attitude is the shared social reason for the collective social action or practice in question. A shared we-attitude represents the (or at least *a*) standard kind of collective intentionality. The idealized, "pure" notion is this: a person has a we-attitude A (say a goal, intention, or belief) if he has A, believes that the others in his collective have A and believes in addition that there is a mutual belief in the collective that the members have A. We-attitudes drive much of human life, because people are social in the sense they involve and tend to take into account in their thinking and acting what others think and do.

A we-attitude can be in the we-mode or in the I-mode. The we-mode involves thinking and acting from the collective's perspective and thus it expresses a central notion of sociality or, rather, collective sociality. Such activities are meant for the use of the members of the collective and in general the members are assumed to be collectively committed to the content of the attitude, whereas the I-mode lacks the mentioned two features of we-modeness and concerns centrally the agent's own benefit (or utility) and action. The distinction between these two modes is important, and it will be further clarified in the book. Collective social actions are actions performed by many persons for a social reason of the precise kind that shared we-attitudes (attitude contents, more precisely) yield. It is argued in the book that the notions of shared we-attitude and (weakly cooperative) collective social action are the central conceptual building blocks of the man-made parts of the social world. My account of social practices accordingly depends on the notion of a collective social action (cf. chapter 4). Note that I speak of "collective sociality," or of the collective-social features of activities, rather than merely of "collectivity" or "sociality" here. This is because there are many kinds of things called social (e.g. thinking of other people) which need not be collective, and there are collective activities which are not social. Consider Max Weber's example of people in the street simultaneously opening their umbrellas when it starts to rain – this is a *nonsocial* collective action. Basically, the predicate "collective" in a pure sense applies to collections of people and their features. The predicate "social" in contrast applies to (mental) dependence between individuals concerned with taking into account others' thoughts and actions. Thus, a collective social action is seen to be an action based on a shared we-attitude.

Let us still consider examples of social practices that are somehow representative. Cases of social practices include (repeated) questioning and answering and other similar speech acts involving at least two people. More generally, doing something together recurrently (e.g. cleaning the house together once a week) counts as a social practice. The joint intention and the relevant mutual beliefs involved in repeated joint action serve as a shared social reason to act, and this reason establishes a strong kind of social connection between the participants. The participants thus have a social reason to participate if they have somehow arrived at a shared understanding (e.g., joint plan) to act together. Another typical practice is that of standing in line to get on a bus or to buy something. As to the more general case of social practice in which no acting together (or joint action of any kind) is needed, we may consider fads and fashions. For instance, some girls may want to buy the latest fashion dress just because the others are buying it. There is thus a shared social reason related to what the others are doing or thinking, and this social reason serves to make a (repeated) action social in the sense required of social practices in the full sense. Yet another example of an informal social practice is provided by some villagers' practice to play soccer on Sunday afternoons. This social practice involves their collective intention to engage in the practice with the appropriate shared or mutual belief that they have this collective intention. (We will return to this example in detail in chapter 6.)

The obvious point should be noted that the activities involved in a social practice may occur in different places and at different times. This presents no problem. As the bond assumed to make the activities elements of a social practice is a shared social reason, this characteristic need not pose any spatiotemporal limitations, except perhaps in special cases. Let me also note that social practices – at least those needed for the build-up of society – are at least to some extent cooperative. Especially, the practices needed for the conceptual and causal construction of society are at least in the institutional case solutions to collective action dilemmas and must therefore be to some extent cooperative. (Here we find a connection to cooperation, in particular to the kind of theory of cooperation relying on two kinds of cooperation, we-mode cooperation and I-mode cooperation; cf. Tuomela, 2000a.)

According to thesis (2) of section 1.1 social practices depend conceptually on shared we-attitudes and collective social actions. This thesis does not as such claim that mind is conceptually prior to action or that action is conceptually prior to mind or that neither of these two alternatives is true, but that there is mutual conceptual dependence. This book does not conceptually depend on any one of these alternatives, as long as the conceptual priority of social practices for the conceptual construction of macrosocial notions such as institutions and organizations is granted. It should be noted here that even if actions (and social practices) are, or were to be, taken to be conceptually prior to mental states (thus we-attitudes), the latter can still be viewed as causes (in my account, "purposive causes") of actions.

To summarize the content of chapter 4, it is a new, detailed account of social practices in terms of shared we-attitudes and defends a number of theses about their nature. Social practices are thus regarded as repeated collective social actions performed on the basis of shared we-attitudes. This serves to define social practices in the *core* sense. In addition, weaker kinds of practices are discussed by means of a variety of examples. Chapter 4 also gives a brief account of institution-dependent social practices and connects customs and traditions to social practices. Customs present a typical case of social practices. Briefly, a custom is a social practice in which part of the reason for performing the included activities is that "that is how things are done." In a tradition the reason is more "historical," so to speak, and roughly speaking has the form "this is how things have been done in the past and we regard this way of acting as valuable." Not all social practices are customs, nor are, of course, all customs traditions.

Chapter 5 shows precisely how the man-made aspects of the social world are created and maintained, and in doing this it defends thesis (4), which is also under consideration in chapters 6 and 7. The account given relies on collective acceptance for the group and involves (at least some amount of) collective commitment to the accepted item. Collective acceptance is analyzed in part by reference to the central notion of a shared we-attitude. The resulting Collective Acceptance (CA) model of collective sociality is discussed at length (cf. Tuomela and Balzer, 1999). Basically the account builds on the aforementioned three features: performativeness, reflexivity, and the I-mode/we-mode distinction (and thus the entailed aspects of forgroupness and collective commitment). Collective sociality – the collectivity and sociality intersection that construction is concerned with – requires a we-mode social reason (we-attitude), which the Collective Acceptance model of chapter 5 (and especially its "CAT formula") provides. The approach is formulated by speaking mainly of the acceptance of collective ideas and thoughts that are assumed to be linguistically expressible so that we can speak of the acceptance of meaningful sentences. The analysis proceeds in two steps. First, a characterization of collective-social sentences or collective-socially used sentences is given by means of the features of performativity, we-modeness, and reflexivity. In the second phase collective acceptance is analyzed in terms of the notion of holding a special kind (or, rather, one of two special kinds) of collective attitude, namely a (shared) we-attitude toward the sentence in question. The Collective Acceptance account clarifies the collectively man-made aspects of the social world and thus defends the wide program of social constructivism.

Note that collective intentionality is not enough for characterizing institutionalized social practices, because they require for their analysis normative vocabulary and such notions as social norm, sanction, and authority. This conceptual machinery is central to chapter 6, which discusses social institutions.

Social institutions, especially, can be argued to be collectively created and maintained in a sense that also requires some collective intentionality. However, there are obviously structural features – that economic theory has taught us about – which are only unintended consequences of individual intentional (and in some cases nonintentional) actions. These two claims are factual claims about our social world as we now have it.

It can be added that, as far as I can see, on the one hand, it is conceptually possible to construct ("design") at least social institutions if not all social structures on the basis of collective decision making, and, on the other hand, it is also a conceptual possibility that they are created and maintained by some kind of invisible hand processes which do not (at least directly) involve collective intentionality.

The Collective Acceptance account also gives an analysis of social institutions. Accordingly, chapter 6 is concerned with my theses (3) and (4). Social institutions form the most important class of collective-social things. Roughly speaking, by a social institution in the broad sense I basically mean a type of norm-based collective activity related to a collectively created and maintained social entity with a special conceptual and social status (e.g., money, marriage, property right). Due to the constitutive social norms, some forms of sanction or pressure will be connected to the institution. The full-blown, ideal notion of a social institution assumes that the "target" people are collectively committed to the instituted thing. The institutional social practices also indicate the collective acceptance (amounting to holding a relevant we-attitude) of the institution in question. Typical examples of social institutions are normatively governed practices of social exchange, religious practices involving normatively governed shared worshiping, normatively governed teaching practices, and the social practice(s) of language use. The social norms which serve to constitute social institutions can be of various kinds. Thus, they can be what I will call "rule-norms." Rule-norms are authority-governed norms and they may be formal (e.g., state law, charter) or informal ("house rules"). Another type are those that are centrally based on the mutual expectations that members of a group have towards each other. These norms need not even be articulated. Let me mention the normative practice of taking turns as an example of a social practice which, in many cases, is governed by this kind of "proper social norm" (although there are of course rule-governed cases of waiting one's turn as well, for instance customers waiting to be served in a bank).

There are also more specific kinds of institutions, as we all know. The central feature of organizations, for example, is their normative positional structure, viz., they involve positions which represent various functions (tasks, jobs) and are normatively governed. I will be speaking of a "task-right system" connected to each such social position. Briefly, a task-right system is a system of obligations and permissions related to a position in a normatively structured collective, like an organization. These task-right systems can be based on rule-norms or on proper social norms. In the institutional case the norms serve to normatively constrain the collective attitudes (shared we-attitudes) and collective social actions which constitute social practices. In general, a task-right system related to a social position functions as a constraint (because of the obligations serving to define the tasks in question) and as an enabling factor (because the permission norms serve to define the rights in question). Examples of organizations are schools, churches, and national postal systems. We may also consider other social institutions which have a normative organization but which in ordinary parlance are called something else. The state is an example of this kind of social institution.

The central cases of institutions discussed in chapter 6 are institutions essentially involving new reflexive concepts, institutions involving in addition new deontic statuses, and, finally, institutions as organizations. Searle's (1995) theory of social institutions is in many respects similar to the CA account and is mainly concerned with institutions in the second, deontic status sense or is actually a subclass of them. A brief scrutiny of Searle's account is included in chapter 6. Also the weak notion, common in social science literature, of an institution as norm-governed social practice is considered in this chapter. Institutions of the first three kinds are argued to satisfy the Collective Acceptance account (with its CAT formula) and thus may be seen to be reflexive notions in a sense which is clarified in detail.

The dynamics of social practices and social institutions is the topic of the last chapter of the book. In it I present a general mathematical model, developed jointly with Wolfgang Balzer, that can be used to describe how social practices and institutions are initiated and maintained. The account shares some features of the "structuration" theory (Giddens), but differs from it in that it builds on we-attitudes and is formulated in precise mathematical terms. That is, it shows how shared we-attitudes serve to initiate and guide recurrent social activities and accordingly how relevant social structures (including centrally normative structures) are created and maintained in a dynamic perspective. Our account also covers social institutions and includes social norms especially in the form of task-right systems related to group positions. Furthermore, this can incorporate intended and unintended (and unexpected) consequences of actions and show what role they can play not only in the maintenance but also in the change and cessation of social practices.

The general importance of a study of group attitudes, collective attitudes, and social practices is that they are central elements of societies and social life. Permanent social structures such as the state and its administrative apparatus, the educational and business systems or structures of a society are thus all dependent on the relevant underlying social practices maintained by the members of the society. This "actional" view of society serves to partially justify the treatment of social structures in the book. The philosophical importance of the present account, the Collective Acceptance account, is that social practices exhibiting collective intentionality are central building blocks of conceptual activity and of social institutions. It also shows how social practices and institutions develop and how relevant social structures emerge and are maintained. This account presents a kind of mechanism for simple cases of institutional and other social change and provides a solid foundation for future research along the lines I have explored in this book.

CHAPTER 2

Collective intentionality

2.1 INTRODUCTION TO COLLECTIVE INTENTIONALITY

Suppose two persons plan to carry a table upstairs together. Their plan will consist of their intentions to carry the table together and their shared beliefs concerning how to do it. There is joint or collective intentionality here about the joint action of carrying the table and about the means for doing it. Thus there is collective intentionality or aboutness related to intending and believing. In the case of joint intending the relevant part of the world has to be (jointly) changed to accord with the content of the intention for it to be satisfied. Thus the satisfaction relation here has the world-to-mind direction of fit. In the case of shared or mutual belief the correctness of the belief is determined on the basis of what the world is like and the direction of fit is mind-to-world (cf. Searle, 1983 and 2001 for this kind of account). In the "fitness" relation the first term is the variable and the second one the constant factor in the situation. We may speak of collective intentionality also in the case of emotions like joy, fear, and shame.

Not only intentions and beliefs but also emotions, such as shared joy, can be analyzed in terms of shared we-attitudes. In the case of shared we-attitudes the social bond between the agents is their relevant beliefs concerning others' attitudes and beliefs concerning them. In the present theory the central "carriers" of collective intentionality will be collective intentions (explicated as shared we-intentions) and mutual beliefs (shared we-beliefs). This centrality will later be argued for in terms of their role as conceptual and causal determinants of social practices. Chapter 2 will accordingly concentrate on collective intentions and beliefs in order to give the reader some background for what is to come later in the book. The notion of shared we-attitude will be seen to be the common denominator between the different kinds of collective intentionality.

17

Social practices will be taken to (conceptually and causally) depend on collective attitudes (more precisely, shared we-attitudes), which all express collective intentionality. As there are collective attitudes of different kinds and, especially, as there are collective intentions and shared beliefs of different strength, the social practices depending on them will also be different.

The study of the central notion of collective intentionality has not been a popular topic in philosophy. While there is a huge literature on intention, belief, intentionality, and related notions in the single-agent case, there is relatively little systematic work available concerning the corresponding joint notions. In recent years, however, the situation has begun to change in this respect – not only in philosophy but in related areas (such as AI, psychology, and linguistics) as well. Some of the relevant research uses the term "social representation" for concepts and views incorporating collective intentionality.[1]

2.2 COLLECTIVE INTENTIONS SURVEYED

There are many kinds of collective and joint activities, as we all know. We can jointly write a paper, carry a table, sing a duet, and perform a toast to somebody. We can collectively conserve energy, vote in elections, and, in general, create and maintain social institutions. Furthermore, crowds and organized groups can behave in meaningful ways – for example, a crowd can try to conquer the Bastille or a business company can take over another. Undoubtedly actions of these kinds typically involve, and are performed on the basis of, intentions – and often not only individual intentions but also joint or collective intentions. The latter kinds of intentions are needed for the explanation of collective and joint action and for the explanation of the social phenomena and structures that rely on collective action. More generally, collective intentions and various other kinds of collective attitudes are relevant to the explanation of social life. Thus, mutual and shared beliefs are typically needed in the context of collective action, as will be seen. When such collective attitudes (basically shared we-attitudes) serve to explain intentionally performed collective action, collective intentions will also have to be ingredients of the explanantia.

Corresponding to the aforementioned kinds of collective activities, the joint or collective intentions on the basis of which they are performed are different. Accordingly, depending on context, collective intentions of different kinds are needed to account for the respectively different kinds of collective activities. Thus the simplest kinds of social practices that will be considered in this book require less than full-blown joint intentions and less than full-blown collective intentions (in sense (2) below). On the contrary, collective social acting together must rely on joint intentions in the we-mode, which entails that the participants must have collectively accepted the joint intentions in question as their collective intentions and must be collectively committed to them.

There are at least three importantly different notions ("ideal types") of a collective intention or goal. Below, I will regard the contents of intentions as goals; this enables me to speak of intentions and intended goals as interchangeable items. Let me list the core notions I have in mind.[2]

(1) "Collective goal" formed out of we-wants (or we-goals).

(2) (Intended) collective goal.

(3) A collective's goal.

Of these, (1) is the weakest notion, which in fact differs in important ways from the notion of a full-blown collective intention. The participants' having a collective goal in this case amounts to their sharing a we-want (or we-goal, the content of the want). The participants' beliefs about others' goals and actions form a central connecting "social glue" here. Thus, some people may have as their goal to see a certain opera performance, believing that the others in the collective (or many of them) have that goal and believing also that this is mutually believed in the collective. The shared goal to see the opera is a shared we-goal. Analogously, all the shoppers at a department store may rush to the entrance when the fire alarm rings. They have the intention to get out of the store as quickly as they can, knowing that the others are trying to satisfy their corresponding intention of the same kind. There is no acting together here – not at least with respect to the intention in question. The collective intention here is a weak one, even when accompanied by mutual knowledge that the others also have the same intention. In section 2.3 I will discuss weak collective intentions of this kind. They will turn out to be central for the developments in this book.

The next, stronger notion is that of an intended collective goal. It involves the participants' intention but possibly not yet their plan-based joint intention to achieve the goal. It also requires appropriate collective goal-directed activity and, in a weak sense, relevant collective "control" of the situation (e.g., the intended collective goal to have an old, historically valuable building restored). An intended collective goal in this sense is based on the participants' shared intention and collective commitment to satisfy the content of the intention by acting together. The "Collectivity Condition" applies to the present notion of satisfaction (but is not required of case (1) concerning we-goals). According to this principle, if one or more agents satisfy the goal (intention content), then necessarily, on noncontingent "quasiconceptual" grounds, it is satisfied for all participants. That is, it is satisfied in part on the basis of the participants' acceptance of the goal as a collective goal, one applying to the collective in question (see section 2.4). The notion of intention here is one that can be adequately applied to the collective of agents in question. The individual agents cannot normally intend the content in question in the standard "action sense" of the notion of intention, which basically requires that they believe or accept that they can satisfy the content by their own action (with some likelihood at least). They can, however, be said to have the content of the collective intention as their (distant) goal, they can aim at its satisfaction and be collectively committed to it, their basic action commitment being to their own contributions to the goal at hand (or possibly their part-performances related to it). I will speak of "aim intention" and "aim goal" in such a case in contrast to standard "action intentions" (not to be confused with "intentions-in-action"). A person has an action intention if he believes or accepts that he can satisfy the intention by means of his own action. A participant's intention to perform his part of a joint action is a species of action intention.[3]

A full-blown (viz., plan-based) joint intention is stronger, indeed the strongest kind of collective intention. In its case each agent we-intends (or, more generally, is at least disposed to we-intend) to perform X jointly with the others. A we-intention is an aim intention, but it entails the action intention to perform one's part of the joint action. The intention to perform one's part has "holistic" content as it involves joint action. This personal (but still "nonprivate") intention is based on the joint intention in question. Joint intentions will be regarded as a subclass of collective intentions of the aforementioned more general kind.

In this situation the participants will be jointly committed to the satisfaction of the intention content. This joint commitment is a strong form of collective commitment (of the kind required in the case of intended collective goals) accompanied by a "social commitment" to be responsive to the other participants' expectations (cf. section 5.4 below).

There are collective goals which are not full-blown joint goals. For instance, some people could share the collective goal of reducing the ozone hole without in any way having planned it together. Nevertheless, this is a collective goal requiring that the people in a weak sense act together, thus cooperate, to achieve the goal. In the case of collective goals there will be many persons (actually or potentially) involved, and the participants also believe this, and they need only accept the collective goal separately (thus without group discussion and communication of their acceptance to the others). Indeed, their goal-directed action is separate and, furthermore, they may not know – or even have specific beliefs about – which other people have accepted the goal. We might speak of a *mere collective goal* when we are dealing with the weaker kind of goal and reserve the term "intended joint goal" for the more specific case which satisfies, at least typically and as default conditions, the *communication of acceptance* condition, the *jointness of goal-directed action* condition, and the *knowledge of other participants' acceptance* condition.

Some further introductory comments on intended joint goals are still pertinent here. Let us start with some agents' intended joint goal to perform an action, X, jointly. Here they must jointly intend X, and this amounts to their sharing a we-intention to perform X, about which fact there in standard cases is mutual knowledge based on communication. Intended joint goals and joint intentions go together in that intention contents can be regarded as goals. Such a goal can be either a joint action or a state. If you and I we-intend – and thus have the joint intention – to build a house together, building the house can be called our intended joint goal. Alternatively, and often more appropriately, the state of the house having been built can be regarded as our intended joint goal. Sometimes a certain kind of activity is inherently involved in an intended joint goal: we may have as our joint goal to jog together. In other cases only the end state matters: we jointly intend to see to it that the house stays warm. Sometimes action goals are not means to a collective end, but they are either ends in themselves (without being means to anything else) or they are means to private ends. To rationally have an intended goal presupposes that the intending actor believes that the goal is achievable with some probability. In the case of a full-blown collective goal, this belief must be a mutual belief of the participants that they by their collective actions can so achieve the goal.

As I have said, intended joint goals in their fullest sense involve shared we-intentions or at least dispositions to we-intend (see Tuomela, 2000a, chapter 2, section 7, for we-intentions and group-intentions). I will regard all joint goals as collective ones below. As to intentionally performed joint action, it is based on a relevant shared we-intention and hence a we-intended goal (for a defense of this view, see Tuomela, 1984 and 1995). Even in cases of joint action with conflicting preferences (desires), such as playing tennis, there is a joint goal (viz., playing tennis). Indeed, there must be a shared collective goal also in cases involving collective action in a broader sense, thus also in cases which are expected to involve – or potentially involve – collective action in which the participants can separately, as opposed to jointly, contribute to the goal (cf. conserving energy or helping to keep the city clean). It can be argued that such collective action nevertheless involves acting together. (See Tuomela, 2000a, chapters 3–4 for detailed discussion of the above matters.)

As to case (3), a social collective can have as its goal or intention to perform an action X (cf. a state's goal to conquer a certain territory). Basically, at the level of the members of the collective, this can involve two quite different things, indicating two basically different senses in which a collective can have a goal in an intentional sense. Firstly, and this is the "normative," group-binding sense, the collective may have a decision-making system by virtue of which the goals are agreed upon for the collective. (The other members need not strictly have the collective goal, but are obligated to accept it at least tacitly.) Secondly, a collective can be said to have as its intended goal to achieve something X if its members – or a majority of them – share a weak we-intention to achieve X (in the sense of our category (1) above). This gives a nonnormative or "statistical" sense of the notion of a collective's goal. (For a fuller discussion of group goals, see Tuomela, 1995, chapter 6.)

Case (1), goals and intentions in the (weak) we-attitude sense, is central for the treatment of social practices as it will be accomplished in this book. I will argue that social practices are constituted by we-attitudes, in particular we-intentions (in a weak sense) and mutual beliefs. Case (2), intended collective goals, pertains especially to institutional practices in a full-blown sense. They represent we-mode cases, cases satisfying the Collectivity Condition, and are thereby involved in the Collective Acceptance model of social institutions, as will be seen in chapters 5 and 6. Case (3), goals attributed to groups, will not be discussed much in this book, but it has clear relevance to full-blown institutional cases.

2.3 SHARED WE-ATTITUDES

We-attitudes are attitudes involving social beliefs in a group, say g, which typically is characterized intentionally (in terms of a property or a description) rather than extensionally (in terms of listing its members). We consider a person's we-attitude, WATT, related to an attitude, ATT, which has content p. Here ATT can be a plain want, goal, intention, belief, and so forth. (We can, in addition, let ATT be exemplified by an action performed with a certain intention or purpose; or from a logical point of view ATT can indeed be any content.)

A we-attitude in its strongest, full-blown sense is defined as follows for a person, say x: (a) x has ATT(p) and (b) he believes also that the others in the group, g, have ATT(p) and he also (c) believes (or at least is disposed to believe) that it is mutually believed (or in a weaker case plainly believed) that the members have ATT(p). Acting for a we-attitude related to ATT(p) entails acting in the right "ATT-realizing" way for the reason content p (cf. clause (a)). It also involves acting for the social reason that the others in the group have ATT(p) and are satisfying it or at least are disposed to satisfy it (clause (b)), and also acting in part on the mutual belief in question (clause (c)).[4] For instance we can have p = "Our club house is beautifully decorated" and ATT = want. When some persons act for (because of) this we-want to have the house beautifully decorated, each person has a composite full reason because of the collective end in question. This full reason "internalistically" described consists of his wanting to have the house beautifully decorated and his believing that also the others want so and his also believing that it is mutually believed that the members want to have the house beautifully decorated.

Whilst I will conduct most of my discussion as if the content p were a propositional content, that is not a central requirement in my theory. Thus p could in principle represent an object by description (cf. x sees a dog) or have a vague, unspecific content (x sees a moving object) or be a nonarticulated content (x sees *this* object), and so forth.

Given the above, a we-attitude WATT that a participant has can be expressed in logical terms as:

$$\text{WATT}_x(p) \leftrightarrow \text{ATT}_x(p) \,\&\, B_x((y)\text{ATT}_y(p) \,\&\, \text{MB}_g((y)\text{ATT}_y(p)))$$

Here B stands for belief and MB for mutual belief, and ATT represents some attitude. The notion of a we-attitude in general, without any qualifications, expresses sociality in the general sense and an action performed because of a we-attitude is social in a broad sense.[5]

A stronger intuitive idea related to we-attitudes is that a person has ATT in part *because* the others have ATT (and perhaps these in turn base their having ATT on the others having ATT) and this is mutually believed in the group. My above definition does not, however, require that this is invariably the case. Surely also the weaker notion can have applications even if they are less social. The stronger notion can be expressed symbolically by using $/_r$ for the reason-relation as follows:

$$\text{WATT}_x(p) \leftrightarrow \text{ATT}_x(p)/_r B_x((y)\text{ATT}_y(p) \,\&\, \text{MB}_g((y)\text{ATT}_y(p)))$$

When discussing social practices I will mainly speak of actions performed because of a social reason, where the social reason is a we-attitude. In such a context it does not normally make much difference whether the standard notion or the reason-based notion of we-attitude is used, and therefore I typically only speak of we-attitudes without further specification. (However, there are "toxin puzzle" type of cases trying to drive a wedge between an intention to perform an action and performing it, and there are arguments against the ubiquitous transitivity of reasons. I will not here discuss these problems; cf. Tuomela, 2000a, chapter 11.)

How can conditions (a)–(c) defining a we-attitude be justified? First, it must be said that they are obviously somewhat idealized in requiring without exception that all the members satisfy the condition. That can easily be remedied, although I will not do it here. As to (a), which may be called the *genuineness* condition, it can be thought of as a rather obvious requirement for distributable (and distributed) group properties, which in principle must apply to all individual group members. This is a central idea when speaking of we-attitudes, since they are basically attitudes that individuals can have – as distinct from group properties like group cohesion. It can be said that we-attitude concepts are group concepts (at least in a weak sense) which have application to both the individual and the group level. Furthermore, an attitude can be held either in the I-mode or in the we-mode. When it is in the we-mode it requires that the participants must hold it qua group members, and hence they must collectively accept it as their group attitude and must be collectively committed to its content, which is "collectively available" to them (or, equivalently, is meant "for the use of the group"). In contrast, I-mode attitudes are not based on functioning as a group member (relative to g) and the person having it is only privately committed. (See the appendix for a more detailed account and see chapter 5 for collective commitment.)

Concerning (b), the *conformity* condition, belief is an obvious element for intentionally "gluing" the attitudes together, as we are speaking of attitudes distributed among the group members. A mere aggregate of facts about people having the same attitude (say fear) is not fully social, because it lacks an appropriate doxastic connection between the participants. This connection here basically consists in the participants' belief that the others share the attitude; and this can be a person's reason (or cause, as the case may be) for conforming and for his continuing to have the attitude. It accordingly seems appropriate to require (b), understanding belief to be the basic cognitive notion for capturing information from the social world.

What about the mutual belief requirement (c), which may be called the *social awareness* condition? The basic idea is that everyone is aware that the others are socially conscious, and are disposed to act on the social, intersubjective consciousness afforded by mutual belief. Thus, a group member will not only believe that the others have the attitude in question but will also believe that the others believe that he has it. Often this creates experienced or believed social pressure, since the agent may also think that the others think he should (continue to) have the attitude in question. A way to defend such a loop belief derives from the assumptions that the others are relevantly similar to him: if he believes that the others have the attitude (assumption (b)), he should also believe that on the basis of such similarity the others believe that he, too, has the attitude; and this reasoning can be replicated, resulting in mutual belief in the sense of replication or iteration (see Tuomela, 2000a, chapter 5). There will also be similar replicable loop beliefs between all group members, at least if the group is small, and our reference point member will believe so (e.g. x believes that y believes that z believes that y has the attitude in question). This is y's belief about a replicable loop belief, and it should be allowed that his belief about such loop beliefs between other members can be wrong. Thus, one can speak of a member's belief that there is a mutual belief that every member has the attitude in question. (At least a fixed-point characterization of mutual belief – cf. section 2.5 – can allow that there be beliefs about mutual beliefs and even mutual beliefs about mutual beliefs.)

Weaker forms of the above notion of we-attitude may be considered. There is the weaker case where the belief in (c) is only about plain rather than mutual belief; and there is the case in which (c) is not satisfied even in this weakened sense. The beliefs and mutual beliefs might be taken to concern only the majority of group members and the mutual belief need not be taken to require that everyone participates in the mutual belief (see section 4.3 below for a discussion of various weaker cases). Furthermore, when speaking of a shared we-attitude, the sharing may be complete or only partial. In the latter case one might speak of percentages and say that p percent of the members of a collective have the we-attitude in question. When I speak below of shared we-attitudes I basically speak in terms of the above standard notion (involving 100 percent sharing). However, almost all of my points will also apply to the we-attitudes with a weakened clause (c) and a great many also to the rudimentary we-attitudes defined merely by (a) and (b). Furthermore, it does not seem necessary to require 100 percent sharing, as that would seriously affect the applicability of my account to real life. What seems a more reasonable requirement is that most group members share the we-attitude in question. This statistical majority criterion entails that the social practice is prevalent, supposing that the people in question indeed act on their we-attitudes. (When needed, other minor changes in the notions can be made. My main interest, nevertheless, is to get the full-blown cases right and not to worry very much about "realisticness.")

Of special interest in the context of intentional social practices will be we-intentions in the present weak sense (which fall short of being joint intentions in a sense entailing jointly held plan). We can actually consider two notions of we-intention based on we-attitudes. The first is a direct application of the above analysis to the case where ATT is intention (I). The second makes the fact that the others intend and the fact that this is mutually believed partial reasons for each agent having the intention. Letting $/_r$ represent the reason relation we get the following two notions of a (weakly) we-intended goal:

$$\text{(i)} \qquad I_{we,x}(p) =_{df} I_x(p) \,\&\, B_x(I_E(p)) \,\&\, B_x(MB_g(I_E(p)))$$

$$\text{(ii)} \qquad I^r_{we,x}(p) =_{df} I_x(p)/_r \, B_x(I_E(p)) \,\&\, B_x(MB_g(I_E(p)))$$

Here $I_E(p)$ means everyone's intending that p, and this can as a first approximation be analyzed distributively in the standard sense of "every member x of g." According to (i), an individual x has a we-intended goal p (viz., we-intends p) if and only if he intends p, believes that the others intend p, and also believes that it is mutually believed that the others intend p. According to the stronger notion (ii), not only is the definiens of (i) satisfied but, in addition, the fact that the others we-intend p and that there is a mutual belief about this is a partial reason for x to we-intend p. The index r in (ii) refers to the intention being a reason-based notion.

2.4 COLLECTIVE INTENTION TO ACT TOGETHER

Intended goals to act together typically are involved in social practices. Consider the following rudimentary case, which represents a social action that may become a social practice. Suppose a person is collecting trash in a park. He sees another person entering the other end of the park and starting to do the same thing. These persons notice each other's presence and action, but neither one need acquire the belief that the other one has noticed him (or her). Not being acquainted with each other, they may just go on with their cleaning without further contact. In a rudimentary sense the persons are cleaning the park together, provided they regard each other as participating in performing the same task. Each is, of course, doing his or her bit of cleaning intentionally, but there is also an element of collective intentionality involved. We can assume that the agents have as their aim to clean the whole park (or a certain part of it) as a kind of joint activity. Notice that in this example the persons need not have prior intentions, "intentions-in-action" suffice (cf. note 2). (In contrast, it might happen that each has instead separately decided – say, beforehand – to clean a certain small area in his part of the park. Then we would have only a case of separate individual actions.)

I will now give a stylized summary analysis of the notion of a shared intention with acting together as its collective content, or, put in other terms, of a shared intended collective goal (I will draw on Tuomela, 2000a).

(*IAT*) You and I share the *intention to act together* in performing an action X if and only if

    (1) X is a collective action type, and this is understood by us

    (2a) I intend to perform X together with you, and on this basis I accordingly intend to participate in the performance of X (or to contribute to X)

    (2b) you intend to perform X together with me, and on the basis of this you intend to participate in the performance of X (or to contribute to X)

    (3a) I believe that you will participate in the performance of X

    (3b) you believe that I will participate in the performance of X

    (4) (2a) in part because of (3a), and (2b) in part because of (3b)

Acting together is the collective activity that comes into existence when our intentions to act together in the above sense are satisfied.[6] In the weakest, "rudimentary" case satisfying (*IAT*) the collective intention is only *subjective* in the sense that it is based on mere first-order beliefs. In the stronger cases it is *intersubjective* (when based on mutual belief) or *objective* and in the "public space" (when based on agreement making and mutual knowledge).

Clause (1) simply states the obvious conceptual prerequisite that the action type involved be a repeatable one allowing many agents as participants. (X might indeed be regarded as a *sequence* of actions, viz., a potential social practice.) Clause (2) is a crucial one. It connects the analysandum notion of acting together somewhat circularly to the participants' intention to act together relative to X, where the intention might also be a policy intention concerning repeated action. The concept of acting together occurs in the analysans (in the intention content) and should be possessed at least in a rudimentary sense by the participants. We are here dealing with intentions having collective content (viz., acting together) and hence with at least subjectively shared intended collective goals. The intention is in part "presuppositionally" based on their beliefs (not necessarily mutual beliefs in a loop-involving sense) that the other will participate, at least with some probability (see chapter 4 for presupposition reasons). We need not here bother about whether flat-out beliefs or only some kind of partial or weakened beliefs should be required. In any case, the participants must actually have the belief about the other's participation, and this is obviously an important motivational factor here.

This said, it should be emphasized that in the rudimentary cases there can be certain "looseness" here. First, clause (2) must be understood liberally so as to allow that the participants need only have an intention-in-action to participate in the collective performance of X. Thus the joint or collective *telos* in their part performances is to participate in acting together relative to X. (The Collectivity Condition, to be discussed below, must be understood liberally enough so that it is satisfied here.) Secondly, (2) is also meant to allow for the possibility of "mixed intentions" in which a participant intends to perform X either together or alone (the latter possibly only if the first disjunct cannot in his view be realized). This is often a realistic possibility, which leads to a shared collective goal and joint action only when the first possibility is realized (which must happen in the context of (*IAT*)). The mixed intention can be conditional on the others' participation in a sense different from the others' participation being a presupposition of joint action. In the former but not in the latter case it would be contingent on what the participant notices about his environment.

Clause (3) requires only simple participation belief. However, if the participants were assumed to believe, in addition, that they cannot perform X alone, for acting together to rationally occur they would have to have a mutual belief about each other's participation – involving at least loop beliefs of the kind "I believe that you believe that I will participate in X" (see Tuomela and Miller, 1988, for a rigorous argument).

More precisely, the loop belief need not be a "positive" one but the requirement can be of the form that a participant is not to have the belief that the other believes that he will not perform his part.

Due to the concept of acting together requiring both to participate, the agents cannot properly have intention (2) without belief (3) and they must believe or at least be disposed to believe that the project they are involved in is properly collective (and thus at least tacitly understand that (1) is the case).

The jointness of the action X makes the participants' intention (goal) of performing X together a collective intention content or goal, viz., makes this intention at least in standard cases satisfy the following Collectivity Condition in the case of a collective or group g (cf. the discussion in Tuomela, 2000a, chapter 2, and 2002a for the restriction to standard cases):

(*CC*) It is true on quasiconceptual grounds that the participants' collective goal (intention) of performing X is satisfied for a member A_i of g if and only if it is satisfied for every member of g.

An intersubjective version is obtained if it is required, in addition, that the above condition is mutually believed in g; and this I will require of normal cases. In general, the content of (*CC*) must be assumed to be mutually known to the participants.

In (*CC*) the qualification "on quasiconceptual grounds" means the following: due to the fact that the participants here have collectively accepted the intention as their collective intention to perform X (note the reflexivity), the intention has conceptually necessary simultaneous satisfaction as its special feature. Collective acceptance here means in a normal case that, firstly, each participant has accepted the intention and thus takes it to be true of himself that he has the aim intention to perform X, that, secondly, there is at least shared belief about the participants' acceptances, and that, thirdly, the participants are collectively committed to what they have accepted. Somewhat more precisely, a collective intention is a common intention which by its conceptual nature is simultaneously fulfilled for the participants, and the simultaneous satisfactions of the individuals' corresponding personalized collective intentions to act together are necessarily connected due to the mentioned collective acceptance. Collective acceptance can vary in strength, so to speak, and range from joint, plan-based acceptance to shared "acceptance-belief" (cf. chapter 5). The stronger the kind of collective acceptance that is involved, the stronger the necessity. It can be noted that the agents need not even have beliefs directly about (*CC*) – the connection can be generated in a roundabout way due to their *de re* beliefs that they are engaged in the same project.

(*CC*) is a distributive version of the following intuitively plausible group condition (which I will not here discuss further; cf. Miller and Tuomela, 2001):

(*CC**) It is true on quasiconceptual grounds that the goal of performing X is satisfied for g if and only if it is satisfied for every member of g.

While in a general sense thinking or acting in the we-mode involves properly thinking or acting as a group member, with collective commitment, in the case of intentions (viz., intended goals) the following explicate, amounting to a strong we-intention, can be proposed:

(*WM*) An agent x's intention to satisfy a content p is in the *we-mode* relative to group g if and only if x intends to satisfy (or participate in the satisfaction of) p when functioning qua a member of g and at least in part for (the use of) g and is collectively committed to satisfying p.

Basically, x's intention is in the I-mode if it is not in the we-mode relative to the group g and he is only privately committed to satisfying it for himself.

A many-person version of we-mode intentions comes out as follows:

(*WM**) Agents $x_1, \ldots, x_m$ forming a group g share the intention to satisfy a content p in the *we-mode* if and only if p is collectively accepted by them as the content of their collective intention and they are collectively committed to satisfying p for g.

In chapter 5 I will discuss the notion of collective commitment. A more detailed account of both the we-mode and the I-mode in the general case will be given in the appendix to this chapter.

The present analysans entails the satisfaction of the Collectivity Condition (as proved in Tuomela, 1999, and 2000a, chapter 2). The notion of collective acceptance is a relatively "thick" notion entailing that the acceptance is for the use of the group. The collective commitment also concerns the inferences the members qua members ought to perform or may perform.

In (*IAT*) there is no assumption of a joint plan or any kind of agreement making. The psychologically essential elements in my analysis are simply each agent's intention to do something X with the others and the belief that the others (or sufficiently many of them) will indeed participate. To illustrate, suppose that some otherwise unrelated agents come to face a physical danger threatening them. A fire may break out where the agents happen to be. They see a joint project in front of them – putting out the fire. They need not confer with each other at all. They act on the basis of their common understanding of the situation, which also involves that a collective activity is at stake.

The intention clause (2) of (*IAT*) in its fullest sense can be understood to entail that you and I intend to perform X together "in accordance with and (partly) because of this very intention." I shall here only give the following short argument for the reflexivity of intention: if an agent intends to do something and does it unintentionally (or the result event of the action comes about due to an external factor), that does not satisfy the intention. He must perform the intended action in the way intended in order for it to be properly satisfied. However, the feature of reflexivity belongs to the concept of intention but not necessarily to its actualized psychological content. Furthermore, the agents need not have more than at best a disposition to come to think of their concept of intention in this way. (Another, but related kind of reflexivity is involved in the requirement that a collective intention must be one which is collectively accepted by the participants as their collective intention; see the appendix to chapter 6 for this feature.)

The main factor connecting the agents – and creating dependence between them – in (*IAT*) is the collective intention content. The participants' part-performances (or "component actions" of X) are rendered "reason-dependent" by the intention content, and when carrying out their shared intention they may of course also become causally dependent (depending on the nature of the action situation).

(*IAT*) may be strengthened in various ways. I will here mention two possibilities. The first, stronger version (*IAT1*), corresponds to (*IAT*) except that the belief requirement in (3) is replaced by the stronger requirement of mutual belief (or expectation) about the other person's participation. The second one, (*IAT2*), requires agreement making. Thus, the agents share the intention to act together in performing X in the sense of the *agreement view* of joint intention (viz., *IAT2*) if and only if they have formed a joint intention to perform a joint action X based on their explicit or implicit agreement (or obligation-involving shared plan) to perform X.

In the case of (*IAT*), we may speak of a collectively shared intention with a collective content only in a weak *subjective* sense: the participants have the intention to act together, but there is only a shared belief about the others' participation. In (*IAT1*) we have an *intersubjectively shared* collective intention. The mutual belief creates unity among the participants, and from (*IAT1*) upwards we are dealing with a proper collective intention expressible by the participants by an intention expression of the kind "We will do X together," viz., here it becomes justifiable to convert "I intend to perform X with you" into "We will do X together." (Here we have to do with collective or joint intentions consisting of *strong* we-intentions in contrast to the *weak* ones discussed in section 2.3.) (*IAT2*) gives a strong notion of an *objectively shared* collective intention to act together. Objectivity here means that the intention is epistemically objective and in the "public space." Let me note that the agreement view (*IAT3*) entails that the agents are *obligated* to perform X together and to perform their parts of X. The obligation is based on the underlying agreement (as agreements are here understood in the "normal," obligation-entailing sense). The collective intention here is accordingly taken to require agreement making, and the event of agreement making is taken to entail the formation of a joint intention. Thus, agreement and collective intention – although different notions as such – go together here, and neither is prior to the other. Accordingly, if the joint intention is annulled, then so is the agreement, and vice versa.

I impose as the central requirement for (*IAT*) that each participant must intend to do something X together with the others, presupposing that all the persons involved, or such and such number of them, participate. This trust-entailing presupposition must be believed by the participants, and the belief must have an effect on their having the intention to act and on carrying out the intention. This kind of "confirmation" of the actual obtaining of the presupposition reason is a requirement of action in standard (full-blown) cases. The joint action here is the participants' shared goal.

It can be pointed out that (*IAT*) can be seen to express a special but typical case of joint intention in the shared we-attitude sense of section 2.3. I have assumed above that (*IAT*) is understood in a "nonpathological" sense in which it concerns a we-mode joint intention satisfying the Collectivity Condition (*CC*). Given this, we can model the central content of (*IAT1*) – the notion involving mutual belief – in logical terms and arrive at an analysis of proper, we-mode joint intentions (JI) to perform a joint action (X) with the present machinery. (This is a notion pertinent, for instance, to an analysis of goals and intentions attributed to groups.) Consider thus the following proposal (where E means every participant and "we" refers to group g):

$$JI_{we,x}(X) \leftrightarrow I_x(X) \& B_x(I_E(X)) \& B_x(MB_g(I_E(X)))$$

This entails that the intention $I_x(X)$ is an *aim* intention of person x, not his proper *action* intention (in partial contrast to the account (i) in section 2.3, in which this is not assumed). Concerning such an aim intention, we may require that the agent x should believe that he together with the other participants is able to perform X (but we do not, of course, require that he believes that he alone can perform X, which would be the case with an action intention).

Now we can continue by defining $I_x(X)$ further:

$$I_x(X) =_{df} WI_x(X)$$

where WI is a we-intention in the sense of Tuomela (1984, 1995) and Tuomela and Miller (1988). In those analyses, WI is given the following stylized semilogical analysis:

$WI_x(X) \leftrightarrow I_x$ (x performs his part of X as his part of it and does it at least in part because of the participants' joint intention to perform X together) & $B_x(JAO(X))$ & $B_x(MB_g(JAO(X)))$

Here JAO(X) means the "joint action opportunities" for the joint action X. (In (*IAT*) the clauses (3a) and (3b) express such joint-action opportunities.) Now, our present analysis may seem circular. Why? Our participant x's intention to perform his part (see the first conjunct) contains reference to the participants' joint intention to perform X together. But that joint intention may seem to amount to their shared we-intention, viz., so that shared WI(X) amounts to JI(X). But matters are not quite so circular. There are two factors that are central here. Firstly, shared WI is a theoretician's construal of the situation, and a participant's pre-analytic conception of a joint intention may be much vaguer. Secondly, this remark is fortified by the fact that the notion of joint intention occurs here in an intentional context, which concretely shows that we are dealing with a participant's belief or view about a joint intention to perform X rather than even of an intersubjectively shared notion of a joint intention. These two points mitigate against the charge of circularity and make the proposed analysis sufficiently informative to qualify as a viable analysis.[7]

2.5 MUTUAL BELIEF

To end this chapter, a brief discussion of mutual beliefs is warranted, as it represents a second important type of collective intentionality on a par with intentions and goals. The importance of the notion of mutual belief has been emphasized by philosophers, economists, sociologists, and psychologists at least since the 1960s (cf. Schelling, 1960; Scheff, 1967; Lewis, 1969; Schiffer, 1972). The central point here is that mutual beliefs serve to characterize social or intersubjective existence in a sense that does not rely on the participants' making agreements or contracts. Thus, many social relations, properties, and events can be argued to involve mutual beliefs (cf. Lewis, 1969; Ruben, 1985; Lagerspetz, 1995; Tuomela, 1995 and 2001). As a simple example, think of the practice of two persons, A and B, shaking hands. It presupposes here that A believes that B and A are shaking hands and that A also believes that B believes similarly; and B must believe analogously. Many philosophers, especially Grice, have argued that communication must involve mutual belief (cf. Schiffer, 1972; Grice, 1989). Furthermore, the characterization of we-attitudes in the sense of this book depends on the notion of mutual belief (cf. section 2.3 and Balzer and Tuomela, 1997b).

The notion of *consensus* – viewed as mutual belief of some kind – has been regarded as relevant to such topics as public opinion, values, mass action, norms, roles, communication, socialization, and group cohesion. Also fads, fashions, crazes, religious movements, and many other related phenomena have been analyzed partly in terms of shared beliefs, consensus, shared consensus, mutual belief, or some similar notions. Such analyses have sometimes gone wrong because they have treated consensus merely as shared first-order belief. Thus, consensus as mere first-order agreement does not properly account for *pluralistic ignorance* (where people agree but do not realize it) and *false consensus* (where people mistakenly think that they agree). Basically, pluralistic ignorance and false consensus are second-level phenomena. A third level will have to be brought in when speaking about people's awareness of these phenomena. Other well-known social psychological notions requiring more than shared belief are Mead's concept of "taking the role of the generalized other," Dewey's "interpenetration of perspectives," and Laing's metaperspectives (see Scheff, 1967, for discussion of the above points).

There are two different conceptual-logical approaches to understanding the notion of mutual (or, to use an equivalent term, common) belief: (1) the *iterative* account, and (2) the *reflexive* or *fixed-point* account. According to the iterative account, mutual belief is assumed to mean iteratable beliefs or dispositions to believe (cf. Lewis, 1969, chapter 2, and, for the weaker account in terms of dispositions to come to believe, Tuomela 1995, chapter 1). In the two-person case, mutual belief amounts to this according to the iterative account: x and y believe that p, x believes that y believes that p (and similarly for y), x believes that y believes that x believes that p (and similarly for y); and the iteration can continue as far as the situation demands. In the case of loop beliefs, there is accordingly mutual awareness only in a somewhat rudimentary sense. As will be seen, in many cases one needs only two iterations for functionally adequate mutual belief: x and y believe that p and they also believe that they believe that p. However, there are other cases in which it may be needed in order to go higher up in the hierarchy. As to the connection between shared we-beliefs and mutual beliefs, the very definition of a we-belief of course uses the notion of mutual belief. Operating within the iterative account, we can see that, apart from the smallest possible difference in the number of iterations, shared we-beliefs are mutual beliefs, and vice versa (see the discussion in Tuomela, 1995, chapter 7).

The fixed-point notion of mutual belief can be stated as follows: x and y mutually believe that p if and only if they believe that p and also believe that it is mutually believed by them that p. No iteration of beliefs is at least explicitly involved here. Correspondingly, a clear distinction can be made between the iterative or the level account and the fixed-point account. Shared we-beliefs can be related to the reflexive or fixed-point account of mutual belief. According to the simplest fixed-point account, mutual belief is defined as follows: it is a mutual belief in a group that p if and only if everyone in the group believes that p and that it is mutually believed in the group that p. It can thus be seen that the account of mutual belief given by the fixed-point theory is equivalent to the definiens in the definition of a shared we-belief. In the *fixed point* approach the syntactical infinity involved in the iterative approach is cut short by a finite fixed-point formula, that is, an impredicative construct in which the joint notion to be "defined" already occurs in the definiens. Under certain rationality assumptions about the notion of belief it can be proved that the iterative approach which continues iterations ad infinitum gives the fixed-point property as a theorem (see Halpern and Moses, 1992, and, for a more general account, Balzer and Tuomela, 1997b).

As compared with the iterative analysis, the fixed-point account is in some context psychologically more realistic, as people are not required to keep iterative hierarchies in their minds. Note, however, that it depends on context whether the iterative approach or the fixed-point approach is more appropriate. Thus, in the case of successful joint action, at least loop beliefs must be required.

A belief, too, can be held either in the I-mode or in the we-mode. The we-mode sense is concerned with believing (here: accepting as true) a proposition or sentence qua a group member. A we-mode belief, expressible by "We, as a group, believe that p," requires that the group in question is *collectively committed* to upholding its mutual belief or at least to keeping the members informed about whether it is or can be upheld. This contrasts with mutual belief in an aggregative individual mode involving only purely *private commitments* to the belief in question. A we-mode we-belief in a group directly or indirectly concerns the constitutive features of the group (viz., the "ethos" of the group; cf. the appendix below and section 6.3).

In the context of a normatively structured group, a group member functions as some kind of position holder or in a certain role, and we may speak of institutionalized, group-binding we-mode beliefs (this concerns at least the sense d) of institutions in the classification to be given in chapter 6. Accordingly, we-mode beliefs of this group-binding kind are central and sometimes constitutive beliefs in structured social groups such as organizations and states. More precisely, according to the "positional" account defended by Tuomela (1995) the group members authorized for belief or view formation collectively accept the views, which will qualify as the group's normative, institutionalized beliefs. These views are we-mode views accepted for the group and are strictly speaking acceptances of something as the group's views rather than beliefs in the strict sense (see below, chapter 5, note 5).

Summing up, therefore, a group can have beliefs both in the institutionalized, normative sense and in the shared we-belief sense. When such shared we-beliefs are in the we-mode, we may speak of group beliefs that people have qua members of a certain group.

The analytical conceptual framework for representing collective intentionality created in this chapter is central for the theory of social practices and social institutions to be developed in later chapters.

APPENDIX: THE WE-MODE AND THE I-MODE

I have given analyses of the notions of we-mode and I-mode in different works and earlier spoken also of the positional mode or the group-mode instead of the we-mode (see Tuomela, 2000a, 2002a, and Miller and Tuomela, 2001, for recent characterizations). I will here generalize the account of we-mode, I-mode, and private-mode goals in Miller and Tuomela (2001) to cover any kind of attitude. The private mode is a special case of the I-mode, viz., a case which denies dependence on any group and not only the reference point group g.

Here are my definitions of the we-mode and the I-mode in their "standard" senses.

(a1) Agent x, a member of group g, has a certain attitude ATT with content p in the *we-mode* relative to group g in a certain situation C if and only if x has ATT with content p and this attitude (thus also the sentence s expressing it) has been collectively accepted in g as g's attitude, and x is functioning (viz., experiencing, thinking, and/or acting) qua a group member of g and is collectively ATT-committed to content p at least in part for g (viz., for the benefit and use of g) in C. (Here g can be either an unstructured or a structured group.)

(a2) Agent x, a member of group g, has a certain attitude ATT with content p in the *weak we-mode* relative to group g in a certain situation C if and only if x has ATT with content p and is functioning qua a group member and is also collectively ATT-committed to content p at least in part for g (viz., for the use of g) in C. (Here g can be either an unstructured or a structured group.)

(b) Agent x, a member of group g, has a certain attitude ATT with content p in the (plain) *I-mode* in a certain situation C if and only if x has ATT with content p and, relative to g, is privately ATT-committed to content p at least in part for himself in C. (Here g can be either an unstructured or a structured group. What is analyzed here is simply acting as a private person relative to group g, but possibly not relative to some other group.)

(c) Agent x has a certain attitude ATT with content p in the *private mode* in a certain situation C if and only if x has ATT with content p and, relative to all groups, is privately ATT-committed to content p only for himself in C.

Action modes can now be accounted for by means of attitude modes and the "because of" relation ("because" in general expressing both reason and cause): an action is performed in a certain kind of mode (in the above sense) if and only if it is performed because of an attitude had in that same mode.

Acting, or more generally functioning, qua a group member is a notion with several aspects, of which only one is acting in one's group position. Let me therefore here summarize the account of this notion I have given in Tuomela (2002a).

In any group it is possible to perform freely chosen actions qua a group member provided that these actions – or, more broadly, activities, including mental ones – are within the realm of "concern" of the group, viz., provided they belong to topics which are of concern or are of significance for the group. Such actions are to be (rationally) socially accepted by the group (either through normative, group-binding group acceptance or through the we-acceptances by the group members or their majority; cf. Tuomela, 1995, chapter 7). The nonnormative acceptance or belief here could be of the form of a we-acceptance within the group, g: ideally, everyone accepts T to be a topic of concern for g, and believes that everyone so accepts and also believes that this is mutually believed in g. So we get a notion of group concern: topic T is within the realm of group g's concern if and only if T is we-accepted to be in g's realm of concern. Group g's (intended) realm of concern C consists of a set of topics $\{T_1, \ldots, T_m\}$. A topic T_i which is within the realm of g's concern consists of a set of contents involving, but possibly not reducible to, content-satisfying or content-maintaining actions or activities (types) X_j; let us call their set $\mathbf{X}_i$. Considering the union of the set of actions $\mathbf{X}_i$, viz., $\cup_i \mathbf{X}_i$, we can classify those actions as follows from the point of view of acting qua a group member, as will be seen.

The general case is that of a structured group with positions (the unstructured case can be regarded as its special case with no specific positions over and above group membership). I will first classify the types of actions within the realm of a (structured) group's concern, viz., actions falling within the realm $\cup_i \mathbf{X}_i$.

(1) Positional actions (related to a group position or role), which include (i) actions (tasks) that the position holder in question *ought to* perform, perhaps in a special way, in certain circumstances and (ii) actions that he *may* (is permitted to) perform in some circumstances.

(2) Actions which other group norms (e.g. norms which are not position-specific) as well as group standards require or allow.

(3) Actions and joint actions that do not, or at least need not, belong to classes (1) or (2) and which are based on situational intention formation or agreement making which has not been codified in the task-right system of g or the group norms of g, but which still are consistent with actions in (1) and (2).

(4) Freely chosen actions or activities (and possibly joint actions) which include actions and activities not within classes (1)–(3), but which are still not incompatible with them and which are within the realm of concern of g and rationally (understood broadly to amount to *reasonably*) collectively accepted by, or acceptable to, the members of g as such actions.

The notion of acting or functioning qua a group member would require much discussion, but to avoid that I will here make some simplifying assumptions. One thing that must be said immediately is, however, that the previous classes are classes of actions. Attitudes can be dealt with similarly. Thus, we may speak of attitude contents and actions within the realm of concern of group g, and in the above classification we may speak also of attitudes in addition to actions. The important thing to notice here is that those attitudes are based on acceptances and thus something that one can acquire by means of one's intentional action.

Basically, acting as a group member is to intentionally act within the group's realm of concern. Such action can be either a successful action or an unsuccessful action. What is required is that the group member in question will intentionally attempt to act in a way related to what he takes to be the group's realm of concern, such that he does not violate the group's constitutive goals, standards, values, and norms (in one word, its "ethos"). Thus, full success will not be required. There may thus be failures due to false beliefs about the group's norms and standards, due to lack of skill, or due to environmental obstacles. *Acting (functioning) as a group member* (relative to group g) in the positional case, viz., in a structured group, is equivalent to acting intentionally, with the purpose of satisfying or at least not contradicting the ethos of g, in one of the senses (1)–(4) or attempting so to act. I will below mean this notion when speaking of acting or functioning qua a group member. Obviously, one can be a group member without *always* acting as a group member, one can act within the realm of the group's concern but fail to obey the constitutive norms and standards of the group, and one can act qua a group member without thereby acting qua the member of another group.

Actions in (1) are of course typical positional actions that accordingly qualify as acting qua a member of g in one's position. Subclass (ii) of (1) thus consists of actions that the holder of a position may choose from. (The task-right system specifying (i) and (ii) may contain r-norms and/or s-norms – cf. chapter 6 for the notions.) However, classes (2)–(4) can occur also in the positional case and in other cases. Note that in the case of unstructured groups, class (1) is empty. The notion of rational collective acceptance in (4) is assumed to take into account what is generally presupposed of action in the community in question. Thus, it will respect the standards and generally accepted criteria of classifying actions within that community.

CHAPTER 3

Conceptual activity, rule following, and social practices

3.1 INTRODUCTION

Several philosophers, most notably Ludwig Wittgenstein (1953) and Wilfrid Sellars (1963), have argued that social practices, qua central elements of "forms of life," are conceptually crucial for conceptual activity. This is because they – or rather some fundamental kinds of them – in some instances are themselves *inherently* conceptual activities. This entails that they are activities which do not psychologically depend on the participants' following rules or meeting standards of any kind. This feature of social practices can be used to argue that the correctness of activities such as rule following and in general the application of concepts to the world crucially depends on the social practices of the community in question. Basic social practices are a kind of "discussion stopper" and form the irreducible and noncircular conceptual *fundamenta* of conceptual activities, according to this line of thought. The same communitarian idea can be applied to argue that language – or rather language use – is conceptually prior to thinking, even if thoughts may be argued to cause action. This is what Sellars (1963) argues. I will conduct part of my discussion within a Sellarsian framework (although without accepting all of his central views). Furthermore, I will not accept strong communitarianism, nor does Sellars.

Let me here say briefly what I mean by action and how I use some central related terms. When I speak of a strictly intentional action, I mean action performed on purpose. Such action is performed in accordance with and (partly) because of the intention to perform that very action or a "closely related" action. The closely related action can be a part of the action in question or it can be a whole of which the intentionally performed action is a part or a means for (see Tuomela, 1991 and especially 1995, pp. 67–73, for detailed discussion and for a wider notion of intentional action).

Consider next an example of a nonintentional action. Suppose a person scratches his nose while talking without paying attention to it. The action was still a meaningful action in the sense of being an understandable action with a teleological point – as contrasted with reflex behavior and the like.[1] The action was under the agent's control at least concerning its movement aspects and thus the behavior was clearly an action from the agent's point of view. Thus, in this control sense it is meaningful, and it is meaningful also in the teleological sense just because the type of action of scratching one's nose is a meaningful action. It was not a mistaken action, or a slip, or anything of the kind. It belonged to a larger pattern of action as an element which was not necessary for the pattern but which was still meaningful and perhaps expressive of the agent's nervousness. The action was not nonintentional in the sense, for instance, that falling or slipping is, or even unintentional in the sense that making a mistake (which is based on an attempt intentionally to perform something right) is unintentional.

In the terminology of this chapter, the present kind of action can be called a pattern-governed activity in a wide, non-Sellarsian sense. As will be seen, Sellars' sense requires more demandingly that there are no intentionally performed tokens, viz., the activity to count as pattern-governed behavior in his strict sense is one which cannot be performed on purpose at all (see section 3.2). I will use the terms "behavior" and "activity" as generic common-sense terms that cover essentially nonintentional movements such as reflexes, fallings down, Sellarsian pattern-governed behaviors, nonintentional but meaningful activities such as scratching one's nose, unintentional mistakes, as well as intentionally performed actions. Strictly intentional actions in my sense correspond to Sellars' actions in the conduct sense. They are actions one performs, and generally can perform, on purpose.

This chapter starts my discussion of the notion of social practice, to be discussed properly in chapter 4. As indicated, my approach to social practices relies on the notions of we-attitude and collective social action, both understood in a specific sense. Briefly, a collective social action is an action performed for a social reason, explicated as a shared we-attitude. A social practice is a repeated collective social action. In this chapter I will be concerned with the questions of the conceptual primacy of social practices and the criteria for rule following and conceptual activities in general. This will lead also to a consideration of nonintentional collective and individual behavior (especially single-agent and collective pattern-governed behavior) as a way of avoiding a celebrated circularity problem, viz., the problem that all rule obeying regressively depends on other rule obeying.

My central concern will be nonintentional behavior in the sense of pattern-governed behavior. I will be looking especially for *collectively* performed nonintentional action (pattern-governed behavior) that exhibits collective intentionality in a general collective aboutness ("meaningfulness") sense. As will be seen, (single-agent and collective) pattern-governed behavior can serve to ground intentional action in the "public realm." As to social practices, they typically involve pattern-governed behaviors, and, conversely, pattern-governed behaviors are often embedded in social practices, as will be seen in sections 3.5 and 3.6.

I will claim in chapter 4 that (a) social practices come about because of shared we-attitudes, where "because of" expresses a reason-giving causal relation (or, in my terminology, "purposive-causal" relation) and that (b) each particular token of a social practice gets its (teleological) meaningfulness from the social reason for which it was performed. Theses (a) and (b) are compatible both with the general view that action conceptually precedes thought and with the converse thesis that thought is conceptually more basic than action. They are also compatible with a third view according to which no conceptual precedence exists in either direction but, rather, mutual dependence. We need not take a definite stand here, as we will be mainly interested in somewhat less general ideas, especially in public-in-principle thoughts and their argued dependence on public conceptual activities. Shared we-attitudes will be taken to be public in principle, and for them the first view has at least some plausibility, as will be seen. A social practice (repeated collective social action) in its core sense may accordingly be understood as expressing the content of a we-attitude that need only be a we-attitude-in-action, which again has as its conceptual model "we-attituding out loud" or a disposition to "we-attituding out loud." For instance, suppose I am doing X for purpose p and believe that the others are also doing X for purpose p and that this is common knowledge among us. The idea here is that from a conceptual (although not causal) point of view we may think of the mentioned psychological notions in an overt sense, as inhering in the overt action, "we-action." The conceptual content of we-attitudes is not connected to their specific ontic status and, especially, does not entail that they are causally real inner mental states or episodes.

The view I will argue for below regards action, especially social practice, as conceptually fundamental. Before discussing my thesis on social practices in detail, some related background material must be covered (in the next section) to see where the important philosophical problems lie. Relying on the view that there is meaningful pattern-governed behavior, sections 3.3 and 3.4 develop a view of conceptual thinking and action that I regard as tenable. The discussion of the collective case will be conducted in sections 3.5 and 3.6.

3.2 SELLARS ON CONCEPTUAL ACTIVITY

The deepest sense in which social practices can be regarded as primary is that they are conceptually the basis of all thinking and all other conceptual activities, viz., thinking and acting on the basis of concepts, especially making inferences involving concepts. If this is right, the notion of a social practice surely is very central not only for social science and the philosophy of social science, but for systematic philosophy in general. What is involved is in part that language use – viewed here as a primarily social practice – is conceptually prior or at least conceptually central to thinking (in the "episodic" sense). I will discuss this problem here in part from the point of view of Sellars' theory (or, rather, a modified version of his theory) and use it to some extent as a basis for my own further theorizing. His theory is the best systematic account and defense of the view that "languaging" is conceptually primary. Sellars views language use as a social practice and so do his followers (see especially the rich book by Robert Brandom, 1994). Famously, Wittgenstein is another champion of the view that language use is conceptually primary, and the communitarian interpretation of his writings makes him also an advocate or champion of social practices (and of forms of life, which largely consist in social practices).

In Sellars' functionalism the framework of thoughts ("thinkings") is introduced as an *analogical* one, the *fundamentum* of which is meaningful overt speech: thinking is (in a certain analogical sense) internalized silent speech.[2] This is contrary to another traditional view, according to which speech is to be construed as overt thinking. Sellars' theory characterizes the semantical and conceptual aspects of thoughts in terms of their analogy to overt, conceptually meaningful action, especially linguistic action ("speech"). Here speech is to be understood in terms of the uniformities and propensities that connect utterances with other utterances (at the same or at a different level of language), with the perceivable environment, and with courses of action, including linguistic behavior (cf. Sellars, 1967, p. 310). I shall discuss the types of uniformities involved later.

What is central for our present purposes is that in Sellars' theory (a) linguistic behavior (activities consisting both of actions and non-actions) is conceptual activity in a primary sense and (b) linguistic behavior is through and through *rule-governed* and thus in an important way involves a *prescriptive* aspect (cf. Sellars, 1974, p. 97). I will below accept both (a) and (b), but construe the notion of a rule in a somewhat broader sense than Sellars. My own account, to be sketched later in the chapter, does not rely on the analogy theory in the Sellarsian sense, but still requires that sense must be made of the idea that meaningful action (including of course linguistic activity) is conceptually the *fundamentum* of publicly expressible thought in the richest sense in which thinking is placed in the "logical space of reasons and of justification." However, my view accepts and emphasizes that there is nonsocial thinking and that not all conceptual contents need to be socially constructed.

Sellarsian semantics will not be properly explicated below and will not be strongly relied on (although I regard it as being basically on the right track). Some remarks on his basic semantical ideas are needed, however. In his theory, to say of a linguistic utterance (e.g., noun or sentential expression) that it means something is not to construe meaning as a relation between a linguistic entity and some nonlinguistic entity (thought, proposition, etc.) but to go about "nominalistically" as follows. Consider, for example, the Finnish common noun "*talo.*" The analysis now becomes: "*talo*" (in Finnish) means house, which has the sense of '*talo*'s (in Finnish) are .house.s. Here ".house." is a common noun that applies to items in any language which play the representational *role* played in our base language (here English) by the sign design that occurs between the dot quotes. The word "means" indicates that the context is linguistic, and it also reminds us that in order for the statement to do its job directly, the unique common-noun-forming convention must be understood, and the sign "house" must belong to the active vocabulary of the person to whom the statement is made. There it plays the same role that the word "talo" plays in Finnish. (Dot-quoted sentences will be used in this book in later chapters; for a nonlinguistic version of dot quotation, see section 3.4.) Sellars' account of thinking reduces intentional aboutness to metalinguistic semantical discourse. The basic idea is that an item is intentional precisely in case this item is the kind of thing which makes *reference* to something.[3]

For Sellars, thinking is ontically prior to speech ("languaging") and, indeed, its *cause*. But in the order of conceiving, speech is the *fundamentum* (but cf. the broader view in Sellars, 1981). To give a conceptual clarification to a piece of linguistic behavior (speech) in his account is to characterize this piece of speech *functionally*, in terms of its linguistic role (broadly understood). Thus, given the analogy account of thinking, to say what a person thinks is to give a functional classification of his thinking and, ultimately, of his linguistic and other intelligent overt behavior. Accordingly, in Sellars' semantical theory the key notion is that of playing a *role* in a language. This functionalistic notion is analyzed in terms of overt speech, that is, in terms of the uniformities and propensities of the linguistic behavior of language users. These uniformities again are based on linguistic *rules* in an essential way that involves the causal efficacy of rule expressions (cf. Sellars, 1967, p. 310).

Sellars argues that a proper understanding of the nature and status of linguistic rules is a *sine qua non* of a correct interpretation of the sense in which linguistic behavior can be said to *be* (and not merely to express) conceptual activity. These linguistic rules may concern world-to-language or language-entry uniformities, intralinguistic uniformities, or language-to-world or language-departure uniformities. But what we are here interested in most is a different type of classification of rules, viz., their classification into *rules of action* (in the first place, *ought-to-do rules*) and *rules of criticism* (in the first place, *ought-to-be rules*). Rules which specify what one ought to do are rules of action. Their prototype is the conditional rule expressible by

(1) One ought to do X, if C.

Rules of criticism, on the other hand, specify how something ought to be. An important type of ought-to-be rules is the following:

(2) Any x ought to be in state S, if C.

It should be noticed here that an x, a subject of the rule, need not (on Sellars' account) have the concept of what it is to be in state S or of what it is for C to obtain.

Before we proceed to a more detailed discussion we need to consider the problem of what it is to satisfy a linguistic norm, or, what it is to follow or obey such a rule. We notice that mere behavioral uniformities ("constant conjunctions" or merely conforming behavior) give at best necessary criteria of satisfaction for rules such as (1) and (2). Thus, for instance, in the case of satisfying (1) we have to say more than that people invariably but "accidentally" do X when C is the case. Here is one common way to do it: to satisfy a rule is to obey it with the intention of fulfilling the demands of the rule. This criterion may be taken to entail the agent's awareness of the rule, his ability to apply the rule in appropriate circumstances, his ability to criticize the rule, the possibility for him to err or to break the rule, and so forth. Furthermore, at least in the case of objectively sanctioned rules, obeying would be taken to entail the recognition of rewards and punishments and reacting to them in one way or another.

This kind of psychological approach to clarifying the notion of satisfying a rule seems not to be available to Sellars on pain of circularity, if the analysis is understood to rely on inner psychological notions (cf. below). Sellars' account, rather, is based on the notion of *pattern-governed behavior*. This is behavior that is more than merely rule-conforming behavior (in a "constant conjunction" sense) but which is not yet rule obeying in the above strong psychological sense. "Roughly it is the concept of behavior which exhibits a pattern, not because it is brought about by the intention that it exhibit this pattern, but because the propensity to emit behavior of the pattern has been selectively reinforced and the propensity to emit behavior which does not conform to this pattern has been selectively extinguished" (Sellars, 1973b, p. 489). It can be said that to "play the game" at the level of pattern-governed behavior is to behave *because* of a system of moves to which these behaviors belong.

Accordingly, for Sellars pattern-governed behaviors (*pgb*s) are meaningful (functionally meaningful and meaningful in the aboutness sense of intentionality) but *necessarily* nonintentional (in the conduct sense) activities by single individuals. (For Sellars, intentionality in the representational or aboutness sense and conceptuality are the same thing.)

As noted, he argues for the conceptual priority of language and linguistic behavior to thinking. If all meaningful human activities were intentional "at bottom," viz., "under a suitable description," and if they, supposedly qua being intentional, had to rely on intentional mental states or processes (like intentions or "willings"), then thinking would, after all, be conceptually (and also causally) prior to linguistic and other actions. Sellars claims that Cartesian thoughts (mental states) in an unacceptable sense would hence have to be accepted (cf. Sellars, 1956, but also see the more liberal view in Sellars, 1981). Their unacceptability allegedly is that, being supposedly cognitive and knowledge-involving while yet non-conceptual, they rely on a rejectable form of the Myth of the Given. At least for this general reason Sellars has emphasized the notion of pattern-governed behavior especially in the context of his analogy theory of thinking. (As is well known, Wittgenstein somewhat similarly opposes Cartesian mental states and relies on overt action.)

Sellars' standard example of relatively elementary, biological, pattern-governed behavior is the "dance" of the bees (the kind of dance exhibiting the direction and distance to a source of food), but there are better examples. Thus perceptual takings (e.g. the perceptual taking that the cat is on the mat), logical inferences (e.g. the pattern-governed use of *modus ponens*), and "volitions" (e.g. the volition that I will now raise my hand) are more to the point.[4] The basic thing in these cases is that pattern-governed behavior is something performed *because of* the whole behaving system's achieving its goal. Thus, in a weak sense, there is a *reason* for this behavior, and this fact distinguishes it from accidental and from systematic rule-conforming "zombie-like" behavior. However, a piece of pattern-governed behavior as such is not an action in a full sense (something one can decide or intend to do). Therefore, pattern-governed behavior is not correct or incorrect in the same way as actions are correct or incorrect. Pattern-governed behavior is subject to ought-to-be rules but not directly to ought-to-do rules. Pattern-governed behavior is still rule-obeying behavior – it is normatively *correct* if it is in accordance with the ought-to-be rule in question, and it is otherwise incorrect. Nevertheless, Sellars takes ought-to-be rules to be connected by entailment to ought-to-do rules: "the connection is, roughly, that ought-to-be's imply ought-to-do's" (Sellars, 1974, p. 96; but cf. below).

Let us next consider a simple example of an ought-to-be rule (cf. Sellars, 1974, pp. 96–99).

(3) One ought to feel sympathy for bereaved people.

Feeling sympathy is not an action in the conduct sense, but it may be taken to involve some activity. (3) does not presuppose that the target subjects have the concept of feeling sympathy.

In what sense does an ought-to-be rule imply an ought-to-do rule? Sellars gives a couple of examples of this. It suffices to consider the following ought-to-do rule corresponding to, and entailed by, (3) (cf. Sellars, 1974, p. 97).

(3′) (Other things being equal and where possible) one ought to bring it about that people feel sympathy for the bereaved.

It is relevant here to consider the underlying source of ought-to-be rules. One such source for them is a community's collective acceptance as its (conditional) goal of what the rule expresses, for example that the collective goal is that an x be in state S if C. In such a case, assuming that indeed a proper we-mode collective goal is at stake, the members of the community are collectively committed to seeing to it that the goal is satisfied, and this may require teaching and requiring the members of the community to be in state S if C or, if that is not possible in terms of intentional action, to otherwise see to it that the goal is satisfied. Here we obviously have an argument for the entailment of ought-to-do rules by ought-to-be rules in the case of collective goals. Whether or not an ought-to-be rule in all cases entails some kind of ought-to-do rule, which is what Sellars claims, seems to depend crucially on the nature of the ought-to-be rule. As said, when the rule is based on a collective goal, relevant ought-to-do rules can be taken to be entailed (cf. chapter 6 for ought-to-be rules in the context of collective goals).

Rules can be conceptualized in a still more liberal way so that every concept has a rule attached to it. Thus, Kant understands concepts as having the form of rules – viz., as being concerned with what one ought to do and what one is responsible for. One can even take a broader view of rules in the context of accounting for conceptuality. Thus, Pettit (1993) takes rules to be "normative constraints that determine that one member – of perhaps one subset – of a set of options is more appropriate in some way than alternatives" (p. 65). This comparative notion of rule seems to fit ought-rules, viz., ought-to-do rules and ought-to-be rules, best. However, it is more liberal, because every ought-rule is a rule in this comparative sense, but not conversely. Thus, we can capture more normative nuances by using the liberal notion of a rule. For example, the concept expressed by the predicate "round" entails a rule concerning the normative use of this predicate: some things are round while others are not (and "round" applies better to some things than to others, even if they are not round in a strict sense).[5]

I will below accept this more general notion of a concept and I will not accept the Sellarsian view that ought-to-be rules invariably entail corresponding ought-to-do rules (but accept the entailment for the discussed case involving collective goals).

3.3 CAN CONCEPTUALITY BE NONCIRCULARLY CHARACTERIZED?

Let me now discuss whether Sellars' account satisfies the noncircularity requirement, viz., the requirement that conceptual inner mental states be noncircularly based on overt linguistic activity. Marras has criticized Sellars' analogy theory on two grounds (see Marras, 1973a, 1973b, and 1973c). First, it is claimed to be circular in that his analysis, after all, relies on inner episodes. Secondly, Sellars' attempt to explicate conceptuality (the having of concepts) in terms of linguistic rules also is circular, as the latter notion presupposes conceptuality.

The argument concerning circularity in the sense of reliance on inner episodes can be reconstructed as follows (cf. Sellars, 1973b, and Marras, 1973b). (1) If the concept of the conceptuality of inner episodes (i.e., thoughts) is to be analyzed by means of the concept of a rule of language, it is essential that the concept of a rule of language does not presuppose the concept of the conceptuality of inner states. (2) However, the concept of a rule of language presupposes the concept of the conceptuality of inner episodes. Therefore, (3) the concept of the conceptuality of inner episodes cannot be analyzed or theoretically explained by means of the concept of a rule of language.

Sellars (1973b) accepts the first premise. (In slight contrast, I would rather say in its formulation that conceptuality involves rules of language, "rule" broadly understood, and say that rules of language can be taken to explicate, rather than strictly analyze, conceptuality.) The concept of rule of language is Sellars' analytic tool for explicating the manifest image framework of conceptual thoughts-out-loud and pattern-governed behaviors in general. Thus, rules are already part of the overt, Rylean framework. Sellars accordingly does not accept the second premise.

We recall that Sellars gives as his examples of *pgb* the dance of the bees, feeling sympathy for the bereaved, making an inference, and so on. The basic point here is that *pgb* is essentially nonintentional in the conduct sense – viz., it cannot be performed on purpose, by forming an intention to perform it. Thus the nature of these behaviors is such that they can only have nonintentional tokens, and the tokens are not even nonintentional tokens of actions in the conduct sense. (An action in the conduct sense must – when "suitably redescribed" – have intentional tokens.) Still, the action can occur in a meaningful context of activities and indeed does normally so occur (recall the examples and cf. below, section 4.1). The context may be one in which the agent is carrying out a general policy intention.

To illustrate Sellars' solution let us consider a simple case of inference (*modus ponens*). An agent is supposed to have two premises, viz., "p" and "if p then q." He then infers "q." This is a piece of pattern-governed behavior (corresponding to *modus ponens*) that is not an action and hence not an obeying of any ought-to-do rule. Yet it is a piece of conceptual activity, which is at least in part governed by the following ought-to-be rule: if "p" and "if p then q" are true, then one ought not to infer "−q," and, furthermore, under epistemically suitable conditions (e.g. when facing the task of determining whether "q" is entailed by the premises) one ought to infer "q." Let us accept that this rule (or something closely similar to it) is indeed causally efficacious. This efficacy here need not amount to more than that the agent is relevantly sensitive to the rule and is disposed to behave in accordance with it; thus the causal efficacy does not at least directly depend on the agent's inner mental episodes.

Now this kind of inference represents a type of activity which (a) has no action tokens in the conduct sense of action (thus not even nonintentional action tokens), (b) has at least some overt "activity" tokens (viz., inferrings-out-loud), and (c) is (more or less clearly) conceptual. (As to (a), there is no corresponding ought-to-do rule – in the sense (3′) corresponds to (3) – that the agent would be obeying when engaged in inferring.) This shows that there then are conceptual activities that do not depend on inner episodes in the circular way conceived in Marras' first circularity argument. Psychological circularity is blocked because *pgb* can stand on its own feet, so to speak, from a psychological and ontological point of view, viz., from the point of view of what actually is going on in the agent's mind and action.

My rebuttal of Marras' argument so far is that Sellars does not accept premise (2) on the grounds that the concept of a rule of language merely presupposes the concept of the conceptuality of thoughts-out-loud (i.e., *pgb*), which are not actions, and whose concept therefore does not presuppose the concept of inner episodes. What is crucial, therefore, is that the concept of the conceptuality of thoughts-out-loud does not presuppose the concept of a rule *if* it turns out that the concept of a rule presupposes or implies the framework of thoughts (whether inner or out-loud).

But how can Sellars hold without circularity that the concept of a rule presupposes the concept of the conceptuality of thoughts-out-loud if it turns out (as one may argue) that the latter concept presupposes the concept of a rule? Since thinking-out-loud is not *merely* a matter of instantiating uniformities, how can its conceptuality be explicated without employing the concept of a rule? (Rules are part of the *fundamentum* according to Sellars; they are already implicit in the very Rylean framework.)

Indeed, Marras argues that Sellars now must face the following dilemma. Thinkings-out-loud (and their subclass pattern-governed behaviors) are not merely behavioral items in some physicalistic sense (movements of the body, sounds uttered, etc.). They can be assumed to have conceptual properties. Thus, as Sellars (1974) himself argues in so many words, they exist in "an ambience of semantical rules" and typically we are not dealing with items like utterances, but with sayings (activities, which need not, however, always be full-blown actions), and this difference is due to the embedding of the latter in a system of linguistic rules. Now, the semantical rules explicating the conceptuality of thinkings-out-loud are either ought-to-be rules (at the level of pattern-governed behavior) or ought-to-do rules (at the level of linguistic actions or rule-obeying behavior). In the latter case the above argument is directly relevant. The former alternative, Marras argues, leads to a vicious circle, too, as soon as one accepts, as Sellars does, that ought-to-be rules entail a related ought-to-do rule, because the ought-to-do rules lead to dependence on conceptual inner mental episodes. Thus, there will be conceptual dependence on inner mental episodes, even if *pgb*s would suffice to block psychological (or ontic) dependence in the general case. (By psychological dependence I mean that they are meaningful pieces in their own right, quite independently of the existence of the inner mental episodes causing them.[6])

Let me next consider a way to block the paradox, although it is not available to Sellars. According to it, it is simply not the case that ought-to-be rules *without further assumptions* entail relevant ought-to-do rules (in the sense, e.g., rule (3) has been supposed to entail rule (3′)). The same people (the targets of norms) are not normally required to bring about that they do what the ought-to-be rule requires, and no other group of persons need to be subject to such a requirement either, unless a proper collective goal is at stake (recall our earlier discussion).

Marras' second charge of circularity simply says in more general terms that Sellars' analysis of conceptual activity in terms of rules of language leads to a vicious circle. This criticism concerns the analyzability of conceptual activity in terms of the concept of rule of language and claims that this cannot be done in a noncircular fashion. As said above, in our ordinary conceptual framework of agency there is a conceptual connection between conceptuality and rules of language. Furthermore, although conceptuality can be illustrated and elucidated in terms of rules, no reductive analysis is possible. Accordingly, I take it that our ordinary framework of agency, and hence Sellars' account, is committed to the view that full-fledged linguistic ability *indirectly*, if not directly, presupposes language as an instrument and that the concept of rule or language and the concept of conceptual activity are mutually intertwined.[7] Rules can be taken to represent the normative aspect (the correctness/incorrectness aspect) of the application of concepts.

Let us still consider the analogous charge of conceptual circularity in the case of *rule following*. The argument here says that when following a rule the agent must meet another criterion or standard, viz., follow a rule in a possibly wide sense that yet involves ought-to-do rules, which launches a regress. However, this charge can be met by reference to pattern-governed behavior, which is rule-governed and meaningful by itself (at least if the general entailment of ought-to-do rules by ought-to-be rules is not accepted). As to the psychological circularity point, in the case of pattern-governed behavior there is, however, no circularity, as all tokens of a type of pattern-governed behavior – in Sellars' strict sense – are meaningful nonactions. Somewhat analogously, in the case of Wittgenstein's (1953) "blind actions" (here understood as types), there is no actual psychological dependence on further rules (here understanding rules in the broad Kantian sense), at least on some occasions (viz., some action tokens). Such blind actions are either pattern-governed behaviors or conduct actions that on the occasions at stake are performed without the problematic circular psychological dependence (cf. section 3.5). Thus, the circle to internal mental states can be blocked either by showing that some intentional actions are meaningful as such and are rule obeyings as such, or, in other cases, that they depend on intendings-out-loud that do not need further intendings-out-loud. Thus, the "buck stops" either at intentional actions of a basic kind or at intendings-out-loud.

My overall conclusion concerning circularity problems is that Marras' first circularity argument (psychological circularity) can be avoided but that the second argument (conceptual circularity) applies to the full-blown case in the sense that rules and conceptual activity are conceptually interconnected to the effect that full-blown conceptual activity cannot be noncircularly *analyzed* in terms of rules of language (even when *widely* understood). Nevertheless, conceptuality can, of course, be elucidated and illustrated in terms of rules of language as long as strict reduction is not attempted.

3.4 ELEMENTARY CONCEPTUAL ACTIVITY

I will argue below that there is *elementary* animal and prelinguistic behavior which is conceptual but which can be understood without speaking of rules and without the target organisms having concepts in a strong sense. In this sense one can say that conceptuality and rules of language do not always go together, and this also means that (strong) communitarian views of conceptuality cannot be quite right, because there is then nonsocially based conceptual activity.

Let us consider elementary cases of conceptuality as exhibited in higher animals (such as chimpanzees) and prelinguistic children. Conceptuality (in the sense of "having" concepts and acting "on" them) comes in degrees and can indeed exist in nonlinguistic beings (Sellars, 1981, in effect makes this same point, which entails departure from strong communitarianism). As to the point about degrees of conceptuality, we may illustrate it in terms of having the concept of table. A rudimentary concept of table is already possessed by an individual even at the conceptual level of a few months' old child. For such a being a table is probably some rather diffuse perceptual entity with some shape, size, color, and texture plus the property of causing pain when it is kicked. The child has only a functional concept of table: at best it tends to exhibit the right kind of overt behavior toward tables, for example it perceives it as something solid and, when able to crawl, tends to avoid bumping into it. Thus it performs relevant "associative," "Humean" inferences (cf. Sellars, 1981, for the quoted notions that do not rely on proper logical inference). This is far from, for example, a scientist's concept of table, which contains both of Eddington's famous tables as its representations and involves his ability to make proper inferences using the concept(s) of table.

As to the much larger and more difficult question of nonlinguistic conceptual thinking, let me say the following. Prelinguistic babies learn to act meaningfully in a teleological or functional sense because they, qua living organisms, have certain basic needs they are disposed to satisfy either due to learning and teaching or other environmental influences or (in part) due to their genetic makeup. So they behave *functionally* and thus exhibit *regularities* in their behavior. We may speak of rudimentary and less than fully conceptual prelinguistic behavior here. Such elementary or rudimentary conceptual behavior can still involve the kind of commerce with the environment that is adequate for the satisfaction of at least some basic needs (moving from one place to another, getting food, shelter, etc.). This commerce can even be based on the fact that the organism represents objects in its environment and portrays them as being thus and so. All this can happen without the organism being reflectively conscious of its thoughts, viz., of the fact that it has thoughts.

The aforementioned regularities – some of which are habits and routines – can be *normatively* classified. That is, some ways of doing things are classified as right (or appropriate) and others as wrong, originally in the case of basic needs simply because the former, in contrast to the latter, enable the actors to reach their goals. What we have is at least *implicit* normativity, which can in principle be made explicit in terms of ought-to-be and, possibly, ought-to-do rules. Linguistic action is a refined and sophisticated form of this kind of functionally meaningful behavior. In its evolutionary beginnings, communicative action was not very sophisticated, as we know, but it evolved into a natural language in our sense, the major step in this process being the invention of a generative syntax or, more broadly, of a representational system such as there is in the case of a person capable of using logic and grammar and making inferences in "the logical space of reasons and of justification."

Let me elaborate further on the problem of understanding others, including nonlinguistic animals. We speak of representational systems that animals such as chimpanzees or dogs have. We can take the semantical features of the items in such systems to be based on the semantical features of the functionally meaningful behaviors of these animals. The functional meaningfulness of such behavior is understood ultimately – to put the matter very crudely – in terms of the animals' being able to satisfy their basic needs and to survive. But the semantical features of such behaviors – roughly, what they can be taken to express – are understood by analogy to our own behaviors, especially linguistic behaviors. More precisely, some states of such organisms represent objects and characterize them as having certain aspects or features. Such states are propositional states, but they need not be linguistic and need not involve subject and predicate terms. In Sellarsian fashion, we take as our conceptual and epistemic starting point functionally classified states of the dot-quoted. This is F. kind. and uses as the functional basis the functional connections that our framework of agency employs.[8] The latter kinds of connections rely on our basic needs, wants, beliefs, intentions, memory, emotions, and even obligations.

Our nonlinguistic meaningful behaviors are semantically characterized by analogy to our linguistic behavior. To take a trivial example, a person x's drinking a glass of water has semantical features in virtue of the semantical characteristics of the sentence "x juo lasillisen vettä" (in Finnish), which plays the role of the dot-quoted ".x drinks a glass of water." with English as the base language. This involves that we can use as our total symbolic base system the system consisting not only of our linguistic behaviors, but also of meaningful nonlinguistic behaviors. And due to this base system we understand other animal species' behaviors. The animals' meaningful behaviors again are the basis for our attributing an operative representational system – a symbolic system – to the animals. So we have this epistemic or epistemic-conceptual order of explication: our linguistic activities → our functionally meaningful behaviors → the animal species' functionally meaningful behaviors → the animal species' operative symbolic system. Which animals or species of animals actually do behave functionally meaningfully to the extent that a relevant representational system and acting on the basis of that system can be attributed to them, must be left for science to determine. In any case, conceptual activities must be based on such representational or symbolic systems, simply as a matter of what we understand by conceptuality. A stronger form of conceptuality – the one that applies to us humans – requires not only the active use of representational systems as a basis of action, but also the capacity to make inferences in a proper sense that amounts to more than associative thinking (cf. Sellars' 1981 discussion of Aristotelian inferences versus Humean associative "inferences").

The above considerations indicate that there is nonsocial conceptual activity in nonlinguistic organisms in an objective sense, although we cannot but use our conceptual system to elucidate and to speak about it. Thus, we have an argument against strong communitarianism. This still leaves the kind of *weak* communitarianism intact that only says that there is – and conceptually *must* be – much socially constructed conceptual activity, which contrasts with strong communitarianism that makes conceptual activity invariably socially constructed. Weak communitarianism is what the arguments of the present chapter will be seen to warrant.

From the point of view of the developmental and evolutionary order of explanation, we now get the following schema to complement the above conceptual-epistemic order: functionally meaningful nonlinguistic thinking and action → linguistic thinking and action → mental states as inner episodes and action based on them. This accounts for mental episodes both in an action sense or conduct sense and also for mental episodes in a weaker activity sense. In the latter case we must understand linguistic action in a similarly weak sense as something like pattern-governed activity (cf. inferring out loud). Thus, the following points can be made: (1) there is conceptual activity that is based on functionally meaningful nonlinguistic action, and (2) one can attribute thoughts to animals on the basis of their similarity to humans.

3.5 COLLECTIVE PATTERN-GOVERNED BEHAVIOR

3.4 has shown that in the case of Sellars' analogy theory of thinking the notion of a pattern-governed behavior (*pgb*) plays a central role and helps to block psychological circularity. A somewhat different argument for the importance of pattern-governed behavior – and group members' learned dispositions to produce them – is this: every action in the full-blown conduct sense has both intentional and nonintentional tokens. We can say that every action is intentional under some description, so to speak, because every action token (viz., a token of an action performable on purpose, in the conduct sense) has an intentional core and a description under which it is intentional. Thus, if intentionally performed actions need intentionally performed conceptual mental events or even any kinds of conceptual (conceptual in the sense of exhibiting intentional aboutness) mental events to ground and cause them, then we do not get an account of the conceptuality of all mental states in terms of overt action (and the analogy theory). But if *pgb*s are available, one can perform the task – or so it can be argued.

I have shown that pattern-governed behavior is behavior that is meaningful in the aboutness sense of intentionality and, which partly explains its representational character, also of being (objectively) teleologically meaningful (recall note 1). Teleologically meaningful behavior is something performed for the sake of a goal or end. This factual feature of the behavior serves as a ground for its semantical meaningfulness in the aboutness sense.

Earlier I discussed Sellars' standard examples of single-agent *pgb*. These example *pgb*s cannot be interestingly (especially nonaggregatively) generalized to the collective human case. For instance, the dance of the bees is not very good for our present purposes, as it is nonhuman behavior. The problem with the sympathy example is that feeling sympathy is an emotional state, and it is debatable whether it can be called an activity performed by an agent. As to making an inference, it seems like a good example per se, but it is primarily an example of mental activity, although one can speak of "inferring out loud" (cf. my later comment on the collective version of it). The case of perceptual takings, for instance seeing a table over there, fares somewhat better. These kinds of activities, while being essentially nonintentional (in the conduct sense), occur in the context of meaningful intentional activities and are themselves fully intentional in the broader aboutness sense of having content. These perceptual examples of course are examples of mental *pgb*, but perceivings-out-loud corresponding to them would be overt actions. (Cf. also my later social example related to conformative perceiving.)

As to the social or collective case, let me first point out that Sellars' account of language use is actually social and that he therefore is implicitly discussing aggregated *pgb*s in a social context. As I shall show, mere aggregated *pgb*s are not properly social and "groupish" and are indeed insufficiently social for the purposes at hand. As *pgb*s in Sellars' theory are in all cases nonintentional (in the conduct sense), they can, at best, be embedded in a collective action that is performed intentionally for a shared social reason.[9]

To block the discussed psychological and conceptual regresses, a collective *pgb* must be taken to be nonintentionally exhibited collective behavior that is meaningful both in the aboutness (representational) and in the teleological sense. In general, in the social case we must require that all the participants share a social reason (a we-attitude content), which, furthermore, requires them to "interact," at least mentally, on the level of their we-beliefs, if not overtly. Such a social reason disposes them to collective social action. I suggest the following account: basically, *collective pattern-governed behaviors are nonintentionally exhibited but representationally meaningful elements (or parts) of collective social actions performed because of relevant social reasons (we-attitudes)*. These meaningful elements can be *essentially* nonintentional in the conduct sense that they do not on metaphysical grounds have any intentionally performed tokens, or they can be nonintentional because of being ingrained and routine. The former case corresponds to strict Sellarsian *pgb*s and the latter to Wittgenstein's "blind" actions, viz., actions which are, or are based on, routine skills due to learning (cf. below for them). As emphasized, pattern-governed behaviors are meaningful in the sense of exhibiting intentional aboutness in a teleologically appropriate sense; and in the collective case they analogously exhibit collective intentionality (aboutness) and teleological meaningfulness (cf. below).

Collective social actions in general are not reducible to aggregates of individual actions (cf. Tuomela, 1995, and chapter 4 below). Neither are collective *pgb*s reducible to aggregates of individual *pgb*s. As will be seen, collective *pgb*s may have different causes, viz., group-related causes, than have individual *pgb*s. This gives reason to think that the concept of a collective *pgb* (which requires a group context) is not reducible to the notion of aggregated individual *pgb*, as individual *pgb*s need not causally or conceptually depend on a group context and thus may not be social to a sufficient extent; this is, of course, not to say that collective *pgb*s in *all* cases amount to more than aggregated individual *pgb*s. (Sellars does not discuss properly collective *pgb*s at all although his emphasis on social practices may suggest that he would give a place to collective *pgb*s in his system, but only in the trivial aggregative sense.)

The general point about my discussion of collective *pgb*s is that, firstly, they serve to ground collective social action in analogy with how individual *pgb*s ground mental states and episodes. As collective social actions and the social practices built out of them will be central for my account of conceptuality and social institutions, collective *pgb*s will also derivatively anchor them in routine patterns of behavior. Accordingly, collective *pgb*s are central building blocks of the social world, especially in the sense of forming the "routine" ingredients in social practices (viz., repeated collective social actions), customs, and institutional behavior. Such routines generally come about because of repetition and learning. Also mental activities can be *pgb*s and, in the case of collective wants, intentions and beliefs, they can form collective *pgb*s, which may also make the mental (motivational and other) elements involved in customs and social practices routine. This can result in collective activities and practices that are, so to speak, routine throughout (cf. chapter 4). Activities that are routine may of course be psychologically functional for agents, as they typically tend to save energy and effort for other, more demanding activities, and they may be societally functional and tend to create social order. Secondly, collective *pgb*s serve to block rule-following circularity also in such collective cases as joint action and institutional acting, especially in the case of the maintenance of social institutions (cf. section 3.6 and chapter 7). In the context of my Collective Acceptance model of sociality, to be discussed in chapters 5 and 6, they will serve to "anchor" the collective social activities required for the continued collective acceptance, viz., maintenance, of a social institution.

Proceeding now to a detailed account of collective *pgb*s, I propose that (1) a collective *pgb* in the strict sense is a collectively meaningful element of an intentionally performed collective social action (in the sense of chapter 4 below), that (2) the collective *pgb* consists of, or is made up of, individual *pgb*s, and that (3) the collective social action in question is performed in part because of a shared we-attitude, at least a shared we-belief to the effect that (a) that is what the participants are doing and (b) that the single-agent *pgb*s either are directly (i) individual part actions or are involved as (ii) elements in the individual part actions serving to make up the collective social action in question. A collective *pgb* understood in this sense is "actionally" nonintentional both in the collective sense (entailing lack of guidance and control by a shared collective intention) and in the individual sense (entailing that the involved singular *pgb*s are nonintentional). Nevertheless, it is collectively intentional in the aboutness sense (recall that the ought-to-be rule governing a *pgb* can be taken to represent a collective goal). However, in principle this does not require that individual participants have relevant representations, e.g. goals, at all. Thus there need not be intentional aboutness on the level of individual participants.

I would like to point out, however, that it is possible on merely conceptual grounds that *pgb*s occur even without being embedded in conduct actions. However, I will assume below that they will always be embedded in intentional actions, partly on the basis of our common-sense knowledge and partly because of the general hypothesis that, whenever awake, a human being is performing some action intentionally in the conduct sense.

A collective social action is a many-person action performed because of a shared we-attitude (see chapter 4). An example would be the collective social action of making a certain kind of pot, which requires a special ingrained skill, say, a special hand movement that de facto cannot be performed without the learned skilled action in which it is embedded. (The hand movement type can be a bodily action type – something that can be performed directly on purpose – but my analysis also allows that it is not an action in this conduct sense.) The *pgb* here can be regarded as the nonintentionally performed hand movement having a certain result. We can assume that every potter participating in this tradition believes that the others are also manufacturing pots in the same special way and believes that this is mutually believed in the group. The pot-making thus is a collective social action in the standard sense. While the embedded special hand movements are *pgb*s, the collective sanctioning (especially disapproval) of, for instance, norm violation might here consist of individual activities that are also *pgb*s (expressions of negative feelings) and of the required we-belief. (This corresponds to the disjunct (3bi).)

Here are some further examples of collective pattern-governed behaviors. Collective practical inferences may sometimes provide such (cf. the mental candidate action expressed by "We believe that p and believe that p entails q; so we believe that q"). Next, conforming perceptions (or "perceivings-out-loud" in Asch-type social psychological experiments) may count as examples of collective pattern-governed behaviors. According to the results of the Asch experiments, some people in a group may influence the perception of, for example, the length of an object by the other agents in the group so as to make these perceptions grossly nonveridical (Asch, 1987). The collective action here may be taken to be the agents' jointly producing a certain distribution of length judgments. This can be, but need not be, an overt action. Here the perceptual takings by the agents that the objects are of such and such length form the collective perceptual taking that is the collective pattern-governed behavior in question.

More generally, group members can be sensitive to a range of other conformity phenomena in a group context (but not perhaps in other contexts). For instance, they might have certain attitudes towards out-group members. This kind of group-sensitive phenomenon could be a disposition to exhibit nonvoluntary *pgb*. Sanctioning in the case of proper social norms can also be of this group-sensitive, nonvoluntary kind and be *pgb*.

My next example of collective pattern-governed behavior in the present context would be "collective yawning" (or, for that matter, involuntary laughing). Yawning and laughing are teleologically meaningful activities of the *pgb* kind such that when started by one person in a group they tend to spread to others so that we soon get collective, many-person yawning (laughing). Another type of case would be collective *pgb* produced by a shared social emotion, such as collective fear, leading to "mass hysteria," panic behavior, and so on.

Yet another example of a kind of social pattern-governed behavior would be "communication" in which the communicating actors, say two politicians from rival parties, so to speak say one thing by their words but another, contradictory, thing by their body language (mimes and gestures) and where they also have a mutual belief concerning what their mimes and gestures express. The body language aspect is nonintentional and may be taken to count as meaningful pattern-governed behavior. Indeed, we have collective *pgb* because of the mentioned (conscious or unconscious) mutual belief. Somewhat analogously there might be perceptual cases exhibiting meaningful patterning in something like the way Gestalt psychologists have mapped these patterns for us (cf. Schlicht, 1998).

The above list of ontically irreducible examples can be taken to represent collective pattern-governed behaviors which do not have any intentionally performed tokens either on conceptual or on factual grounds. While the interpretation of examples is a tricky matter depending on one's background views, still the examples can be regarded as strict cases of collective *pgb*s, viz., cases with no intentional tokens.

In contrast, in the "non-Sellarsian" cases of collective *pgb*s the singular *pgb*s can themselves be even intentionally performed – while still being ingrained "basic actions." In this case the collective social action may accordingly be composed of this kind of *pgb*s, assuming that the collective social action is performed because of a shared we-attitude. Accordingly, I will explicate social reasons in this particular context as we-attitude contents. It is not necessary below to require in all contexts that *pgb* be *essentially* nonintentional (viz., that *all* – actual and possible – tokens of a *pgb* necessarily be nonintentional). While Sellarsian *pgb*s serve to block psychological circularity, even a single behavior token that is independently meaningful (viz., which does not require preformed intention for its performance) would suffice.

Wittgenstein is famous for his view that forms of life – consisting to a large extent of social practices – are the locus of meaningfulness of human activities (cf. Wittgenstein, 1953). Put in terms of the "communitarian" interpretation of Wittgenstein, rule following (and in general having concepts and acting on them) is made meaningful in terms of a collective's consensus or agreement as exhibited in social practices. Wittgenstein would hardly say that following a rule is, or can be, justified in terms of social practice. For him there are no such things as justified criteria for how to use language and how to engage in conceptual activities on the whole. Nevertheless, in his view social practices are the conceptual and metaphysical foundation of thought and indeed of agency and conceptual activities in general. In this case skills ("blind" actions) will be the kinds of behavior that block the regress paradox of rule following. These Wittgensteinian blind actions are assumed to be meaningful per se. This can be taken to mean that they – when intentional – are actions involving an intention-in-action. Such an intention does not require iteration or its being somehow based on some meaningful inner mental episode. In the collective case we can speak of a "we-intention-in-action" or, more generally, of a "we-attitude-in-action." For example, we could have the meant kind of intentional "basic" collective action if every participant were performing a "basic" action X, we-believing that also the others are performing (viz., believing also they are performing it and also believing that this is mutually believed in the group). As said, such a token of collective action would suffice to block psychological circularity. In section 3.6 I will claim that there is also another route that does not require the existence of intentional blind actions of the Wittgensteinian kind. This other solution uses pattern-governed behaviors in an important way.

We may also consider other weaker kinds of *pgb* that may sometimes be intentional. Teleologically meaningful activities involving an "invisible hand" are a case in point (cf. chapter 7). If we are to believe economic theory, under certain ideal conditions with agents as price takers in a situation of "supply and demand," a global Walrasian equilibrium of demand and supply is created. The agents only mind their own business, trying to maximize their profits, and do not have as their shared collective end to produce a global equilibrium. Here we have a case where as a matter of contingent fact the collective activity is never based on a collective intention. The agents do not (or need not) aim at achieving a global equilibrium. Similar cases from the field of functional explanation can be considered. Thus, in a native tribe the function of witch hunting may be to decrease intragroup hostility. The latter takes place, we assume, but in the collective activity of lowering intragroup hostility the end is neither collectively nor privately intended.

I will not here systematically discuss collective *pgb*s in the wider cases, as they are not needed for the purposes of the present book. Let me just say that in general a collective *pgb* is a goal-directed or *teleologically meaningful* (performed for the sake of a goal) piece of nonintentionally exhibited collective behavior. The nonintentionality here refers to the conduct sense and involves that the behavior is not based on a collective intention. The participants can be taken collectively to have a goal (or at least their collective has a goal) and act towards it, but they nevertheless need not in general have a representation of this goal and need not intend to achieve the goal in question (cf. invisible hand cases). In contrast to the strict Sellarsian cases, the pattern-governed behaviors (when viewed as types rather than as tokens) can have intentionally performed tokens (which, however, are not *pgb*s).

We can characterize the "genesis" and initiation of a collective *pgb* partly in terms of *ought-to-be norms* (in Sellars' sense). Thus, a given collective *pgb* would be the content of an ought-to-be norm, and when obeyed it would become a social practice in the collective. Both biological and environmental determinants can result in *pgb*. Upbringing, education, and teaching will of course typically (or often) play a major role in the rise of *pgb*. The target actors of these ought-to-be norms will typically be parents and other educators, but we can perhaps speak of these norms in a more abstract sense without specifying exactly who or which are the persons (or groups of them, or institutions) made responsible for fulfilling the norms. In any case, both strong and weak cases of collective *pgb*s are in general dependent on cultural and social values, traditions, norms, and the like, as their basic ingredient is the learning of novices (e.g. children) based on expert teaching (by, e.g., parents or skilled specialists).

As to the initiation problem, there can be collective *pgb* as a type of activity which requires both relevant individual and collective intention to be initiated, although the intention is "forgotten" if the activity gets fully routinized. Alternatively, there can be collective *pgb* that requires only relevant individual intention to get initiated.

We may take collective intention in the above cases to be a shared "weak" we-intention (either in the I-mode or in the we-mode), where a weak we-intention is a social intention in the we-attitude sense (cf. chapter 2). It seems that I-mode collective *pgbs* (of collective social actions involving collective *pgbs* in the Sellarsian case) would suffice for both Sellars' and Wittgenstein's account. The central claims about social practices in this book apply both to I-mode and we-mode social practices, understanding social practices as repeated collective social actions performed on the basis of a shared we-attitude. In the above cases my theory (or Wittgenstein's account) need not assume that the possibility (expressed by "can") is conceptual, whereas Sellars' account is based on that assumption (which, however, is grounded on factual or ontic impossibility).

As seen, collective social practices (repeated social actions performed on the basis of shared we-attitudes) can consist of *pgbs* or, in the collectivized Sellarsian case, have them as their parts. Minimally we are then dealing with "we-actions," viz., collective social actions based on shared we-beliefs, which are not performed on purpose (and hence are not intentional in the core sense). Note that certain strongly ingrained habitual behaviors might be quasi-Sellarsian in the sense of not having intentional tokens on factual psychological grounds (think of habits related to communication, for example body language and gestures while in face-to-face communication or of wording and pronunciation in various dialects).

Earlier I presented two kinds of reasons for the central role of collective *pgbs*, the first of which relates to collective *pgbs* as anchoring repeated social activities, viz., social practices, customs, and institutional activities, to routine behaviors while the second deals with the blocking of circularity problems in cases of joint action (in parallel with singular action). Furthermore, it was noted above that the important – both from a social-theoretical and a practical point of view – invisible hand kind of activity can be regarded as *pgb*. To the same category belong implicit social norms of a certain kind, and possibly tastes and feelings. The view that I advocate in this book basically is compatible with all of the above notions of collective *pgbs* of various strength.

There are also other philosophical reasons for emphasizing the role of something like *pgb*, nonintentional behavior, and social practice. Thus Heidegger (1927) argued for the importance of nonintentional activity (activity not being based on intentional mental states) in contributing to the breakdown or to the abolition of the Cartesian subject–object relation (also see chapter 4 below on Bourdieu). This view is based on the centrality of "readiness at hand" objects and activities (in Heidegger's

Zuhandensein sense as opposed to the Cartesian–Husserlian *Vorhandensein*, "present at hand") and the assumed primitive intentionality and teleological nature of our common-sense world. Heidegger's point can be based on weaker kind of *pgb* than the strict Sellarsian one. Even totally unreflected but yet intentional action seems to be able to block the Cartesian subject–object dichotomy at least in a psychological sense, for in such a case there is in the psychological sense no subject in the picture. I cannot go into this large topic here except to note my general doubts about the claimed ontological as opposed to conceptual-epistemic nature of Heidegger's *Zuhandensein* entities, which after all are human artifacts constructed in terms of collective acceptances (at least as I see this matter). This latter point, if right, would seem to make his account similar to both Sellars' and Wittgenstein's ideas and would hence also resemble my present account.

This section has shown that collective pattern-governed behaviors form a central element in the "Background" abilities and skills required by collective intentional activities (cf. Searle, 1995, chapter 6). The background needed in the present theory, of course, must contain the standard elements, beliefs, and presuppositions that any account of intentional activities is based on (cf. Searle's list in the mentioned work and notice that there is nothing resembling *pgb*s in his account; also cf. section 3.6 below). This background is also what a rational agent must take for granted when acting.

3.6 ARE SOCIAL PRACTICES REQUIRED FOR CONCEPTUALITY?

3.6.1 General background theses on conceptual activities

In this section the problem of the *criteria of correctness of rule obeying* and, more generally, the *criteria of correctness of concept use and conceptual activity* will be briefly investigated. Especially central will be the question whether social practices have a conceptually central role in accounting for conceptual activities. In what follows I will concentrate on *language use* as the prime example of conceptual, activity. However, also inner mental states can be conceptual, even if they need not literally involve language use. Furthermore, the use of any propositional representational system capable of expressing elementary logical relations and reasons will do. Thus, nonlinguistic higher animals become candidates of beings capable of conceptual activity. To avoid clumsy qualifications I will, however, mostly speak only of language use below.

Here are some central general theses and presuppositions concerning conceptual activity and language use that will be elaborated and defended in what follows:

(1) Conceptual activity in its full-blown sense (such as exemplified by speech acts) is intimately based on language use – or is itself language use. (However, there is elementary nonlinguistic conceptual activity; recall section 3.4 and cf. thesis (2) below.)

(2) Solitary language is in principle possible. That is, language without social construction of content is possible, although such language *cannot* be *full-blown* language in the sense the contents of linguistic items in a social language are. Thus, there are conceptual activities, although somewhat rudimentary in nature, in the case of which conceptual contents are not socially constructed but are largely based on the causal contribution of the external world (cf. primitive perception of shapes, color, movement as examples).

(3) Language is commonable ("public"; cf. Pettit, 1993, for commonability), viz., language users must be able to use linguistic phrases in a way that is in principle accessible to anyone in the linguistic community. This applies not only to our social natural languages, but also to all human languages including solitary ones. Private languages in the strong sense Wittgenstein discussed them are not possible.

(4) Social language (viz., language used in a community of people) is the standard case – and indeed its sociality is what our standard concept of natural language noncontingently entails. This kind of full-blown language involves, both on conceptual and on causal grounds, the social construction of content, where, for example, social speech acts such as giving and asking for reasons, commanding, and informing require such social construction of content. In this case, a kind of "negotiation" model explicating the processual aspects of content construction in the case of conceptual activities is required. This will entail that in such cases the contents of thought are socially constructed.

(5) The correctness of rational concept use and conceptual activity in general requires (entails) the following on conceptual grounds:

(a) Conceptual activity in the full human case must (both in the conceptual and causal sense of "must") in general be based on social practices of a suitable kind (although "in general" allows also for nonsocial construction of certain kinds, e.g. perceptual contents). These social practices will have to involve the exchange of reasons between the parties of communication concerning the topics in question and will affect not only the truth of the statements and claims made, but also the meanings of the concepts used (hence the correctness of concept use). Conceptual activity here concerns the use of language in communication and in thought. In the latter case we are, of course, dealing with the conceptual and linguistic aspects of thinking.

(b) The correctness of conceptual activity requires in the full case (with the exceptions indicated above) that there be some interaction-based consensus among the people in the linguistic community in question as to what correctness in each case involves. (Which particular words to use requires such consensus in all cases for an optimal result.) We may speak of *implicit* negotiation here, as explicit negotiation may be too strict a requirement. Such implicit negotiation need not even be expressed in language in all cases, and it can be based on social sanctions rather than "official" sanctions, but it still needs to be reason-based. It is assumed to lead to some degree of agreement, thus making the use of language and communication functional. A unique, fully shared agreement in the community concerning concept use is a desideratum, but communication and thinking may be sufficiently functional (concerning the success of communication) also without it.

(c) Concept use must be, and can be, accounted for in noncircular terms.

(6) There are various factual capacities, conditions, and preconditions that successful and correct conceptual activity require – see below.

In chapter 6 I will discuss social institutions. In that context it will be seen that:

(7) Language as used in a linguistic community is a social institution (in a general sense, viz., (a) or (b) in the classification of chapter 6).

Of the above theses and assumptions, (1), (2), (3), and (5) are conceptual assumptions that underlie the present treatment. Thesis (4) is a partly factual, "dynamic" thesis that will carry a heavy burden in my overall argument; thesis (6) is a kind of factual presupposition; and (7) is a conceptual philosophical thesis (to be discussed in chapters 5 and 6). (Contrary to the Background in Searle's sense, the above assumptions need not be made by the agent whose conceptual activities are being discussed.)

Let me next comment on the commonplace background assumptions about human beings related to thesis (6). One central assumption is that human beings as language users must have the capacity to use symbols, viz., the "symbol function." It is the general and initially nonspecific capacity to symbolically represent things by means of language, thoughts, and other similar means (also overt meaningful action). The representations represent something distinct from themselves. Accordingly, people have the ability to understand the basic idea of ostension (e.g. "this object is a ball"). As a consequence, they are also able to create new concepts and ideas in the context where the environment cooperates. We can also say that the symbol function is the capacity to create new meanings and to impose new "satisfaction conditions" on items that already may be representational and have some kind of satisfaction conditions (cf. Searle, 2001, and below chapter 5, note 2). The full capacity of imposing conditions of satisfaction on conditions of satisfaction seems unique to human beings, as far as we know. This mainly biological capacity makes for the conventionality of language. In the case of natural human languages, communication is, of course, a central element (although above I have downplayed it and emphasized the more fundamental representational aspects of language). The need for communication can be assumed – at least there are good instrumental reasons for this assumption. Communication requires a language with public and publicly ascertainable meanings (uses) of representational items (Pettit, 1993, speaks of "commonable" meanings and concepts in this connection). Such a language is social in the sense of being usable by a community of people.

We can say that a central social aspect of the symbol function is given by the existence of speech acts such as assertives, directives, and commissives. Part of this is represented by the kind of social "performativity" capacity to be discussed in chapters 5 and 6. There I will speak of the kind of "collective acceptance" of an item that creates a new conceptual status to the item. For instance, to mention my paradigm example, a collective of people may collectively accept that squirrel fur is money, and thus give a new conceptual and deontic status to squirrel fur.

Another factual background assumption that we need here is the commonplace that human beings are social and are disposed to cooperate and act in groups. We have learned from biology and ethology that such factors as "kin altruism" and "reciprocal altruism" can ground cooperative behavior in animals. In the case of human beings, we think somewhat similarly but in more general terms that people are social. This sociality is a many-faceted thing, which involves at least that people on the whole need, and enjoy, the company of other human beings. This kind of dependence can be intrinsic (sociality as an irreducible basic want or need) or instrumental (related to features like self-respect, honor, pride, etc. or to various things that they want to achieve but cannot alone achieve). What is highly relevant for the purposes of this book is the feature of sociality that people in their thinking and acting tend to take into account what others think and do (recall the analysis of we-attitudes in chapter 2). Thus others' approval and disapproval of one's ways of thinking and acting form an important motivational element, and all this induces an element of conformity and cooperativity (at least "harmony") into human life in a social context. Furthermore, this sociality feature serves to ground the need for communication and we-mode activities (see below, section 6.3.2).

Needless to say, for the aforementioned capacities to become realizable, there must be the right kinds of social environmental influences. They include teaching language use and conceptual thinking by parents and other educators, and such teaching is assumed to lead to the successful learning of skills and linguistic knowledge. All this presupposes that we are dealing with sufficiently normal human beings from a biological point of view: they must have the right kinds of basic needs – such as hunger, thirst, sex, security, curiosity, power, sociality – and the elementary behaviors needed for fulfilling them.

3.6.2 Elaboration and discussion of the theses

Before discussing the above theses in more detail, I will sketch a programmatic, "baby-level" account, expanding on section 3.4, which should make more plausible my general claim of the need of social practices for rational conceptual activity.

A baby has certain basic needs, and it learns by means of its reflexes and due to its parents' teaching to satisfy those needs. Here pattern-governed behaviors arise and are further developed through training and education. The baby's behaviors rely on genetically based pattern-governed behaviors – e.g. some of its bodily movements, such as directing its head and sucking, needed for the satisfaction of its primitive needs. Biologically developed behaviors and, especially, dispositions to behave – we can speak of "adaptations" here – and training (environmental influences) work together to produce "basic" actions (routines), which either are or involve pattern-governed behaviors as their elements. A psychologist can be expected to give an account of how such basic activities develop – referring to evolution, perhaps, and to various environmental factors including teaching and learning (especially social learning, imitation). In section 3.4 I argued for the following developmental order of explanation of conceptual activity from weak conceptuality to strong conceptuality: (1) functionally meaningful nonlinguistic thinking and action → (2) linguistic thinking and action → (3) mental states as inner episodes and action based on them. Level (1) is central for my present account and its function is to present a level of human (and other) activity that is meaningful but need not involve conceptual thinking on the part of the behaving organism.

We do not really need here the details of the above account, but only its final output – that people acquire certain basic skills, an action repertoire, for doing things in various circumstances. These basic actions and skills are Wittgensteinian blind actions. So we would arrive at the result that there exist such "buck-stopping" basic skills, as they stop ontological regress and circularity on a token-by-token basis in the sense of section 3.3. Thus there could be meaningful actions and practices that do not factually require (further) rule following for them to be teleologically meaningful. In this sense we would have a factual criterion of correctness for the action or practice in question. Actually the requirement of meaningful blind actions seems not to be necessitated at all. If there are such intentional blind actions, that is fine. But, after all, they are not required on conceptual grounds. The situation could be more holistic or, so to speak, "coherentist." There simply might not be any intentional actions that do not conceptually require other actions or other rule following. Here (collective) pattern-governed behaviors will help. For even if they are (or were) always embedded in suitable kinds of actions in the conduct sense, they would make the system functional. The underlying requirement is that people should be naturally so equipped (due to evolution and learning) such that they are able to exhibit the pattern-governed behaviors (e.g. the elementary directed movements) that make the system run, so to speak.

Thus, it would not matter if there were holistic conceptual circularity of the kind that all conceptual acting entails at least the dispositional or "presuppositional" presence of some other conceptual activity. Being anchored in *pgb*s, our bionic machine (the organism) would be able, so to speak, to compute its program (especially the conceptual psychological part of that content, comparing the conceptual framework of agency to a program).

Nevertheless, neither of the above ways of dealing with the conceptual circularity problem entails a general conceptual or philosophical criterion of correctness (applying to types and not only to tokens of actions). In

more or less full-blown cases of rational conceptual activity, people base
their thinking and acting on reasons, and in those cases we can make use
of "games of giving and asking for reasons" (emphasized by Sellars and
Brandom; see below). Here the conceptual centrality of social practices
for advanced cases of conceptual thinking and language use can be seen.

To discuss criteria of correctness, I will first consider social institutions,
such as money, language, and property. Their creation and maintenance
clearly involves special conceptual activity. I advocate the philosophical "nonsolution" line in the general case, viz., I do not assume that *on
conceptual grounds* there has to be shared agreement or collective acceptance of what is – and what is not – correct concept use, even if consensus
would be arrived at on factual grounds. However, in the case of social
institutions I claim that the negotiation model (or, as some theorists say,
communitarian agreement) can give a satisfactory philosophical solution due to the "performative" creative powers of people. (Whether they
indeed exercise those powers is, of course, a factual problem.) In this
case we can start from the view that people and perhaps some higher
animals have the symbol function and are able to create new concepts
and ideas. Here we can speak of performative creation, borrowing a
term from speech act theory. Thus, the familiar device of performative
christening is an example of the creation of a new conceptual and symbolic item (here a name) by means of the use of language. We are here
dealing with collective acceptance and creation of a new symbolic status for some entity. This is *social* and *collective performativity*. For instance,
that squirrel fur is money (money not only in the barter sense but also
in the "fiat" sense) can be created in this way. Squirrel fur then gets a
new conceptual, social, and deontic status as a result. We have thus a
social criterion – indeed, both a sufficient and a necessary condition –
of correctness in terms of collective acceptance for a concept here. Collective acceptance is both necessary and sufficient for institutional facts
such as that squirrel fur is money (see chapters 5 and 6 for detailed
discussion).

The case of language is analogous. The members of a collective might
decide that "abracadabra" is to be their new word for squirrel money
(or whatever). Joint decisions are of course to be obeyed in order for the
right results, viz., correct concept use, to occur in a nonaccidental way.
Furthermore, there is the (contingent) social requirement that they be
sanctioned, that is, either approved of or disapproved of. The next step on
our way to a weaker account is to imagine that there is no joint decision
but only a weaker kind of collective agreement or consensus that is the

outcome of some kind of negotiation process or, more generally, a suitable communicative interaction process (whose precise nature can be left for communication theorists and social psychologists to study). Instead of actual agreement making, it suffices that people have internalized and act on the idea that they ought to think and act as if there were a contract. This idea can plausibly be regarded as a shared normative we-belief. It can be suggested that it is a kind of *meme* which is spread by means of imitation and teaching, and so forth. The so-achieved consensus or collective acceptance results – or may result at any rate – in the same actions and dispositions to act relative to the collectively created things such as squirrel fur money. The action here is maintenance and renewal action, perhaps correction, too.

In the general case my model gives only necessary conditions for the correctness of language use, but is still rich enough to generate a relevant ought-to-be rule: people ought to have such and such action dispositions (know-hows, skills), and they ought to be able to appropriately use these skills. I also assume criticizability, which is already built into the negotiation model in the idea of exchange of reasons for claims. People are thus assumed to be prepared appropriately to criticize and sanction each other's actions. Sanctioning can in principle be pattern-governed behavior (or it can be a mixture of *pgb* and intentional action). Basically, people are assumed to have been trained and educated in such a way that they spontaneously think that a response is right or wrong – in the case of social rules and norms – and also utter their thoughts and perhaps non-intentionally perform (verbal or nonverbal) sanctioning actions on the basis of their taking the response to be right (reward, approval) or wrong (disapproval, punishment).[10] Note that the correct use of language and criteria for it are things different than the correctness of conceptual activities such as perception and other cases in which conceptual activities are at least partly naturally (nonsocially) determined. However, social institutions and other related social cases (thus also the conceptual contents of institutions, for instance) are "totally up to us." There are also mixed cases, but I will not here try to botanize them.

This, then, is my sketchy preliminary account of the primacy of action and blind action, especially if we assume that the realization and maintenance of the above kind of ought-to-be rule in the community is based on training and learning resulting in its first stages (in the case of children, for instance) in pattern-governed behaviors. We have here an account of both rule following and the correctness of language use and other conceptual activity. If people indeed act according to the negotiation model and the case is one in which it is up to them to decide about conceptual contents, this account accordingly also gives a "social-performative" justification for the normativity of action. My account can be taken to yield collective acceptance of what is the right way of thinking and doing things for the discussed situations (including e.g. social institutions). Accordingly, I will speak of the Collective Acceptance (CA) model (see chapters 5 and 6) and take it to include the negotiation model as its central component. In the case of rational people and rational conceptual activities, the negotiation model is a game of giving and asking for reasons (cf. below).[11]

Let me further elaborate on some of the mentioned points, discuss the tenability of the theses presented at the beginning of section 3.6.1, and state finally what the Collective Acceptance model really has accomplished for the case at hand. As such, theses (1)–(7) serve as a sort of *background theses*, rather than properly defended theses, in my present treatment.

The first thesis presented in section 3.6.1 claims that conceptual activity is intimately based on language use or is itself language use, for example, in the sense of Sellars' analogy theory of thinking. This thesis is needed to broaden the discussion of language use to conceptual activity in general and especially to conceptual mental episodes. I will here accept this conceptual assumption without further discussion. As stated, this thesis concerns full-blown conceptual activities and is compatible with the existence of less than full-blown nonlinguistic conceptual activities.

The second thesis claims that the existence of an (essentially) solitary language is possible. The third thesis claims that a language must, nevertheless, be commonable on conceptual grounds. The fourth thesis makes nonsolitary (viz., social) language the standard and the full-blown case. Indeed, it is de facto the only type of case of natural language we know of. This excludes Cartesian private languages. Theses (2), (3), and (4) hang together to the extent that they can be fruitfully commented on together.

Language is commonable ("public"), viz., it is required that language users be able to use linguistic phrases in a way that is in principle accessible to anyone in the linguistic community. This entails that personal languages must be translatable into a commonable basic language or be intertranslatable in terms of similarly accessible "translation manuals." Communication of conceptual thoughts in general is not possible without a commonable language, and the same point holds for language teaching. (Ought-to-be rules for novices such as children and their counterpart ought-to-do rules for language teachers can be placed in this context.)

Personal commonable languages that are used by totally isolated single language users are also possible to a somewhat limited extent. Thus, a totally socially isolated person can have a personal language, use it in his thinking and even communicate with himself on different occasions (e.g. write memoranda to himself). That is fine as such, but such a language always seems to be based on a preexisting, commonable language (and indeed necessarily is, if Cartesian private languages are impossible).

In the solitary case, one and the same human being can be thought of as metaphorically not only one but many language users (or "temporal slices of himself") or, perhaps rather, as the player of different roles in language games. Thus, he may ask for reasons and give them, he may even in a restrained sense issue orders and obey them, and perhaps even, as a highly problematic limiting case, make insincere promises to himself. He may thus have to face the hard task of taking on roles with different epistemic statuses (e.g. questioning and answering) or different authority statuses (commanding and obeying). Here the person in question must not only be playing different roles, but must also socially (causally as well as informationally or epistemically) interact with himself (his earlier and later selves) on different occasions. However, assuming that in the case of a standard natural language the language users indeed have different social perspectives due to their different histories (and whatnot), the personal (viz., one-person) language we are talking about here is rather limited, because it is based on the social perspective of only one person. Even with the mentioned limitations, we can still take the isolated personal language to be based on the social practice of giving and asking for reasons. Thus, solitary language use can be an activity which belongs to "the logical space of reasons and of justification" (as discussed by, e.g., Sellars, 1956, and Brandom, 1994).

However, social language (viz., language used in a community of people) is on contingent grounds the standard case and indeed the only case in the actual world, as far as I know. As said, in the general case we use the negotiation model for constructing contents of thought, as the different social perspectives on content have to be reconciled somehow. This can happen by people doing it intentionally (e.g. by making agreements based on negotiation) or by there being a suitable causal process, which, without collective intentionality, leads to a sufficient amount of consensus (e.g., via some kind of invisible hand mechanism). Explicit negotiation is not needed, but some kind of corrective procedure and sanctioning, be all this based on intentionally performed actions or not, are required. All this entails that the contents of thought are socially constructed and collectively accepted in general. This is not only a contingent matter, as there are social speech acts that necessarily require many participants, and in such cases the social construction of conceptual content is required on conceptual grounds. There may be partial exceptions to the contingent part of my thesis – for example "dictatorial" cases based on coercion – but even here we can speak of social construction to some extent.

According to my thesis (5), the correctness of rational concept use and conceptual activity in general requires that rational and correctly performed conceptual activity must rely on a suitable kind of reason-based social practice that involves interaction in the sense of the negotiation model. These social practices will thus have to involve the exchange of reasons between the parties of communication and will affect not only the truth of the statements and claims made, but also the meanings of the concepts used (hence the correctness of concept use). This is a refinement of the collective acceptance idea and the accompanying dynamic negotiation account leading to collective acceptance. As indicated, Brandom (1994, 2000) has presented a version of such an account – viz., the game of giving and asking for reasons. His central assumption is that "a performance deserves to count as having the significance of an assertion only in the context of a set of social practices with the structure (in Sellars' phrase) of a *game of giving and asking for reasons.*" This assumption I take to be basically right for full-blown language use. However, one has to notice that it is a very strong assumption that serves by itself to make all language use and conceptual thinking social. Games of giving and asking for reasons are central in the case of the social construction of content, but there seem also to be cases of giving and asking for reasons, for example cases concerning the nature of the nonsocial world, in which the contents of thoughts are in part externally determined (think of a person perceiving a red, hard surface, for instance). More generally, as argued earlier, there are cases of conceptual activities involving at least partly a natural, nonsocial construction of content. Furthermore, in contrast to what Brandom's account requires, one can argue that weak kinds of intentions (e.g., spontaneous ones) and beliefs do not involve commitments to their contents.

As noted, a community of language users or of "linguistic roles" is conceptually necessary for commonable meanings and, hence, for communication in many cases, such as social speech acts. As Brandom has emphasized, different social perspectives must be involved in games of giving and asking for reasons. Similarly, I make the assumption that language users have only "finite" perspectives (e.g., there is only a finite number of reasons they can invent for justifying a claim) and that their perspectives – although they must be assumed to be overlapping – are in general more or less different (cf. here Bloor's, 1997, "meaning finitism"). The finiteness of language users' perspectives entails that a commonable language (especially commonable uses of language) can be achieved only as a suitable mixture and perhaps as a "compromise" of the various social perspectives involved.

All this fully applies to the cases that are "up to us" (and to which the Collective Acceptance account of chapter 5 will be argued to apply). In these cases, meanings and in general the correctness of rule following and of rational activities are, or can be, conceptually based on games of giving and asking for reasons. This view is grounded, firstly, on the idea that rationality must involve reasoning and, so to speak, moving around in the logical space of reasons. Secondly, it is grounded on the finiteness of perspectives assumption, and, thirdly, on the requirement of a commonable and sufficiently common language (or conceptual representational system, more generally). As also Brandom might say, the correctness of language use and of conceptual activity in general depends on people following norms, which are in turn based on and largely constituted by games of giving and asking for reasons. Such games or practices can be viewed as social practices based on shared we-attitudes (cf. chapter 4). For instance, I participate in the language game of questioning and answering when I act either in the role of a questioner or that of an answerer and believe that you do similarly in a role complementary to mine and also believe that this is mutually believed by us; and analogously for you. However, we must add that in order not to violate the noncircularity criterion, it seems that collective pattern-governed behaviors must be present in some cases (recall section 3.3). They are not by themselves conceptual games of the kind we are talking about here, although they may be "elements" of such games (collective social actions) in the sense discussed earlier.

Commonability requires that the language users can understand – and use – ostension to the degree that they can speak of the same kinds of things and the same kinds of properties of things (and so on, whatever that exactly involves). They can thus form at least partly the same *de re* beliefs about things, although they may attribute different properties to those things. Thus, if one language user has an ostensive *de re* belief about a rabbit and another one of undetached rabbit slices, these two language users can communicate about the same thing via a shared translation manual ("rabbit" in the first user's sense is a composition of "rabbits" in the second user's sense). (Cf. Brandom, 1994, 2000, for this kind of use of *de re* beliefs, although I do not assume that this can give more than a necessary condition of the objectivity of contents in general.)

Clause (c) of thesis (5) says that the normativity criteria for language use and conceptual activity should not lead to a vicious regression and claims that this criterion indeed can be fulfilled. Such a regression is avoided, if using language correctly – and, more generally, having the conceptual thought that something p is the case – need not in all cases be based on doing something (usually something else) on the basis of the intention to satisfy a relevant criterion or standard of correctness. This problem was earlier basically solved by means of activities or skills that people perform as pattern-governed behaviors, and I refer the reader to earlier sections of this chapter. There it was argued that psychological circularity can be avoided by means of *pgb*s and that while conceptual circularity exists in the full-blown case, there are elementary cases of conceptual activity that are conceptual (meaningful) in a functional sense – which, furthermore, is presupposed by the full-blown cases.

One of the factual presuppositions (assumption (6) above) was that people need to communicate with each other by means of their representational systems. Their reasons may even be intrinsic, but on the other hand there are many instrumental reasons to support this claim. (I will not here consider the evidence for (6) in detail.) Then, assuming that the difference in social perspectives matters for conceptuality and assuming also the tenability of all the other constraints incorporated in the theses or assumptions made in the beginning of this section, the negotiation model can lead to a socially constructed commonable and common language and indeed will plausibly do so. This is mainly because it is a rational outcome to be striven for. On the other hand, even if people do not rationally aim at such consensus, it may come about, as it were, by means of an invisible hand process, given the guidance of the agents' need to communicate (recall my earlier remarks to this effect).[12]

3.7 CONCLUSION

Perhaps the most basic conclusion of the present chapter is that there are central cases of activities in which the conceptuality of the activity is socially constructed and constituted. These cases include advanced cases of thinking and communication – such as activities that are based on giving and asking for reasons. However, there are primitive cases involving nonlinguistic animals and prelinguistic children where conceptuality is not socially constructed and analyzed in terms of rules of language. Even if full-blown conceptuality cannot be understood independently of rules of language, the primitive cases of conceptuality show that at least in some cases the psychological and conceptual regress problems can be avoided. This kind of evolutionary foothold into objective conceptuality was accordingly emphasized in this chapter. The considerations relating to primitive conceptuality also support the view of the importance of *collective* pattern-governed behaviors – over and above other background factors – as grounding conceptual activities. Later, especially in chapter 4, these kinds of behaviors will be shown to be important elements of social practices, especially routine practices and customs.

An account of social practices

4.1 INTRODUCTION

Social practices are often spoken of in social science literature, but I have not found comprehensive conceptual accounts of them in that literature (with the partial exception of the elucidations by the sociologists Giddens and Bourdieu).[1] In philosophy, the recent rich book by Schatzki (1996) contains interesting discussions and can be recommended.[2] In this book I will, however, make a fresh start. The basic idea is that social practices in their core sense are activities performed for social reasons of a certain broad kind, viz., shared we-attitudes (either in the I-mode or in the we-mode). My approach has as its starting point the philosophy of social action and it is quite different from previous work in this area. Using the terminology of chapter 1, the nature and role of social practices is crucially central for arguing both for the "wide" and the "narrow" constructivist programs in my sense.

The phrase "social practice" is used in many different ways, and social practices will form a very broad category of activities. For instance, there are work-related institutionalized practices. These include banking practices and teaching practices of various kinds, as well as practices for building sailing boats or violins. These practices typically involve specific and widespread techniques or ways of doing things. Accordingly, there are skills embedded here and thus better and worse ways of performing the activities constituting the social practices. Various standards may accordingly be involved and many (but not all) social practices can be rated according to the internal excellence standards involved (cf. MacIntyre, 1985). This also applies to "properly" social practices, viz., practices performed for social reasons, whether or not they are related to work or are important for the "external" ends they purport to achieve. Examples are practices performed in part because of a fad or fashion, customs, and traditions (e.g. celebrating New Year's Eve, bathing in the sauna on

Saturday afternoons, the tempi used in playing music at various historical periods).

I will below develop an account of "core" social practices that is meant to cover all social practices carried out at least in part for a social reason (roughly, because others are doing it and expected to do it, or because it is somehow socially important for the participants). Social reasons here can be explicated basically in terms of (shared) we-attitudes. Social practices of this kind are central because there is then, so to speak, a conceptually in-built social ground for the activities in question. This presupposed ground need not appear in the participants' deliberation and reflection. When it does, we typically are dealing with the agent's motive or disposition to conform to what others expect of him (in a descriptive or normative sense). However, the conformity idea is in the underlying ground, and thus the participants of a social practice may be at least to some extent also motivated by a nonconforming motive, for example the motive to distinguish oneself; cf. section 4.4. I will call a social practice performed for a we-attitude a social practice in the core sense or a *core social practice*. Customs and traditions will be argued to be or involve social practices in the core sense. My account concentrates on intentionally performed core practices, which also include activities that have become routine and skill-like. I will also briefly consider social practices in weaker senses, which only require social awareness (belief) of what is being collectively done or involve a shared goal such that the sharing need not be mutually known.

My approach to social practices accordingly relies on the notions of we-attitude and collective social action, both understood in a specific sense. Put in other words, social practices conceptually and causally depend on collective intentionality. Thus, they are in an important sense man-made and man-maintained. When claiming that collective intentionality is central for social practices it is important to distinguish between two different senses of collective intentionality. Firstly, we have the general sense, in which collective intentionality means collective representation or collective aboutness (or "meaningfulness" in a conceptual sense). Secondly, we have the specific conduct sense of collective intentionality, in which a collective or joint action is collectively intentional. This is the sense requiring that the participants performed the action in question in some sense collectively on purpose and jointly controlled the action. Each social practice in my core sense will have to involve collective intentionality in the first sense, but not necessarily in the second sense.

Before proceeding to a detailed discussion, let me summarize the basic arguments for the importance of studying social practices that were considered in chapter 1. These arguments of course concern any field of research aiming at a correct description and explanation of social life.

(1) As argued in chapter 3, social practices can be regarded as the central elements of "forms of life." They are conceptually crucial in that they – or rather some fundamental kinds of them – can be intrinsically meaningful activities. Most centrally, it was argued that the concept of correctness of such activities as rule following and in general rational conceptual activities crucially depend on the social practices of the community in question. As shown in chapter 3, this "weakly communitarian" view can be used to argue also that language – or rather language use – is conceptually prior to full-blown conceptual thinking (even if thoughts – as propositional states or events – may be argued to cause action).

(2) Social life centrally contains recurrent social activities – social practices such as business practices, educational, religious, and political practices – as everyone knows from personal experience. Social practices, thus, are part of the domain of investigation of social science. This includes the study of multiagent systems in artificial intelligence, insofar as it attempts to capture – even approximately – the important aspects of the social world.

(3) As many sociologists have argued, social practices are factually central for the creation, maintenance, and renewal of social systems and structures. Giddens' (1984) structuration theory can be cited as perhaps the foremost current advocate of this approach.

I will start by giving a brief exposition of the notion of a collective social action in section 4.2. The concept of core social practice will be conceptually built out of the notion of collective social action. Section 4.3 gives my basic account of social practices, and section 4.4 presents a number of central theses on core social practices and defends these theses. Section 4.5 discusses "presuppositional" reasons and "routine" practices. Section 4.6 focuses on some further kinds of social practices.[3]

4.2 COLLECTIVE SOCIAL ACTION

What kinds of collective social actions are there? Can we somehow carve the social world at its joints to achieve a workable classification of collective action? I have elsewhere tried to provide a detailed answer to these questions and have created a kind of map of the territory of collective social action (see Tuomela and Bonnevier-Tuomela, 1997, from which I will draw below). I will here present a brief introductory sketch of my earlier account – the reader will be referred to the mentioned paper for arguments, further distinctions, and illustrations.

Our common-sense framework uses a great variety of social and collective notions related to action. Thus, some persons can be said to perform joint actions, act together, act in concert, act collectively in pursuit of a goal, cooperate, struggle against each other, and so on. To begin with, I will list a number of representative examples to be clarified by means of the analytic framework to be created.

Consider thus the cases described by the following sentences.

(1) Some girls are buying a mini-skirt because practically every girl in town is wearing one this spring.

(2) Finns go to the sauna every Saturday.

(3) We are crossing the street on the green signal.

(4) Dinner guests bring flowers to the hostess.

(5) The two of us are going to a concert, given that the other one will be going there.

(6) When walking in the street I (like other people) try not to bump into others.

(7) I am trying to fill a big hole with sand (there have been many accidents because of the hole); you show up, too, and start acting similarly.

(8) We conserve energy by lowering the room temperatures in our houses.

(9) I am now cleaning this yard together with you.

(10) We are singing a duet together.

All of our examples have to do with collective social action (cf. chapter 5 on "collective-social" features). Here "collective" entails, roughly, that several persons are somehow involved and "social" entails that the actors' reasons for acting must somehow take into account other actors' thoughts or actions, even if perhaps in a codified – e.g., institutional – form. Below I will classify tokens of collective social action, such as the above examples, into different categories by means of some variables which seem to me conceptually crucial. Only collective activities consisting of intentionally performed actions will be considered here. Furthermore, the emphasis is on "distributed" collective actions by noncollective agents as contrasted with actions performed by groups (see Tuomela, 1995, chapter 5 for the latter).

A collective social action can be characterized by means of an action predicate such as "imitating other people," "making a carnival happen," "conserving energy," "cleaning the yard," "joint singing." I will deal in principle with all kinds of conceptually possible collective action predicates and assume, as usual, that the extensions of action predicates can be given by a (possibly highly culture-dependent) criterion or rule of use associated with the predicate. The application of the criterion shows which singular collective social actions qualify as satisfying the predicate and which do not. We can speak of the criterial features in the actions by virtue of which the action predicates correctly apply or fail to apply to them. These might be called the conceptually in-built criterial result events or states.

Collective actions are actions involving several agents exercising their agency. Joint agency or collective agency (at least in a strong sense) is not needed, however. The weakest possible kind of collective action consists of spatial-temporally connected actions by actors who perform an action of the same type – think of people going to lunch at the same restaurant independently of each other. Recall here also Weber's case of people simultaneously opening their umbrellas when it starts to rain, where each actor has as his private personal reason that it is raining and that he does not want to get wet. The actors are not socially connected in the sense we require, for they do not open their umbrellas even in part for the reason that the others do so. These actors could even share the mutual belief that each one is opening his or her umbrella, but as long as this is not a (partial) reason for one's own action, we are not dealing with a collective social action.

What makes a collective action social, thus, is that the agents must be socially connected in the right way. In the present context the idea of social connectedness can simply be taken to be explicated by the notion of acting in part for the same social reason. Reasons will here be understood in a broad sense as states of affairs or "contents" (cf. Searle, 2001; Tuomela, 2000b). Having a reason is having a suitable attitude (e.g., want or belief) towards this reason (content), and acting for such a reason entails realizing the attitude towards the reason. In order for a reason to be a person's motivational, action-guiding reason and for him to act for that reason it must obviously enter and be processed by him in his intentional cognitive system. Accordingly, we here deal with reasons from each agent's intentional horizon and pick out the effective social reason within it. Thus the reasons for which the agent acts will in the present account be believed to exist and, in order to keep things simple,

I will normally assume that they are also objectively existing (viz., that the beliefs are correct). While one may have as one's private social reason for one's action to impress others, here we are after the notion of the *same* social reason. When some agents act for the same social reason in the context of collective social action, they must believe that the others act similarly or act for that same reason (which may be a social fact or state of affairs) and generally also believe that this is mutually believed among them. When acting for the same social reason the participants' component actions can, however, be of different kinds.

Consider example (1). The members of a collective, for example, the teenagers in a town, dress in similar ways, for example, wear mini-skirts. This is a collective social action performed for the shared social reason of wanting to wear similar clothing. For the reason to be social the agents must believe and in part act on the belief that the other girls are acting similarly and are mutually aware of all this. Imitation in the primitive sense of "I do X because you do X" is possible without beliefs about others' mental contents, except possibly that the others are performing X intentionally.

The different case of the girls wanting to distinguish themselves and, instead, dress differently from each other could also be a collective social action, if they accepted the idea of dressing differently and having the right social beliefs about it. However, some girls might not act on the social belief that the others are dressing nonconformingly and might even want to dissociate themselves from any group thinking, be it conformist or nonconformist from a more general point of view. Rather, they would just perform their individual actions based on their possibly different personal goals. This kind of social behavior is of course very common, but it is not collective social action. Next, suppose all of us (perhaps regularly) perform a kind of action (e.g., eat plenty of fiber each morning or go to the sauna twice a week) for the reason that "one should do this." This (and the involved "we") need not be social, the "should" can be merely an instrumental one. All of us could act for this reason, but the resulting collective action would not be social. It would be social only if each participant's reason for acting would be in part that he (correctly) believes that others are acting in the same way or for the same reason.

The agents' component actions in a collective social action may be dependent on each other or independent in a kind of game-theoretic sense. The essence of dependence is "necessity" in the sense that it is necessary for a participant to take into account the other's actions for an optimal or satisfactory achievement of his goal. The social reason might even be constituted by the dependence as viewed (believed) by the participants. Thus, in the "walking in the street" example (6) of collective action the agents may be said to act for the social reason (we-belief) that they are in a specific way physically dependent on the other agents – or at least believe so. In a situation of dependency of this kind one cannot leave the situation except by giving up the whole setup. Note that there are two ways of becoming dependent: one can voluntarily make oneself dependent in some cases (instances of interaction situations including, e.g., joint action), but in some other cases the dependence is somehow externally imposed, for example due to the physical demands of the situation (cf. example (6)).

I restrict my account to intentionally performed component actions (actions performed for a reason) and basically add the requirements that the reason must be the same and must be socially connected via the agents' beliefs. These features give the unity to collective social action that is needed. Whatever private goals and reasons – in addition to the required same social reason – the agents may have when acting does not affect the treatment. My explicative thesis is that having a social reason amounts to having a we-attitude in the sense of chapter 2.

Consider an example related to the familiar fact that an action can be individuated in several different ways. If a person is crossing a street (where crossing is required for him to reach his goal) his social reason may be the norm that one should cross if (and only if) the green light is on (cf. example (3)). Believing that this is a social norm in force in his collective, he intends to cross the street on the green light and, believing that it now is on, starts to cross the street. (There is a myriad of similar examples in which different social norms come into an agent's psychology, depending on the specific "governing intention.") We describe the component actions, such as street crossings, of a collective action in terms of their "largest common reason" so that the result-state is a state satisfying the shared social reason in question, thus something like having crossed the street on the green light, as one should do. The social reason is the point or the rationale of the action type. This social reason must be (at least) a part of the full reason for which each participating agent acts when performing his component action. This also gives a psychological and social psychological limit to what kinds of conceptually possible social reasons people act for in actual life.

The notion of an individual or single action as opposed to a collective (or many-person) action satisfies the following obvious necessary condition: it is at least conceptually possible that a single person can satisfy the action predicate in question; in the case of a purely individual action any of its tokens must be performed by a single agent. This is compatible with a single action's being factually dependent on other persons' actions. When we say that a collective social action is composed of or consists in single-agent actions the only connecting feature in the most general case is the sameness of the social reason for which each agent performs his component action. The agents normally have to be aware of their social reasons as in the case of any intentional action.

Let us still consider our numbered examples to get more insight into the variety of social reasons and actions. In example (1) the actors have a social reason for acting, that of imitating each other. Thus each person performs his action partly because the others are doing it (and because they do not want to be different or act differently). Social imitation is a powerful incentive, as we all know, much of social learning (including language learning and the learning of social norms, practices, customs, and traditions) being in part based on it. Social imitation (in the intentional sense, which is our main concern here) is typically based on the desire to be similar or to act similarly to others. Thus, in our example we can say that the girls have the same social, other-involving reason for their action. In stronger cases of social imitation there can be a social norm reinforcing imitation (e.g. "Use clothing similar to what other young people wear in distinction to what members of the older generation use"). The people involved may or may not have a shared or a mutual belief that the others are also analogically imitating each other or some "reference persons." (Of course, trying to be distinguished and different from others can also be an important motivational factor; cf. section 4.4 below.) Case (2) is concerned with taking part in a traditional institution. Examples (3) and (4) differ from the previous ones in that the participants in the collective actions in question base their actions on a social norm (in the case of (3) on a law, thus "authority-based norm") and in the case of (4) on a "proper social norm" (see chapter 6 for the notions).

While in examples (1)–(4) the actions of the participants are independent in the sense of being performable independently of what others do, in the rest of our examples the actions are dependent on other agents' actions. Thus in (6) the agents' actions are causally dependent or at least believed to be. Their goals are to avoid bumping into the other one. In (5) the other person's performance of an action basically is a social reason, in some of its instances even a necessary and sufficient condition, for the other person's action. Action dependence here is thus "self-imposed" as against case (6) with its "other-imposed" and physically based dependence. In case (7) there is a goal related to a bounded physical state – the road being repaired – and the participants' actions are connected by this same goal, which they share in a weak sense. Example (8) can be understood similarly, but it can also be understood in the stronger sense of involving a collective goal requiring that the people in question believe that they should all be involved in the joint project of conserving energy. Examples (9) and (10) concern respectively a (weak) kind of acting together and joint action. I will not here comment on them in detail, as the focus of the present chapter is on weaker kinds of social action.

In Tuomela and Bonnevier-Tuomela (1997) a classificatory schema for collective social action is created such that the degree of sociality ("social glue") involved in collective action increases when moving higher up in the schema. It was argued that all intentional collective social actions can be fitted into our typology. Before presenting the schema, a remark on the kinds of sociality is due. Two kinds of sociality can be distinguished. First, there is group-based sociality or "g-sociality." By g-social thoughts and actions we can mean thoughts and actions conceptually and causally affected by social groups or group features – such as norms or general behavior expectations. Group action and other group features (assumed to be things that one is not in this case in face-to-face contact with) are part of the presupposed framework of agency and serve to "constitute one's social world" both conceptually and causally, and – what is central here – may in addition also causally affect one's actions through one's mental states. Accordingly, one's thoughts are socially laden in a conceptual sense, and they also causally depend (via one's mind) on group features. Social structures, institutions, and norms are of course involved here, as are social values and traditions. Agents can be socially connected in the sense of acting for the same g-social reason. Secondly, there is individual-based sociality or "i-sociality." Roughly speaking, if what you think and do affects my actions and thinking we say that the latter are i-social. More precisely, my actions and mental states are i-social if the mental states or actions of other particular individuals with whom I am in face-to-face contact or in a causal relationship causally (or causal-conceptually) affect them. The agents taking part in a collective action may be socially connected in the sense of acting for the same i-social reason (sameness possibly allowing for permutation of individuals).

It is worth emphasizing that the framework of agency also concerns various structural group notions and institutional notions in addition to notions related to single agents. Social institutions are norm-based and created by collective acceptance, and are constantly getting renewed and possibly reformed through people's collective activities (see chapters 5 and 6). Money, language, and principles of justice (e.g., ownership rights) are general g-social institutions, as are institutionalized religion, politics, and education. There are also g-social phenomena, such as various fads and fashions, which are less stable.

To proceed to my basic classification of collective social action, it explicates the social connectedness involved in the kinds of collective action under scrutiny in terms of the notion of the same social reason. The classification schema is claimed to be capable of handling all collective social action in the indicated sense. The schema makes some simplifying assumptions. For instance, it concentrates on intentional cases and cases in which the agents are in a symmetric position (although this is not a limitation in principle of the account). The classificatory scheme consists of three main classes of collective action, termed classes A, B, and C. These classes are disjoint and also meant to exhaust the field. Within these main classes or categories there are subclassifications, which I will not discuss in the present sketch. The first main category, A, is concerned with collective action consisting of independent personal action and is capable of dealing with examples (1)–(4). The catchword here is commonality. The second main category, B, concerns collective action consisting of mutually dependent personal actions (by two or more persons), and is meant to deal with cases such as our (5)–(8) (I-mode mutual dependence). Category C is important in that it concerns cases of acting together (examples (9) and (10)). This category deals with proper jointness. It includes both rudimentary cases and more complex and more full-blown cases of acting together. The strongest subcase in category C is concerned with cases that can be termed joint action in the fullest sense, viz., joint action based on an explicit or implicit agreement by the participants to act.

What are the social reasons serving to define the collective social actions in these categories? A person's having (and respectively acting for) a social reason in the discussed criterial sense amounts to his having (and respectively acting because of) a "we-attitude" (at least in a rudimentary or in a weak sense). Some persons' having, and acting for, the same social reason accordingly amounts to their sharing, and acting because of, the same we-attitude.

I now claim this:

(i) In category A the social reason involves a shared undivided goal (viz., a goal which has not been divided into parts). More precisely, the social reason is the content of an undivided shared we-goal (in a weak noncollective sense, without we-mode).

(ii) In category B the social reason is based either on a mutual dependence belief, viz., a we-belief about dependence, or on such a we-belief plus a shared divided we-goal in the I-mode.

(iii) In category C the social reason is basically a shared intended collective goal to act together (a shared we-mode we-goal), with entailed action dependence.

As argued in chapter 2, a person has a we-attitude (for example, a desire) in the core sense (relative to his group) if and only if he or she (i) has (or shares) this attitude, (ii) believes the group members have it, and also (iii) believes that there is a mutual belief that the members have this attitude. A shared we-attitude (viz. content) is a shared social reason for which the agents perform the actions that constitute the (intentional) collective social action in question. The reason need not enter the agent's conscious reasoning, but may function as a kind of presuppositional and unreflected ground serving to characterize the very activity in question (cf. section 4.3). But even in such a case it will have some, albeit perhaps minimal, motivational power.

To make a point about cooperation and harmony, consider still another example. People may share the we-goal of putting lit candles in their windows on Independence Day: each agent's (or, perhaps family's) goal is to light candles and each such agent believes that the others in the community also share this goal (and, let us also assume, share it in part because of the others having that goal) and that this fact of sharing is mutual knowledge. The people then satisfy their shared we-goals by lighting the candles and putting them in their windows. They act collectively in part for the social reason that all the others put lit candles in their windows. Acting on the shared social reason will yield some collective harmony (in goals and actions) and that action can be regarded as weakly cooperative. In general, this holds for analogous cases as long as the participants' goals and preferences in the collective social action are not incompatible. While collective social action excludes major conflict, it still need not amount to cooperation or deserve to be called "cooperation" as such, for the participants need not be connected in the right way. In the Independence Day celebration case there is sufficient connection to give us a case of cooperation in the sense of coordination related to the agents' (private) goals, for the agents in this type of case take into account what the others are doing and, in principle, are prepared to adjust their actions to others' actions (e.g., if the time of lighting the candles is changed due to some sudden mutually known fact requiring social attention). However, there are similar cases in which there is not enough dependence. It used to be a custom in at least rural Finland to take a sauna bath every Saturday afternoon. Even if it were mutual knowledge among Finns that everyone thus goes to the sauna, this would not yet create cooperation even in a weak sense. But if their reason for going to the sauna were in part that others also go (so that they also would not go unless the others go), we have an element of cooperation or "harmony" involved, as the participants take other participants suitably into account (e.g. sharing means with them) even if sharing a collective goal in a full sense need not be involved. However, people acting merely in order to reach the same kind of goal, perhaps mutually believing that they do so, does not suffice for even this kind of individual-mode cooperation.

To summarize, the present account of collective social action gives three basic kinds or categories of collective social actions (CSAs), viz., actions performed for a social reason (a shared we-attitude). The first category is characterized in the following terms: collective social action consisting of mutually independent single actions performed in part for the same social reason. Examples would be people lighting candles on Independence Day or girls buying (and wearing) a mini-skirt at a certain point in time. The second category, one that involves action dependence, is characterized as follows: collective action consisting of mutually dependent i-social single actions performed in part for the same social reason. An example of this kind of CSA would be people walking in a crowded street and suitably adjusting their movements so as not to bump into each other. The third category, which also involves action dependence, is: strong collective action consisting of acting together (with action dependence and a shared collective goal). Examples would be carrying a table jointly (plan-based joint action) and villagers keeping the streets tidy (shared collective goal which need not be explicitly agreed-upon). An institutional example would be people cashing checks at a bank teller's window. Figure 1 illustrates the classification scheme.[4]

4.3 WHAT ARE SOCIAL PRACTICES?

I will now present my central account of social practices; this is done in part by formulating some general theses about social practices. The point of this exercise is, of course, to try to achieve a better understanding of what social practices are from a conceptual point of view. It is, however,

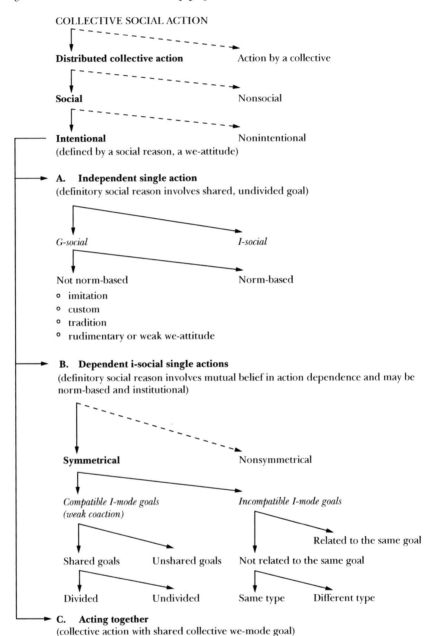

COLLECTIVE SOCIAL ACTION

Distributed collective action   Action by a collective

Social   Nonsocial

Intentional   Nonintentional
(defined by a social reason, a we-attitude)

A.   Independent single action
(definitory social reason involves shared, undivided goal)

G-social   *I-social*

Not norm-based   Norm-based
o imitation
o custom
o tradition
o rudimentary or weak we-attitude

B.   Dependent i-social single actions
(definitory social reason involves mutual belief in action dependence and may be norm-based and institutional)

Symmetrical   Nonsymmetrical

Compatible I-mode goals   *Incompatible I-mode goals*
(weak coaction)
        Related to the same goal
Shared goals   Unshared goals   Not related to the same goal
Divided   Undivided   Same type   Different type

C.   Acting together
(collective action with shared collective we-mode goal)

Fig. 1 Collective social action

helpful to begin by considering examples that are somehow representative (be they cases of institutional or noninstitutional practices).

As pointed out already in chapter 1, cases of social practices include (repeated) questioning and answering and other similar speech acts involving at least two people and, more generally, doing something together recurrently (e.g., cleaning the house together once a week). The "games of giving and asking for reasons" (emphasized by Sellars and Brandom; cf. chapter 3) can be regarded as social practices, for the participants share the intention to repeatedly take part in the shared activity, negotiating or otherwise exchanging reasons for action or thought. Furthermore, institutionalized social practices are central as well (cf. greeting by shaking hands or, more generally, greeting in the way it is done in a certain group). To take another example, part of a group's reason to clean the house every Saturday (a social practice) may be to meet the general cleanliness standards or expectations in the surrounding society.

Social practices consisting of joint actions based on joint intentions are common. The joint intention and the relevant mutual beliefs involved in repeated joint action will serve as a shared social reason to act, and this reason establishes a strong kind of social connection between the participants. (The reason need not be primarily motivational, but may rather be a presuppositional reason, to be discussed in section 4.5.) The participants here have a social reason to take part if they have somehow arrived at a joint plan or shared we-intention in a weaker sense to repeatedly act together. In the general case, there may be complex actions involving coordinated acting on a shared plan (cf. Tuomela, 1995, chapter 3; Sandu and Tuomela, 1996). In this kind of case the we-attitude will be an intention to realize a joint plan involving a general policy, viz., an intention to realize the plan recurrently (or according to some specific schedule). Then the joint plan is a plan for a social practice, and its satisfaction will consist of a sequence of performances of collective social actions.

Another kind of an example is provided by Kuhnian paradigms, taking them to be "exemplars" showing how to operate, for example, when making measurements and observations in a laboratory. Such paradigmatic exemplars also serve to generate social practices, viz., acting in accordance with the paradigm and the social awareness in the group concerning it (cf. Kuhn, 1963). Furthermore, customs (such as wearing a certain kind of a dress or eating certain kinds of food on suitable occasions) form a typical case of social practices. I will argue that they are core social practices.

We can say generally that doing something repeatedly for a shared social reason (basically for the shared reason that others are doing it and expect everyone in the group to do it) qualifies as a social practice, whereas mere repetitive doing of the kind of thing in question would not suffice for a social practice (even if it may causally induce the habit of performing the action in question). This brings up the idea that social practices must have a cooperative aspect that shows up as conformity (although it need not be based on the agent's conscious motive to conform). The conformity in action is in part due to the nature of the social reason operating here, viz., a shared we-attitude. Acting on a we-attitude involves that what others are doing or thinking affects a person's action in the conformity sense that she will to some extent act (and think) similarly. In addition to this kind of conceptually presupposed conformity, there may also be conformity in a psychological sense, and this may be due to the participant's personality trait related to conformity that has become activated (e.g., due to his perception of what the others are up to) and/or it may be due to social pressure due to the other's normative expectations. Nevertheless, the motive or disposition of conformity need not be involved, as long as the discussed conceptual presuppositions of the social practice are satisfied.

As to the more general case of social practice in which no acting together (or "joint" action of any kind) is needed, we may consider fads and fashions. For instance, some girls may want to buy the latest fashion dress just because others are buying it. There is thus a shared social reason related to what others are doing or thinking, and this social reason serves to make a (repeated) action social in the sense required of social practices in the full sense. Let me emphasize that the social reason must involve that the others' thoughts or actions are reasons for one's action in a social practice (in the core sense), even if the participants need not consciously think of them. A custom – the social counterpart of an individual habit – is an example of an activity which is typically routine action. (We may say that in routine practices reasons for action have also become routine, viz., the reasons are routinely used without resulting from deliberation and strategic calculation.) If the people simply happened to share the same goal (e.g., take a walk at a certain time or to go for lunch to the same restaurant) or belief (e.g., that it is starting to rain; cf. Weber's umbrella example) and they took this goal or this belief to be a central part of their reason for action, that would not yet make the practice a properly social practice. Thus, if these agents would not do what they do even in part because the others are doing the same thing, then they would not share the same social reason, and their repeated activities would not constitute a social practice.

The phrase "social practice" is sometimes used in a more general sense to cover cases where people recurrently do a certain thing without doing it even in part because other people do it or think that that activity is the thing to do in the circumstances in question. Let us consider in more detail Weber's case of people opening their umbrellas (or, if a more elementary case is wanted, seeking to cover themselves in a certain way from getting wet) when it starts to rain. Here we have a case in which many people do the same thing in the same circumstances, but they need not be doxastically connected in a reason-based sense. By their not being relevantly doxastically connected I mean that even if they perhaps know full well that the others also are doing the same thing (viz., opening their umbrellas) they might not care about what the other people are doing. In fact, they do not act for a relevant social reason at all. Thus we do not have here a social practice in the core sense.

As already noted in chapter 1, for something to be a (collective) practice there must, furthermore, be a conventional element involved. The acceptance and the performance of the practice must be up to them, both in a collective and individual sense. For example, people use conventional means to keep dry when it rains. Thus, they do not try to rob other people of their overcoats so as not to get wet, nor do they take off all their clothes so as to keep their expensive clothes dry. These people could have found some other way to keep themselves dry, but they did not. Here we have a conventional element which serves to make the recurrent umbrella use a practice, although not yet in the core sense.

There are practical collective activities that resemble the original umbrella case but are somewhat more social. These often involve the use of social artifacts – implying social functions and uses – or a mutual awareness of others acting similarly. For instance, people recurrently brush their teeth, get on the bus at a specific time to go to their work, go to the same place for lunch, and so on. These activities are collective activities and some of them are institutionally based collective activities and for that reason also at least minimally social activities. For instance, people taking the 7:30 a.m. train to Helsinki every weekday morning to go to their workplace are engaged in conceptually institution-dependent social activity. They do not perform their actions because the others are doing so. However, unless they were living in the present kind of society and working in Helsinki they would not do what they now do, the explanation for this being that the society is institutionally organized in such a way that people work somewhere on a daily basis with more or less fixed working hours (etc.). This makes the social activity a conceptually (as opposed to merely causally) institution-dependent social activity. If you like, these kinds of activities can be called social practices in the weak sense. However, at least a minimal social element such as a shared or mutual belief about the activities in question is required to mark the difference between plain collective practices and weak social ones (cf. below). We may want to coin phrases like "conceptual infrastructure" (codifying conceptual presuppositions) and "normative infrastructure" (codifying underlying normative presuppositions, ought-to-be, ought-to-do, maybe, and may-do norms of various kinds). As seen, even social practices in the weak sense may depend on a conceptual and even on a normative infrastructure, and those kinds of infrastructures may factually depend on the existence of a suitable material infrastructure (e.g. roads, buildings, telecommunication facilities, etc.).

Independently of the question of the normative infrastructure of social practices we can consider whether there need to be norms to participate in a social practice once it has been formed and whether the very contents (viz., the collective social actions involved in the practice) are normatively grounded. The answer to both questions is negative. For instance, the social custom in Finland of eating *mämmi* at Easter (or pea soup on Thursdays) is not normative in either sense. Thus there is no social norm obligating people to eat this dish, and the activity of eating it is not governed by social norms. (Of course, there is the weak normativity concerning whether one's activity is or is not correctly describable as eating *mämmi* and, more interestingly, also concerning whether eating *mämmi* is the appropriate thing to do at Easter and is not appropriate at other times.)

As said, the core sense of a social practice is a repeatedly performed collective social action (CSA) because of a certain shared we-attitude, where the we-attitude must be a "primary" reason for the repeated activity, one without which the agents would not take part in it. For example, the actions involved in a social practice such as the practice of (repeatedly) avoiding bumping into others when walking on a sidewalk might have arisen as actions based on strategic thinking (cf., "I have to move right in order not to bump into that pedestrian"), but the primary reason for the resulting social practice, for example the custom to walk on the right-hand side of the sidewalk, would be a we-belief (with the content that others in general intend to avoid and avoid bumping into other people by walking on the right side and that this is mutual knowledge). The we-attitude is a conforming reason while the other possibility would be the strategic reason concerned with maximizing one's utilities relative to what the others are expected to do. The strategic thinking "allowed" by the we-belief would concern how to coordinate one's movements (bodily actions at the "zero-order" level) so that bumping into others ("first-order" level) is avoided. The kind of strategic thinking that could be involved here, assuming the existence of the aforementioned custom ("second-order" level), is calculation and deliberation concerning whether to act in accordance with the custom or not. However, the we-belief in question excludes this way of reasoning.[5]

How can the weaker cases of social practices be classified and analyzed? A social practice in the weak sense can be regarded as a practice performed with but not for a shared we-attitude (not even in the presuppositional sense to be discussed below). In these weak social practices (in the present technical sense) each participant performs a certain kind of action purely individually but with awareness (and indeed mutual awareness) of what the others are doing. What might be termed an "ultraweak" social practice would be one in which there is no mutual awareness but only a plain belief that the others are doing the same thing or whatever is at stake. Brushing one's teeth in the morning falls within the category of a weak (or perhaps ultraweak) social practice. Social practices presupposing institutions like taking the 7:30 train to Helsinki in the mornings are practices codified by rules of suitable kinds. Such codified institution-dependent practices can from the participants' point of view be weak social practices and I-mode activities. However, the institutional design underlying this kind of practice may be regarded not only as an institutionalized recommendation to act recurrently because of a shared we-attitude, but as a recommendation to do it even in the we-mode, although here we are speaking of "because of" primarily in a presuppositional sense that typically does not require conscious reflection of the matter.

There are, in addition, recurrent actions performed for other-regarding reasons which are kinds of social practices. Thus, the practices of using a deodorant or a lipstick every morning or driving with one's Mercedes on the main street in the evenings yield a minimally social practice in which the believed "positive" social effect of one's individual effort makes the action social. The social reason here, however, although under a certain description it is the same, is not a shared social reason in the sense required by social practices in the core sense, nor need it involve the belief that others are doing the same thing. The collective practice here consists of individual practices with certain intended social effects.

In this book I will concentrate on the core sense of social practice. To repeat, social practices in the core sense are activities which (a) involve many people and which (b) are performed at least in part for (viz., because of) a shared social reason (here, a shared we-attitude). Furthermore, (c) the we-attitude must be a primary reason for the activities involved in the practice. Point (a) I take to be obvious. We must require that several people are actually involved and not only believed (e.g., by a certain participant) to be involved. Point (b) is central and point (c) has already been commented on. I will discuss it below in more detail and also qualify it to some extent. The obvious point may be noted here that the activities involved in a social practice may occur at different places and at different times. This is no problem, as the bond assumed to make the activities elements of a social practice is a shared social reason – which need not pose any spatiotemporal limitations, except in special cases. Furthermore, social practices of course can involve task division. This applies especially strongly to rituals and ceremonies. I will not press this point in the following discussion and will often speak as if the participants were taken to perform actions of the same type.

The we-attitude sense gives the full meaning of a social reason, and a (repeated) collective activity performed for this kind of collective reason is a social practice in the full sense, or so I will argue. However, another sense of sociality was mentioned above, namely sociality in the sense of conceptual dependence on institutions. This sense, which often only yields weak social practices, will also be discussed below. (Normally people must have this institution dependence at the back of their minds as something presupposed when acting, e.g., getting on the 7:30 a.m. train in our example.)

To emphasize the significance of core social practices, let us still consider the following example. What does the social reason amount to in the case of several people buying a Mercedes in part for the reason that others are also buying one? In speaking of we-attitude content we now use the so-called reason version of a we-attitude. Thus: I buy my Mercedes for the reason that (I believe that) the others buy one and that (I believe that) it is a mutual belief in the group that the members will buy (or have bought) a Mercedes. This case is to be contrasted with the case where I buy my Mercedes in order to be able to brag about it. Suppose that you and I both buy a Mercedes in order to brag. However, our reasons here need not be connected at all. The reasons are of the same type, to be sure, but that is not enough. They should be socially connected in order to give a shared social reason. But they are not, because I do not have any belief about your buying a Mercedes or, if I have it, it is not my reason for buying a Mercedes. Only if I buy my Mercedes in part because (I believe that) you have bought one, and if the same holds for you, do we have the required kind of social reason. Thus, while bragging does serve as a social reason for both of us, it is not the kind of shared social reason we need to take into account in our present context.

In other words, strong social practices are in the present account related to collective social actions (CSAs) and understood as repeated CSAs (recall section 4.2). Let me further illustrate the view of social practices as repeated CSAs in terms of our earlier example. Suppose (a) it is our goal to celebrate the Independence Day of Finland and that (b) we all believe that others in the group share this goal and that (c) we believe that there is a mutual belief in the group about the existence of this goal. Our goal to celebrate the Independence Day is a we-goal, and it is a we-goal in the reason sense if (b) and (c) form a partial reason for (a). The social reason here thus is our goal to celebrate Independence Day in part because of the assumed fact that the others also have the goal to celebrate Independence Day and that this is a mutual belief in the group. This characterization can obviously be extended by analogy to cover all attitudes.

We can in fact categorize social practices using the same categories as in section 4.2 above. Their application to the case of repeated CSAs gives these – here more briefly formulated – descriptions:

(1) repeated independent actions performed in part for the same social reason (*commonality*)
(2) repeated dependent i-social actions performed in part for the same social reason (*I-mode mutual dependence*)
(3) repeated acting together performed in part because of the same social reason involving joint intention or intended collective goal (*we-mode jointness*)

In accordance with our discussion, the same social reason is to be understood here in terms of the same shared we-attitude content (cf. the qualifications made in section 4.3.2). The earlier examples of CSAs in the various categories can be used here for illustration when the assumption of their repetition is added. It is, of course, assumed that the social reason stays the same (or more or less so) over time for the participants.

Before proceeding to a more detailed discussion of social practices in the core sense, a couple of remarks are due. As social practices as repeated CSAs depend on we-attitudes, we can consider the question of how we-attitudes are formed and expressed in artifacts. This is a very broad question, and I will not try to answer it here, except to make some simple points. What I wish to emphasize is that much of the environment in modern technological communities consists of human artifacts. For instance, houses, chairs, spoons, cars, and traffic lights are dependent on social institutions and practices, which determine their functions accordingly. Similarly, what kinds of food and clothing (etc.) are available at stores may depend on social practices determining demand. We may figuratively say that artifacts (or artifact-involving states) accordingly incorporate or reflect we-attitudes because of this presupposed feature. Such a presupposed, often codified we-attitude will also to some extent tend to motivate people when they are in the right circumstances. For example, a red traffic light can be taken to presuppose the following kind of we-attitude: I believe that I should stop and I also believe that others in this situation believe so (some of those others similarly face a red light, while some others – coming from a different direction – face a green light), and I also believe that it is a mutual belief that I should stop (while those coming from another direction and facing a green light should drive on). Notice that the mutual belief part is needed: suppose I only believe that you – coming from the other direction – believe that I should stop, as I am facing a red light. Then you might still not believe that I believe that I should stop on red, and you might consequently hesitate to drive on even if you are currently facing a green light. The we-attitude of course need not actually figure in the agent's conscious thinking, although it must be to some extent also his guiding reason (see section 4.5).

More generally, it can be said that the artifactual parts of our environment form a kind of (epistemically) objective conceptual infrastructure that is supposed to function at least as a conceptual presupposition or set of presuppositions for us qua thinking and acting cultured and social beings. Persons who have truly internalized these notions will also actually think and act accordingly, for example form the right kinds of contextual we-attitudes, such as those discussed above in connection with acting in institutionally regulated traffic conditions.

As to problems of genesis, CSAs and social practices often seem to arise "memetically," viz., due to people imitating some special agents who enjoy popularity. For instance, the practice of going to the market to sell one's goods or the custom of going to the sauna on Saturday afternoon may have been initiated by a certain group (perhaps a very small group), and others have collectively accepted this by imitating them. Fads and fashions such as wearing a certain kind of hat or some other piece of clothing may have arisen due to imitation. Imitation involves a conformity aspect, as does of course acting on the basis of a shared we-attitude. Fads (including intellectual ones) are social practices – at least when they are sufficiently stable; I will soon discuss them in more detail. Many customs, such as taking off one's hat when entering a building or eating a special dish at Christmas, also belong to social practices that may have arisen and become widespread because of imitation. Some of the more instrumental kinds of imitation may be only weak kinds of social practices. Thus individuals in a certain Stone Age tribe might have manufactured their stone axes (or baked their bread, prepared their meat, etc.) in a certain way on the basis of solely the instrumental reason that a certain procedure will produce a desired result.

4.4 THESES REGARDING CORE SOCIAL PRACTICES

4.4.1 The basic theses and their defense

Related to the idea that (shared) we-attitudes drive much of human life, we can also claim importance for social practices in the core sense (cf. chapters 1, 3, 6 in particular, in addition to this chapter). To discuss the latter in more detail, we distinguish between activities such as social practices, which are in the I-mode, and those that are in the we-mode. We can use the rough-and-ready criterion for we-modeness discussed and elaborated in chapter 2, according to which a social practice is in the we-mode when collectively accepted by the group for the "use" of the group, assuming also that the group is committed to the social practice in question. Note, too, that in the case of a we-mode social practice the social reason (we-attitude content) serving to partially define it will have to satisfy the analogue of the Collectivity Condition (*CC*) formulated for any we-attitude content.[6]

Consider now some simple but central theses about social practices. To begin with there is a thesis explicating the notion of a core social practice.

(1) X is a social practice in the core sense if and only if X is a repeated CSA (collective social action).

Here, repeated CSA is taken to be a sequence of CSAs, viz., a sequence of collective actions performed because of a shared we-attitude (thus for a shared social reason). Going to the sauna every Saturday afternoon (a ritualized practice in the rural parts of Finland) during a sufficiently long period of time – years, decades, etc. – would constitute such a sequence. Similarly, the custom of having a morning swim at one's summer cottage is equally a social practice of this kind. Briefly, a sequence of CSAs means CSAs repeated over time and possibly in different places under relevantly similar circumstances. Consider now the following subtheses: (a) if X is a repeated CSA, then X is a social practice in the core sense; (b) if X is a social practice in the core sense, then X is a repeated CSA. Of these, (a) would seem acceptable, provided that social practices can also be in the I-mode (which clearly is possible). (b) is acceptable too, but its analogue dealing with social practices in the weak sense fails, for, as I pointed out above, social practices in this wider sense allow for repetitions of the participating individuals' actions (such as brushing one's teeth in the morning) that are not performed because others do so, too.

In this line of thought, I propose that we regard (1) as true and as definitory of the notion of a social practice in the core sense (the sense involving the right kind of social connectedness). I will concentrate on this notion, in part because I find the wider notion rather uninteresting, at least from a conceptual and philosophical point of view.

The following theses – taken to deal with conceptual possibilities in the first place – also seem true.

(2) There are both (a) we-mode social practices (in the strong sense) and (b) I-mode social practices (in the core sense).

(3) (a) There can be no we-mode social practices in the weak sense, but (b) social practices in the I-mode are possible also in the weak sense.

(4) Each we-mode social practice requires collective acceptance of the social practice in question in the sense that the group members collectively accept that it is correct or appropriate (in a deontic sense) for the group members to perform the social practice (or, better, the activities that it consists of). In addition, the members must be collectively committed to upholding the practice in the we-mode case.

(5) All we-mode social practices are normative in the weak sense of correctness or appropriateness (e.g., it is correct even if not obligatory – at least without further qualifications – to go to the sauna on Saturday or to eat *mämmi* at Easter). (This thesis is entailed by (4).)

(6) There are both normative (in the strong sense) and nonnormative I-mode social practices.

(7) The strongly normative practices are by definition based on social norms (not always on proper social norms in the sense of Tuomela, 1995, chapter 1) that are in force and in general involve not only obligations to act but also permission to act. Thus, permission to play soccer on the pitch on Sunday afternoon is the intended norm; there is no obligation to play soccer, of course. The strongly normative social practices are weakly institutional, because they involve norm-governed, recurrent activities (cf. sense (a) of institutions of chapter 6). (In addition to social norms in force, we may have normative practices based on norms which may not yet quite be in force but are still typically observed by at least some people in the community.)

(8) There are I-mode social practices in the weak sense that are conceptually institution-dependent (and thus in this special sense normative) even if they need not be normative in the mentioned weak "correctness" sense (cf. thesis (5)) or in the strong norm-governed sense (cf. thesis (7)).

(9) There are actions that are not elements of social practices and do not conceptually presuppose the existence of social practices of any particular kind.

(10) There are weaker versions of core practices obtained by weakening the social reason, viz., shared we-attitude, for which the practice is performed.

(11) Customs and traditions (when also the latter are viewed as practices) are core social practices (but the converse is not true).

(12) Social practices may, but need not, be subject to "standards of excellence" and involve skills that are to be judged with reference to them.

Let us now consider the tenability of the above theses. On the whole, they are rather obvious, given (1). Thus (2) is true simply because a CSA can be performed either in the we-mode or in the I-mode fashion. The same obviously holds true of repeated CSAs. Thus, given (1), (2) is true. According to thesis (3) there can be no we-mode social practices in the weak sense. We recall that in the weak sense the doxastic social connections are rather minimal. However, in the we-mode case the participants collectively accept the practice as the right thing and are collectively committed to the activity in question. I take this to entail that they are performing the practice for the reason that "we are doing it," the we-thought here being explanatory of their action. This gives an argument for (3)(a). (3)(b) is obvious, as the I-mode does not as such require any doxastic connections. (Recall that we-attitudes need not be involved in this case.)

Thesis (4) is true basically on the grounds of (1). A we-mode CSA is based on collective acceptance. Here the plausible additional premise needed is that repeated CSAs in the we-mode must be based on collective acceptance. As repeated CSAs also are CSAs, then if CSAs require collective acceptance (which I will assume), social practices (repeated CSAs) in the we-mode require collective acceptance. (As to the "appropriateness" aspect in (4), see below.)

In thesis (5) the normativity comes from the CA model of collective acceptance (briefly considered in chapter 1 and to be discussed in detail in chapter 5): a sentence or proposition is accepted for the group if and only if it is correctly assertable in the context of group activities by the group members; and the group members are indeed collectively committed to relevant obligations and permissions. Accordingly, they are collectively committed to using an accepted sentence in appropriate contexts; for instance, they are committed to answering the question whether the earth is flat by an affirmative answer if the group in question is the Flat Earth Society. Here an affirmative answer is correct or appropriate, while a negative answer is not. This shows that social practices in the we-mode are normative in a weak sense.

As to thesis (6), I-mode social practices can be normative for instance when based on a proper social norm such as that one ought to take off one's hat when entering a house. This is (or can be, if the norm is in force) an I-mode social practice, as there need be no collective commitment to the norm in question. The norms are typically taught to the group members as children (or when they enter the group), and they need only have accepted the norm in a personal sense and be privately committed to it. (Normativity in the case of thesis (6) may be also due to prospective social norms that are not yet ingrained in the group.) As to nonnormative social practices in the I-mode, there are practices that are not (not yet or no longer) deeply ingrained in the group, and often such practices are nonnormative. For one thing, people may have learned to make roofs to their houses in a certain specific way or to solve some other practical problem by imitating others. This may amount to a we-belief concerning how to do these things and to accompanying action based on the we-belief and we-goal (concerning what the instrumental belief expresses a means to). Thus we arrive at a recurrent CSA, hence a social practice, which, however, is not normative. The Finnish practice (custom) of eating pea soup and pancakes every Thursday is another example of a nonnormative practice (although it can be regarded as normative in the weak sense of "appropriateness").

Thesis (7) is rather obvious, and the example cited in it already serves as an argument for it (also cf. the discussion related to theses (5), (6), and (8)).

Thesis (8) tries to capture a typical sense of norm dependence or institution dependence, which is different from (a) weak normativity in the sense of thesis (5), (b) strong normativity in the sense of thesis (6), (c) mere presupposition of underlying normative institutions, and (d) causal (or "instrumental") dependence on institutions. This conceptual institution-dependent sense was earlier illustrated by the social practice of taking the 7:30 a.m. train to Helsinki every weekday morning. This social practice is not – or need not be – (socially) normative in the weak sense. (An agent may conclude his practical reasons by "I ought to take the 7:30 train" relative to his premises, but that "ought" is a merely personal one, not one "for the group," which would be required even for normativity in the weak sense.)

However, note that institutions may of course causally affect people's social practices. Thus, we may suppose that in olden times going to the sauna on Saturday afternoon was practically the only possibility, as performing the sauna ritual was not possible during weekdays for lack of time, and Sunday was reserved for institutional religious and recreational activities. (Note that the sauna practice – as probably most social practices – also has an obvious instrumental function as an institution related to cleaning and hygiene.)

In defense of thesis (9) it suffices to cite a suitable example. Suppose I twist my arm in a certain unusual way and, responding to this, you do the same thing. We have socially interacted, yet we have not participated in any social practice, and there does not seem to be any particular social practice presupposed by our interaction. Here I am assuming that you spontaneously responded to my action, and thus you are not taking part in any general responding-to-other's action practice, which indeed does not exist.

Let us now discuss thesis (10) and the "rudimentary" core practices in which the social reason involved is not a full-blown shared we-attitude but only a "part" of a we-attitude (as to stronger, reason-based we-attitudes, recall section 2.3). To see what weakening possibilities there are, let me formulate a version of a we-attitude (WATT) about some specific content as follows:

(*WATT**) A person x has we-attitude ATT if and only if

(1) x has attitude ATT

(2) x believes that the group members or the majority of them have ATT

(3) x believes that it is mutually believed in the group that the members of the group or the majority of them have ATT.

In (3) mutual belief need not be analyzed individualistically as requiring that everyone in the group has the belief (that something p) if there is a mutual belief (that p). It suffices that mutual belief means that it is generally believed in the group or that the majority of the group members believe that p and have appropriate iterated beliefs. This and the additional relaxation of the content of the mutual belief that it need only concern the majority of the members gives suitable leeway for analyzing a number of interesting phenomena. Let me now consider some possibilities of weakening (*WATT**), which will result in respectively weaker kinds of social practices. (In my analysis I assume that the members of group g do not think directly in terms of we-attitudes, but rather in terms of the ingredients (1), (2), and (3).)

Consider thus all the logically possible, nonempty combinations obtained by omitting one or two of the elements in the analysans of (*WATT**): (a) 1 & 2; (b) 1 & 3; (c) 1; (d) 2 & 3; (e) 2; (f) 3. Of these, (a) represents a rather common situation. Suppose ATT is the attitude of having a goal. Then (a) says that x has the goal to achieve something, say p, and believes that also the others in the group or a majority of them have the goal p. This we-attitude is assumed to be fully or at least widely shared in the group. Now suppose that people "imitate" each other and have as their goal to attend a certain event, say a rock concert. This can be a case of (a). Speaking in general terms we might say that x's disposition to conform is activated by his belief, and he starts imitating others in the group. What is lacking in (a), as compared with the full case, is higher-order beliefs concerning others' beliefs. As a consequence there will be no acting on the basis of what others expect of one, thus social pressure in this sense is lacking.

Next consider (b). Here the belief that the others share the attitude or psychological feature is missing. This is possible in view of condition (3), for x could simply lack the belief that the others have ATT (toward p) while still believing that the other group members believe that the others have ATT. All or most persons x in the group could consistently believe that there is a mutual belief (e.g. in the sense that all the others iterably believe or that the majority iterably believe) that the group members have a certain goal or will do something without really believing that they themselves have that goal (or that they will do that thing). Notice, however, that case (b) is doxastically inconsistent if the mutual belief is analyzed in a strictly individualistic sense covering agent x himself, for then the base content in the mutual belief would be that the others have ATT, and x would have to believe that the others have ATT in order to be a participant in the mutual belief while still – inconsistently – lacking that belief (viz., this is a case of $B_x(p)$ and $-B_x(p)$).

Case (c) reduces to the nonsocial case and can immediately be omitted from consideration.

As to (d), it is a possible case even when the agent x is taken to believe that he has ATT if we use the mentioned weaker interpretation that (2) does not concern (1). More interestingly, we may here have a case where our agent x aspires to get ATT on the grounds that the others have ATT and are mutually believed to have ATT. Analogously, in the case of alternative (e) the fact that (2) is the case might activate x's disposition to conform. The final case (f) is psychologically close to case (b). Here, too, x might aspire to get ATT even if he does not assume that the others yet have it. This is possible especially if (the agent's belief about) mutual belief is taken to exert pressure to conform, for example when ATT concerns a certain goal or action. (The mutual belief could be a normative one, but it need not be to create pressure.) If, for instance, it is rumored that a new fad will be to acquire some specific object, this may motivate action and indeed create a social practice, even if nobody yet has performed the action in question. Buying the newest kind of skirt, car, CD player, could be the trendy thing which has the character of a social practice with the underlying reason expressed in case (f).

Theses (11) and (12) will be discussed in section 4.6. It can be pointed out here that there are social practices that give a new conceptual and social status to an item (e.g. activity) in a sense to be clarified in chapter 6 in the context of institutional practices. As will be seen, customs belong to them.

4.4.2 Fashions

Consider next an extension of this theory of core practices. I will start with an idea put forward by the sociologist Georg Simmel (1971) in his discussion of fashion.[7] According to him there are explanatory factors in fashion: the need for conformity and the need to distinguish oneself from others. For fashion both factors are required and a certain balance between them. This observation leads me to make some comments on social practices on the basis of the notions of conformity and distinction without assuming that they are needs. It suffices here to understand them as general pro-attitudes, which tend to be involved in social practices. Note that at least in the case of the want or pro-attitude to distinguish oneself we may consider it either in a purely personal sense (the typical sense) or in the sense that one qua a potential or actual member of a group seeks to distinguish himself.

I will distinguish between (1) the (or a) group of which a person actually is a member, (2) the person's (ideal) reference group (the group whose member he would like to be), and (3) the group or groups from which the person qua a group member of (1) or (2) would like to distinguish himself from. Group (1) can also be called a person's in-group while (2) and (3) may be and often are called his out-groups. Note that there is the special case that when one's in-group is the ideal reference group, the out-groups are groups from which one distinguishes oneself, supposing these out-groups are different from the in-group in a relevant respect. Groups are intensionally characterized here by means of the group members' attitudes. To keep things simple, I will concentrate on one particular reference individual and assume that he has one in-group (group of kind (1)), one ideal reference group (group of kind (2)), and that he intentionally concentrates on only one out-group (e.g. a "competing" group of kind (3)).

As to the example of fashion, it lies in the area of compatibility, although the mentioned two wants or "needs" sometimes are in conflict. There may be conflict for instance when a person, x, wants to conform to his own group but also wants to distinguish himself as an individual group member from other members of his group. Suppose now that agent x's in-group is g, his ideal reference group is g^*, and that the out-group from which he seeks distinction either as an individual person or as a member of group g is g^{**}. By the assumption that g^* is x's ideal reference group, he is disposed to do something X if he believes that the members of g^* would do X and that X is an "important" action in group g^*. Given such an X, there can be assumed to be a mutual belief in g^* that one should do X or that everyone in g^* does X, or at least it can be assumed that x believes that there is such a mutual belief. Accordingly, x might also do X in part because he believes that there is such a mutual belief in g^*. However, it may simultaneously be the case that x also believes that in g^{**} the thing to do is-X and (perhaps) that this is mutually believed in g^{**}. This represents a case of distinction of course, but notice that conformity and distinction are here strongly group-relative (and correctly so).

There are several ways conformity and distinction can operate in the present set-up. Conformity can be considered relative to the in-group g (which is the standard case) or with respect to the ideal group g*. For instance, x might conform to g qua a group member but as a private person might want to conform to g*. In fact it is a conceptual or near-conceptual truth that for some actions X, a member of g qua a member of g must be disposed to perform X on the basis of a shared we-attitude and possibly some collectively accepted (viz., in g) additional assumptions entailing or "implicating" X. It is equally a conceptual truth that when conforming relative to g with respect to an action X, a member, x, distinguishes himself from any out-group, hence also g**, supposing such an out-group is relevantly different (viz., requires not-X to be performed). On the other hand, to the extent that x is disposed to conform to his ideal reference group g*, he will come into conflict with what his actual group g demands in contexts where the demands of g and g* differ.

It is accordingly a conceptual truth of course that if there is conformity with respect to one group, g, concerning a certain social practice, then there will be a distinction relative to all other groups that differ from g concerning this social practice. However, it is central here whether all this relies on intentional action, viz., on whether the persons take both the conformity reason and the distinction reason or only one of them as their central reason for action. The conformity reason must always be there to some extent, given that we are dealing with a social practice in the core sense. But also the distinction reason might matter. Thus some group members may tend intentionally to distinguish themselves from out-group members (without caring much about conformity relative to their fellow in-group members) while some other group members may tend consciously to conform to their in-group (and not think much about out-groups).

The ideal reference group g* cannot be the same as the distinction group g**, but g* can be identical with g. There is also the possibility that g** is the same as g, and in such a case a person will be disposed to distinguish himself personally from his fellow group members and may come into conflict with the demands of g. Depending on the case, a conflict is not inevitable, however, for the person in question may be able to find a balance between the different elements. However, one may speculate that, qua a member of g he in many cases is not likely to be successful in the long run, because, as seen, the qua-locution implies conformity, and g may not ultimately allow for much variation. (Assuming collective commitment, acting as a group member amounts to as acting in the

[weak] we-mode while acting as a private person can be explicated as acting in the I-mode, all these locutions being taken relative to a certain group; recall the appendix to chapter 2.)

To conclude, the conforming reason was seen as more central than the distinction reason in the case of social practices in the core sense, although, behaviorally speaking, conforming actions and distinction actions are two sides of the same coin when viewed in the in-group/out-group context (we have X in g and, automatically, distinction from the assumed $-X$ in g^{**}). While there is this "automatic" connection (viz., conceptual truth) from a functional point of view, the actors need not act for that reason. When they act primarily for the distinction reason (the we-attitude to do $-X$), that reason seems mainly to have the function of explaining the conforming we-attitude to do Y, where Y is taken to be the relevant action exemplifying $-X$ and where X is the action performed by the out-group (or the group from which distinction is sought). How the agents weigh these reasons is of course a contingent matter beyond the scope of philosophical research.

4.5 PRESUPPOSITIONAL AND MOTIVATIONAL REASONS

4.5.1 Presuppositions and routines

My requirement has been that we-attitudes are a partial reason for the performance of core social practices. I would like to make this more precise by drawing a distinction (not a dichotomous one) between motivational reason and "presuppositional" reason. The qualification I now make is that the we-attitude content does not have to function as much more than a presuppositional reason. A presuppositional reason for an activity is conceptually presupposed by the activity in question and is psychologically something that need not, and typically or mostly does not enter the agent's conscious reasoning at all, as long as "things go well." As emphasized, even the agent's typical motivating reasons (which may be nonsocial) need not always be consciously entertained. The main philosophical distinction here is that a presuppositional reason is constitutive of the activity in question.

In the case of proper performances of activities belonging to routine customs, it even seems essential that the we-attitude contents – representing the element of sociality in the custom – are not reflected on (at least in general), and this applies both to motivational and presuppositional reasons. My rough slogan here has been that routine action can be, and typically is, based on routine motives (routine ways of thinking – wanting, wishing, believing, etc.). Such routine motives need not be focused on when acting, and in this sense they are also not in the agent's motivating consciousness. What I call presuppositional reasons function somewhat similarly. A presuppositional reason in the first place concerns (in a constitutive sense) what is being done and the participants' understanding of this.

Considering core social practices, let X be the activity (CSA) to be repeated in the social practice, for example X could stand for having a family lunch on Sundays, eating baked ham at Christmas, or having a regularly meeting study group for discussing research-related matters of common interest to the participants. Understood this way, X will typically be an activity that is instrumental for some further purpose. Thus our family may want to meet on a regular basis, and Sunday lunch will serve that purpose. Eating ham relates to olden times and to the idea of Christmas being an important festival. Ham was then a somewhat scarce commodity and suited for this kind of occasion, where serving good food was important. As to the study group, the idea resembles the family lunch – the researchers want to find a systematic way for conducting their discussions. So understood, X is or can be a means for some suitable end such that often the manner or way in which X is to be performed is central, too.

The notion of a core social practice is one that involves not only the idea of repeating X in suitable circumstances, say C, but also a social element; that is, the element which makes the practice, such as a custom, social. This element is the participants' true we-belief or, better, we-knowledge concerning the fact that X is repeatedly performed in C in group g. This shared we-knowledge, call it SWK, and its content give the concept of a (core) social practice (CSP): CSP(X) ↔ SWK(X is repeatedly performed in C in group g). A custom would be slightly stronger and involve a "touch" of normativity: the content would be "X is the way to act in C in group g" accompanied by "raised eyebrows" (but not necessarily stronger "sanctions") in the case of the performance of some X^* (distinct from X) in C.

The shared we-knowledge (content) shared by the members of g (perhaps with some exception, e.g. novices) need only be an unreflected presuppositional reason.[8] Do any other we-attitudes have to be involved in a CSP as conceptually required elements? Not as a general conceptual requirement, it seems. However, in the case of special kinds of CSPs, such as joint actions, shared we-intentions are a conceptual requirement.

The shared we-intention initiating such an action (e.g. the joint intention to have family lunch on Sundays) may have as its content the practice in question or its explicit content may be a related activity of some kind. Nevertheless, or so I argue, a we-intention-in-action concerning the practice action, too, must be involved.

In the case of routine practices there will typically be (collective and single-agent) pattern-governed behaviors involved. Insofar as the routine elements are nonintentional they will of course be *pgbs*, although they do not have to be *pgbs* in the strict Sellarsian sense. So, while it perhaps is conceptually possible to have a core social practice consisting only of fully intentionally performed collective social actions (e.g. basic actions by the participants), typically social practices, nevertheless, involve nonintentional *pgbs* (recall especially the examples of collective *pgbs* from chapter 3). In all, routine actions and *pgbs* are closely connected, as they tend to have *pgbs* as their elements.

Also a constitutive and unreflected presuppositional reason motivates, but need do so only to a minimal extent. Thus, when the agent's performance is conceptually wrong or incorrect, a normally rational agent is supposed to come to believe so, and this process (his acquiring that belief) is due to the causal functioning of the presuppositional reason. Figuratively, such a reason is a strange beast in that it generally remains in hiding when things go well and shows its head only when things start going wrong in the sense that what is being performed changes into something else. This is based on the fact that a we-attitude is an agent's dispositional state, and such a state need not become conscious at least very often (perhaps only seldom in the case of routine actions). We-attitudes can thus function as dispositional, "sustaining" causes. The relevant we-attitudes (e.g. we-beliefs) might in the limiting case be regarded as dispositions to acquire the we-attitudes, which themselves are dispositions. (Cf. Audi, 1994 for a detailed account of this in the single-agent belief case spelling out the relevant release conditions, assumed to be operative here.)

The present section has shown that social practices can be routine and based on routine motives. This involves the possibility that some such social practices are not only unreflected, but to a substantive extent subconscious, even if the agents must know what they are doing "under some description" and in this sense be conscious of the contents of their intentions and beliefs (although not necessarily of the fact that they have those intentions and beliefs). While in the case of routine actions the agent must be conscious of his surroundings, he need not focus on his performance of the routine action, and typically does not so focus, and he need not have reflective consciousness of his motives (beliefs, desires, intentions) nor of its being he who is acting. Thus he need not have manifest thoughts of the kind "I believe (desire, intend) that p" (where p is or is suitably related to X) nor "I am doing X here," where X is the routine action under a suitable description. When the agent is not focusing on X he may be doing it unconsciously (viz., not being explicitly conscious of performing X at all) and accept only afterwards that he was engaged in a practice (like scratching his head when lecturing or, to have a social example, a captain's "mechanically" greeting the people coming on board while being engaged in doing something else). Still, all these cases may well have been cases of intentional action, viz., of action performed on purpose. Routine actions typically are unconscious actions in the sense of not being focused on but typically they are not unconscious in the sense of being repressed (cf. Freudian cases like acting because of repressed hatred).

4.5.2 *Routines and the habitus*

My account relies heavily on the notion of a we-attitude and especially the notion of a we-mode we-attitude (involving a general notion of social position) and, because of this, it bears some functional similarity to Bourdieu's (1980) account. His central notion is the noncausally operating notion of *habitus*, viz., "a system of durable, transposable dispositions which functions as the generative basis of structured, objectively unified practices." However, a direct comparison is somewhat difficult to make, as my account relies more on the kind of conceptually parsimonious pragmatist philosophical background exemplified by Sellars (and Wittgenstein) than on the phenomenological background Bourdieu's views depend on (most notably the work of Heidegger and Merleau-Ponty). In view of the popularity of his theory, let me make a brief excursion to it.

Bourdieu's (1980) key concepts are habitus (a dispositional mental state) and social field. According to him, a field consists of a set of objective, historical relations between positions anchored in certain forms of power (or capital), while the habitus consists of a set of historical relations "deposited" within individual bodies in the form of mental and corporeal schemata of perception, appreciation, and action. "To speak of habitus is to assert that the individual, and even the personal, the subjective, is social, collective. Habitus is a socialized subjectivity" (Bourdieu and Wacquant, 1992, p. 126). According to Bourdieu the proper object of social science is

the relation between two realizations of historical action, in bodies and in things. It is the double and obscure relation between habitus, i.e., the durable and transposable systems of schemata of perception, appreciation, and action that result from the institutions of the social in the body, and fields, i.e., systems of objective relations which are the product of the institution of the social in things or in mechanisms that have the quasi reality of physical objects; and, of course, of everything that is born of this relation, that is, social practices and representations, or fields as they present themselves in the form of realities perceived and appreciated ... The relation between habitus and field operates in two ways. On one side, it is a relation of conditioning: the field structures the habitus, which is the product of the embodiment of the immanent necessity of a field (or of a set of interacting fields, the extent of their intersection or discrepancy being at the root of a divided or even torn habitus). On the other side, it is a relation of knowledge or cognitive construction. Habitus contributes to constituting the field as a meaningful world, a world endowed with sense and value, in which it is worth investing one's energy. (Bourdieu and Wacquant, 1992, pp. 126–127)

The habitus accounts (noncausally, in contrast to my "purposive-causal" account) for nonintentional and unconscious behavior, and is not based on intention.

The conditionings associated with a particular class of conditions of existence produce habitus, systems of durable, transposable dispositions, structured structures predisposed to function as structured structures, that is, as principles which generate and organize practices and representations that can be objectively adapted to their outcomes without presupposing a conscious aiming at ends or an express mastery of the operations necessary in order to attain them. Objectively "regulated" and "regular" without being in any way the product of obedience to rules, they can be collectively orchestrated without being the product of the organizing action of a conductor. (Bourdieu, 1980, p. 53)

The habitus is a disposition generating both thoughts and behavior of a certain meaningful kind:

As an acquired system of generative schemes, the habitus makes possible the free production of all the thoughts, perceptions, and actions inherent in the particular conditions of its production – and only those ... Because the habitus is an infinite capacity for generating products – thoughts, perceptions, expressions and actions – whole limits are set by the historically and socially situated conditions of its production, the conditioned and conditional freedom it provides is as remote from creation of unpredictable novelty as it is from simple mechanical reproduction of the original conditioning. (Bourdieu, 1980, p. 55)

Given the above, we can say that the habitus "expresses" (internalizes) the social group in the human mind or that the habitus is a mental disposition accounting for the social or social-collective part of the human mind and behavior. There is some similarity with dispositions to pattern-governed behavior here and to we-attitudes, especially we-mode we-attitudes, which serve to account for the collective social actions and practices that have ingrained (collective) pattern-governed behaviors as their elements. Those we-attitudes are also dispositional mental states. Thus the totality of a person's we-attitudes, or perhaps rather the we-mode ones, serving to generate activities including (collective) pattern-governed behaviors plays a role in my theory that is functionally somewhat similar to the notion of habitus in Bourdieu's theory. However, there are two important disanalogies. Firstly, at least from the point of view of my theory, Bourdieu's account operates with one level too many, for he has the levels of habitus (mental dispositions), which generate thoughts and other mental states (except for intentions and aims), which again serve to generate (unconscious and nonintentional) behavior. My account only needs the two levels of relevant mental states (such as we-attitudes) and the activities (including as their parts pattern-governed behaviors) generated by them. Secondly, in Bourdieu's theory there are no properly *joint* habituses (only aggregative "class" habituses; cf. 1980, p. 59). But if my arguments in chapter 3 are tenable, we need joint and collective pattern-governed behaviors and dispositions to them ("skills," as emphasized in chapter 3). Over and above these two points, I claim that my more parsimonious theory is conceptually clearer, more easily applicable to concrete examples, and capable of handling the data – our intuitive examples of social practices and the like – at least as well as Bourdieu's theory. (A critic of this thesis must produce concrete examples that Bourdieu's theory can handle but my theory cannot.)

4.6 CUSTOMS AND OTHER KINDS OF SOCIAL PRACTICES

4.6.1 Customs and traditions as core social practices

In this section I will consider some seemingly other kinds of social practices and make some additional comments on social practices. More precisely I will consider (1) customs and traditions, (2) social practices involving standards of excellence (cf. MacIntyre, 1985), (3) instrumental social practices, and (4) practices based on strategic thinking.

In this chapter an account of social practices has been given. "Social practice" is a broad umbrella term according to this account. Yet it is clearly informative, as it is able to exclude a great many recurrent activities – especially those which are not "sufficiently social," viz., are not performed in part because of a shared we-attitude (or perhaps with a shared we-attitude with the mutual awareness component missing). The reader may want to ask where such common-sense activities as customs and traditions belong. "Custom" is also a very broad term denoting the social counterpart of (individual) habit. Basically, an action belonging to a custom or a repetitively performed action realizing a custom is performed because of a past-related we-belief which has, roughly, the content "this is the way we do things in this group" (cf. Gilbert, 1989, p. 404, for a related view).[9] This past-related constitutive presuppositional group reason often is an unreflected and undeliberated reason in the case of intentionally performed custom action (recall section 4.5). A custom often involves the specification of the manner in which the action is to be performed (cf. below).

A custom can be regarded as a core social practice (at least in the rudimentary sense of thesis (10) with the mutual belief component missing), where the social reason is the past-related constitutive reason that this is how things have been done and are generally done in the present group. Often the manner or way in which an action is performed is central (cf. greeting in a certain manner or eating with the fork in your left hand, the way you applaud, and when, in a concert). Such manners may involve skills and may not even be fully intentionally performable – except indirectly in a context that would make the manner aspect analogous to pattern-governed behavior (cf. intonation and pronunciation in speech). What this involves is that the participants in a custom must believe that some action, say X, is the appropriate action to perform in a certain manner, m, in the circumstances in question because that is believed to be so in the group. (I could equally well have defined "action X performed in manner m" to be an action of kind Y, for manners can be built into action descriptions.)

More exactly, supposing a full-blown we-attitude is at work, a participant's reason in part consists of his intention to perform X in manner m based on his belief that the others in the group generally perform X in manner m in these circumstances and that this is, at least in the fullest case, mutually believed in the group. So, whatever other reasons are operative, at least this kind of reason must be involved. It in part serves to define X performed in manner m as an appropriate action, although there need not be any normative expectations toward the participants to perform X in manner m. The mutual beliefs may of course develop into normative expectations accompanied by social sanctions (approval, disapproval), and then the custom changes – or begins to change – into an institution (at least according to my classification). However, in the elementary cases of custom there is only the weak kind of normativity involved that the action in question is appropriate or "the thing to do" in those circumstances. In this sense a custom has a special conceptual and social status (see below section 6.4.3 for an analysis of this notion). The claim of nonnormativity thus means the lack of a full-blown, sanctioned social norm, although there may be weak normativity, viz., the appropriateness demand, and although we can allow that there are even normative social expectations (e.g. that one ought to do X in C) involved, while nevertheless social sanctions (disapproval, approval) in the full sense are lacking; in the case of a custom, people might still be surprised at finding that a custom is not followed by someone and maybe try to correct the person in question. Furthermore, there may be personal, nonsocial norms (concerning the performance of the relevant action X) involved.[10]

To sum up, the intentionality aspect of customs and their "social historicity" entail that they involve an element of conventionality, viz., the people might have chosen – not necessarily collectively intentionally – another way of doing things. The historicity aspect is that the past is somehow collectively involved, the customary action is something initiated earlier and that fact in part gives the explanation "This is how we do things in this group" of custom action. There cannot be customs that are essentially nonintentional, although their manner aspects may be skill-involving and not always intentionally performable. Customs are often routinely performed and involve pattern-governed behaviors as their elements (some of the latter may be collective ones). Collective pattern-governed behaviors were discussed in section 3.5 and were also briefly considered above in section 4.5, and the reader is referred to these sources.

There are intermediate cases between (weak) normative expectations and expectations based on social norms (cf. chapter 6 on social norms). I will not here study such cases. It seems reasonable to regard the aforementioned cases with weak normative expectations as customs while regarding practices governed by social norms as institutional practices, as I will do in chapter 6.

While all customs, then, are core social practices, not all core social practices are customs. There may be practices requiring special instrumental skill (e.g. how to build a sailboat), which should not be regarded as customs. The reason for building a boat in a certain way may simply be that it results in the (instrumentally) best sailboat rather than that way is how to do things in the community in question. This kind of instrumental practice – typically only weak social practices in my sense – may be based on "technical" norms: if you want to achieve X you ought to do Y, where X is a goal state and Y an instrumental action (cf. below section 4.6.3). In contrast, a custom has a more clearly social content and, plus or minus a bit of stipulation, amounts to core social practice (including core practice in the rudimentary sense) and does not involve established social norms.

Traditions involve the historical reason for the activities that they should be appropriately performed because they have earlier been so performed on the occasions in question. The notion of a tradition is not a very clear one. Here I will concentrate on traditional social practices and will below mention some central or typical features that apply to them without attempting to give a strict definition of the notion (or of its subnotions). One central element is that a tradition typically is or involves an old principle which is followed and respected in the group precisely for the reason that it is such a highly regarded principle. Thus a tradition in this sense can be a system of values, beliefs, and symbolic actions adhered to by the group such that the group members engage in certain activities because of the mentioned kinds of values or beliefs. We can speak of a university's tradition of having inaugural speeches by newly appointed professors. A family can observe the tradition of "*noblesse oblige*," although the family is very poor and without extra resources today. Being historically ingrained, a tradition often involves a norm concerning participation in the social practice or practices involved, the norm here being typically a proper social norm, which, however, may sometimes be codified into an authority-based norm (or rule-norm, in the terminology of chapter 6). A case in point is that today inaugural speeches by professors are regulated by a university rule.

In general, it can be said that traditions are or involve social customs (or complexes of "primary" customs or customs involving normative expectations), except when codified to become formal rituals, ceremonies, or something of the kind. Tradition is, however, a richer notion. First, it concerns principles that are relatively old in the group's scale of time, whereas normal customs need not be that old or following them need not refer to "olden times." A tradition is regarded as valuable in the group. There seems often to be a proper social norm (indeed, metanorm) in the group with the content that "one should adhere to traditions." Standard customs need not be regarded as valuable, and there is a comparable proper social norm with the content that "one should follow this custom" only in special cases. Next we can note that when a system of interrelated customs is meant, the word "tradition" is used. A tradition in this sense is a practice involving actions performed in a certain way such that this practice has been adhered to by the group for a long time. For instance, a group's Christmas traditions qualify as examples here. Such traditions involve customs, ways of habitual social acting. For instance, these customs can consist of certain cooking and eating practices (e.g. making ham and gingerbread) and religious practices (e.g. going to church on Christmas Day morning). Traditions may change their contents in the course of time, and this change may be so substantial that only the "spirit" but not the "letter" of an old tradition is preserved today.

Practices, customs, and traditions are related notions, even if it is difficult without stipulation to be precise about their interconnections. Roughly put, the notion of social practice is a broad action concept, which includes my weak and core social practices as defined in this chapter and thus includes instrumental social practices (e.g. social work practices, such as how to build a house or prepare a certain kind of soup). Customs are conventional and lack the "instrumental necessity" that often accompanies social practices; cf. section 4.6.3. Traditions involve customs (or, in some cases, normative counterparts of customs) but are richer, for example in that they involve valuing the past, the "olden times," and they may also involve values and general beliefs about the social environment as well as symbolic activities. As seen, while customs and traditions can be regarded as (or, if you prefer, as involving) core social practices, not all core social practices involve customs (or traditions); recall thesis (11) of section 4.4.1. While social customs have been taken not to involve participation norms, some traditions do involve them. This warrants regarding those traditions as social institutions.

The "concept" sense of institutions, to be discussed in chapter 6, covers the case of customs and traditions which, when conceptualized in a socially entrenched sense (with a norm to conceptualize them so in appropriate circumstances), become "concepts" or, better, activities requiring a certain concept for their correct description or naming. Thus institutions in the concept sense can alternatively be said to fall within the border area between (typical) customs and (typical) institutions. Nevertheless, we can notice that customs and traditions also involve a new conceptual and social status of some activities, such as some constitutive we-beliefs as "This is what we do in this group" or "This is our traditional way of doing things in this group" express (the notions of conceptual and social status will be clarified in chapter 6).

4.6.2 Social practices and excellence

MacIntyre (1985) discusses social practices in a sense which at least seemingly is very different from my sense of a core social practice. He does say, however, that his use does not completely agree with current ordinary usage. The following quotation gives the gist of his view (p. 187):

By a "practice" I am going to mean any coherent and complex form of socially established cooperative human activity through which goods internal to that form of activity are realized in the course of trying to achieve those standards of excellence which are appropriate to, and partially definitive of, that form of activity, with the result that human powers to achieve excellence, and human conceptions of the ends and goods involved, are systematically extended.

MacIntyre continues: "Tic-tac-toe is not an example of a practice in this sense, nor is throwing a football with skill; but the game of football is, and so is chess. Bricklaying is not a practice; architecture is." We can see that a social practice is supposed to involve goods which are internal (essential) to the practice. These internal goods or values (typically social or communal values) involve standards of excellence that are used for evaluating the activity in question. The second factor is cooperative activity involved in a practice. The third factor, which is not explicit in the quoted passage but which becomes obvious from MacIntyre's emphasis of the fact that social practices have history, is the repeated nature of the activity involved.

Although MacIntyre's definition could be analytically sharper, we can see what he is after. The key idea is the standards of excellence involved in a social practice striving to realize some shared goods internal to the practice. The supposed existence of internal goods serves to distinguish social practices from mere instrumental practices, which by definition strive to achieve some external goals. Thus I take it that even if bricklaying involves standards of excellence, those standards are purely instrumental and concern the solidity of the brick wall, or whatever, to be constructed.

It seems plausible to regard MacIntyre's notion of a social practice as a special case of a social practice in my core sense. This is because a practice in his sense is cooperative activity. I do not know what exactly the sense of cooperation here is, but in any case MacIntyre says that the internal goods related to a practice "can only be achieved by subordinating ourselves within the practice in our relationship to other practitioners" (p. 191). It seems that there thus must be a social reason for the activities involved in a social practice and that this social reason must refer to what others are doing in that kind of context. Thus at least a rudimentary kind of we-attitude must be involved (e.g. I am doing what I am doing because others are also doing it, or because that's how we do things in this group, or because this is my part of our cooperative activity). As criteria of excellence in an intrinsic, noninstrumental sense are involved in a practice in MacIntyre's sense, it is a special case of a core social practice. Notice, however, that his examples of nonpractices, such as bricklaying or throwing a football skillfully, are not core social practices either.

MacIntyre's "excellence practices" form an interesting but rather limited subclass of social practices, at least for the purposes of the social sciences. Furthermore, there are core social practices that do not involve excellence standards. When a way of doing something is involved, that seems to entail that standards of excellence are involved. But there are social practices such as greeting or drinking tea in the afternoon which do not involve criteria of excellence. This supports thesis (12) of section 4.4.

4.6.3 Instrumental practices

Let me next consider "purely instrumental" practices or, as I would like to call them, pure work practices. For instance, we may think that farming practices might be such. In order to grow potatoes, say, you ought to do such and such things (X) to be maximally effective. Suppose some farmers then start regularly doing X so that it becomes a practice. Is such a work practice a social practice in some interesting sense? For example, Schatzki (1996) takes business practices and farming practices to be full-blown social practices. But there seems to be the problem that the kind of arbitrariness or rather conventional element that there is in, for example, customs is lacking in the case of work practices, at least in "pure" work practices (viz., practices not performed with a social reason but only with an instrumental, "material" reason). It should be noted that in actual social life most if not all collective work practices have social aspects related to the manner in which the activities are performed. To the extent that this is the case, there need be no conflict here. But there is a conflict relative to pure work practices, no matter whether they ever occur in real social life. Pure work practices are not social practices in my core sense, as they are not, or need not be, performed because of shared we-attitudes. They are, however, typically weak social practices (in my technical sense), as there is typically the we-belief in the collective that people are performing the kind of activity in question although the we-belief is not a reason for the activity. (External standards of excellence seem always to be involved in their case.)

4.6.4 Strategic thinking and practices

Strategic considerations also may matter in the case of social practices. They can give reasons for the formation of social practices – for repeatedly and conventionally doing things in one way rather than another. Some comments related to this were already made in section 4.3 (recall especially note 5). Let me illustrate this matter. The first concerns people buying shares in part because others are buying. They then act because of a we-belief. Do we then have an example of a social practice? People would buy when the majority of them buy a certain share or certain shares (e.g. shares of high-tech companies), and this would be recurrent behavior. This may indeed be a social practice. It is, if it is a fad to buy these shares. However, buying shares because of a we-belief does not count as a social practice when it is based primarily on strategic thinking (cf. note 5). When it is in this way based on strategic thinking, a person's primary motive is that he will maximize his expected utility by buying because the others are buying (or in some often more realistic cases that he will maximize his expected utility by selling because the others are buying). Then the social reason is not primary. A prudentially acting person would not care about what the others are doing unless it happens to affect his expected utilities. In our example the person is buying because the others are buying; that they are buying is a good sign for him that the share value is going up. However, he might also be buying if he received the same information from another source, for example that the recent results of the company are excellent and its future expectations are great. He would believe that other people are also going to buy its stock because of that fact. That the others are buying or can be expected to start buying would not be his primary reason. (He could hope that not too many others are buying now, but will be buying soon after him.) In my account of social practices it is assumed that the social reason (a shared we-attitude) is essential to the action in question. Only then do we have a social practice, otherwise not.[11]

4.7 CONCLUSION

In this chapter an account of social practices has been given with an emphasis on the kind of sociality that must be involved in them. The main thesis of the chapter has been that, while the notion of a social practice in ordinary talk and thinking is vague, a central notion of a social practice is that of a recurrently performed collective social action (CSA). Such a repeated activity is performed because of a social reason that can be explicated as a (shared) we-attitude. This reason (we-attitude) must be the primary reason of the activity and it basically excludes strategic reasoning as the rational basis of that activity. Several theses about the nature of social practices in this sense, called the *core* sense, were defended in the chapter.

Core practices are the most central kinds of social practices, but also many other kinds were discussed. Collective practices without any sociality at all are the weakest practices. Thus, there can in principle be pure work practices devoid of any sociality. The weakest kinds of social practices that were considered are "weak" social practices, the social element here being a mutual belief, and "ultraweak" social practices, based on mere shared belief. Social practices with intended social effects (e.g. using lipstick) were also mentioned. As to more interesting kinds of social practices, customs and traditions (when considered as activities) were argued to be (or at least involve) core social practices.

Customs, which are the collective counterpart of habits and can be highly routine, were taken to concern the right or appropriate way of doing things, where the appropriateness is based on the group-specific reason that that is how to do things in the group in question. However, customs do not involve full-blown participation norms, although I have allowed somewhat stipulatively the presence of normative social expectations related to them. When customs have evolved to the point of involving social norms in the full sense, then the term "institution" is more appropriate than "custom." Traditions are based on the historical reason that things have long if not "always" been done in such and such a way. They can be strongly normative, and when they are (in the sense of involving a social norm to participate) they are also institutionalized practices.

Other notions of social practice were also discussed. Among them are institution-dependent practices, purely instrumental practices, certain strategic activities, and social practices as ones involving intrinsic goods and standards of excellence.[12]

CHAPTER 5

A Collective Acceptance account of collective-social notions

5.1 INTRODUCTION

Many social properties and notions are collectively constructed. Some rather obvious, broadly factual theses about collective construction and maintenance of social structures or social "order" are the following. (a) Collective intentionality is required for the creation and maintenance of at least some social structures, most importantly, social institutions. (Especially, the maintenance of social institutions will be argued in chapter 6 to require strong collective intentionality.) (b) Nevertheless, there are structural features – that especially economic theory has taught us about (recall chapter 3) – which are only unintended consequences of individual actions. These latter two claims are factual claims about our social world as we now have it. We can add to them the parallel and equally obvious factual theses that (c) collective intentionality does not generate all of society (social structures) and that (d) invisible hand mechanisms do not as a matter of fact generate all of society. However, as will be seen, it is conceptually possible to construct ("design") at least social institutions – if not all social structures – on the basis of collective decision making and thus collective intentionality, and, as we all know, many of our institutions have in fact been so created. On the other hand, it is also a conceptual possibility that they are created and maintained by some kind of invisible hand process that does not involve collective intentionality. Thus, collective order can in principle (as a conceptual possibility) come about either by collective intentionality or by unintended consequences of I-mode intentional and nonintentional action (in the I-mode cases, perhaps due to some kind of social evolution; cf. Mantzavinos, 2001).

The present chapter is central for my defense of the wide program of constructivism. It will be argued below that the Collective Acceptance model to be created will explicate conceptual construction in the social case. It shows how collective acceptance, explicated in terms of holding a relevant we-mode we-attitude, will serve to create social items and to account for sociality in the relevant constructivist sense.

Let us now consider collective social construction. There are two important features of the collective creation of some central aspects of the social world that have previously been emphasized in the literature – by such authors as Barnes (1983), Bloor (1997), Kusch (1997), and Searle (1995). The first feature is that of the *performative* character of many social notions. Social things and their characteristics are in many cases performatively created and, in the case of their maintenance, recreated by "us" (the group members).[1] For example, we may collectively bring about that certain pieces of metal qualify as money. Secondly, some central collective and social concepts have been regarded as *reflexive* in roughly the sense indicated by saying that money is not money unless collectively accepted to be money. Although the features of performativity and reflexivity have been discussed earlier (especially outside philosophy), little attempt has been made to give a precise analysis. The present chapter aims at a precise elucidation of these notions. Furthermore, my account adds to this list a third important feature, the *we-mode–I-mode* distinction. In accordance with chapter 2, the we-mode aspect can be explicated largely in terms of a "thick" notion of collective acceptance which is *"for the group"* such that the group is committed to the collective social items it accepts. In my account we-mode collective acceptance will involve performativity and reflexivity in addition to we-modeness (thus forgroupness and collective commitment). Understood in this way, collective acceptance explicates social construction.

I will below mainly discuss acceptance in the sense of acceptance of a sentence or proposition as *true* or as *correctly assertable*. This is to some extent a philosopher's technical notion (cf. my discussion in Tuomela, 2000c). There are other notions of acceptance such as the common-sense notion of acceptance concerned with acceptance of something as good or as satisfactory (but, arguably, even in these cases at bottom something propositional is accepted as true).

Related to the wide program of social constructivism, I will below offer a precise account of "collective sociality," including the two features of performativity and reflexivity. I will speak of "collective sociality," or of the "collective-social" features of things, rather than merely of "collectivity" or "sociality" here. This is because there are many kinds of things that are called social (e.g. thinking of other people) which need not be collective, and there are collective activities that are not social (recall Weber's umbrella case from chapter 4). Basically, the predicate "collective" in a pure sense applies to collections of people and their features. The predicate "social" in its core sense concerns "taking into account others' thoughts and actions in one's thinking and acting." What is more, I will be concerned with the socially constructed, artificial aspects of the social world. The intersection of collective, social, and constructed aspects forms the set of social features or properties that I will be interested in below. This is an analysandum which is intuitively relatively clear and has social institutions as its prime instance. When I below use the compound adjective "collective-social," I mean "social" in a collective context (in contrast to an individual context) and take "social" in this context to express a constructive element. Somewhat generally, for an entity, a property, or a relationship to be social in my "responsiveness" sense, it must enter the "intentional horizon" (thoughts) of these people qua group members, and their thoughts (e.g. beliefs, desires) about the item in question must of course be capable of affecting their intentional action as at least partial reasons for acting, and suitable feedback may also be required (cf. chapter 7). Sociality in the wider sense involving social forms such as groups, institutions, and organizations is a derivative sense of sociality, to be accounted for in terms of the Collective Acceptance model.

Section 5.2 discusses the basic features of the Collective Acceptance account of sociality and sections 5.3 and 5.4 serve to make precise some central aspects of the account. My discussion proceeds in two steps. The Collective Acceptance approach will be formulated by speaking mainly of the acceptance of collective ideas and thoughts, assumed to be linguistically expressible so that we can speak of the acceptance of sentences (with certain meanings or uses, explicated e.g. as Sellarsian dot-quoted sentences). I will first characterize "collective-social" sentences or "collective-socially" used sentences by means of the features of performativity, we-modeness (collective acceptance with forgroupness and collective commitment), and reflexivity, viz. the features which will in one way or another be involved in collective acceptance. In a second phase, in section 5.6, I will analyze collective acceptance in terms of the notion of holding a special kind (or, rather, one of two special kinds) of collective attitude (we-attitude) toward the sentence in question. Section 5.5 discusses the scope of the account.

5.2 THE BASIC FEATURES OF THE COLLECTIVE
ACCEPTANCE ACCOUNT

Consider a person's making a promise by saying "I promise to bring the book back tomorrow" or giving a name to a ship by saying, in appropriate circumstances, "I hereby give you the name *Nautilus*." This person is here doing things by words, in a sense, and it is the performative linguistic (propositional) activity rather than its verbal nature that is central here (recall above section 3.4 for wider perspectives). That is, the actual use of language (verbal activity) is not central, as other meaningful activities may suffice. In the case of promising, agreement making, and related acts, new states of affairs involving obligations and rights are necessarily created by these activities. For instance, promising entails the obligation to keep the promise.

An activity of the above kind is performative in the achievement sense that an obligation is created. I claim that a similar performative element is often present in the case of social properties and entities and always present in the case of social institutions, although here the central idea is that a group of persons collectively do "things," by means of linguistic items (typically sentences), and thereby create as well as maintain social items (e.g. give a new social status to some previously existing kind of item). I use the phrase "Collective Acceptance account" for my view (cf. Barnes, 1983; Searle, 1995; and Bloor, 1997 for resembling ideas).

Money is an example of an entity that gets its collective-social status by being collectively created. Basically any kind of physical entity can in principle become money through the members of the collective in question accepting and using it as money. (In order for the acceptance to be rational, further conditions, e.g. on the scarcity and size, etc., of the physical entity may of course have to be imposed.) Thus we are told that squirrel fur was money in medieval times (up to the fourteenth century) in Finland. This was based on the members of the society regarding it as money. As soon as they ceased to collectively accept it as money and to mutually believe that it is money, squirrel fur lost the status and functions of money. Here the acceptance in the case of single individuals amounts either to accepting out loud (e.g. simply by saying "I accept that such and such is the case") or internal mental acceptance that would have been accepting out loud had it been overt. Acceptance can be intentionally performed and it must result in its objects becoming accepted (achievement aspect).[2]

While squirrel fur cannot be money without being mutually believed (and thus mentally accepted) to be money, there must also be proper actual use of money. Quite possibly, a rudimentary social practice of exchange by means of squirrel furs can have given rise to the mutual belief that squirrel fur is money and to other related cognitive activities. This mutual belief (or shared we-belief, in the terminology of this book) with the cognitively more full-blown exchange activity then serves to "define" money for the community in question. Here overt social practice could be central not only in manifesting mental collective acceptance, but also in the psychological genesis of collective acceptance. (We often have a kind of contingent diachronic "chicken–egg" problem here; cf. chapter 7.)

When speaking of collectively created and maintained notions (institutional and other collective-social notions) and the sentences by which they are being expressed, I will mostly employ the term "collective acceptance" in this chapter, as it covers both creation and maintenance. We can often also speak of collectively "taking" something to be the case (e.g. collectively accepting that squirrel fur is money, where the collective acceptance makes the "is" constitutive and normative), or use the phrase "counting as" (e.g., squirrel fur counts as money). Collective acceptance is taken to amount, in this connection, to coming to (collectively) hold and holding certain collective thoughts or ideas (viz., we-intentions and/or we-beliefs), and being disposed to act, both collectively in a recurrent, social practice sense and individually, on those ideas.

My analytical apparatus will mainly consist of the notion of acceptance of meaningful sentences (thus expressing or being propositions, which in my construal are Sellarsian dot-quoted sentences) and derivatively of predicates and terms, the notion of sentential attitude, as well as the notions of correct assertability and truth, of which truth is a special case applicable to descriptive sentences.[3] We also need to speak of correct assertability and truth "for the group," as we will need collective acceptance in the we-mode.

We must of course distinguish between (a) collectively creating an idea, (b) collectively holding and maintaining it, and finally (c) collectively realizing it or carrying it out. Collective acceptance relates to (a) and (b) in the first place. Of these, (a) is an event or a process and (b) is a dispositional state. I argue that those collective social reasons, viz., reasons for which collective social actions in general are performed, are special kinds of we-attitudes. As will be argued in section 5.6, *collective acceptance basically is coming to hold and holding a relevant we-attitude, either one in the intention family of attitudes (having the world-to-mind direction of fit) or in the belief family of attitudes (with either the mind-to-world direction of fit or the world-to-mind direction of fit – the latter when the belief is a constitutive institutional one).*

My account will mainly be concerned with (either collectively or merely individually) intentional acceptance, but it must be remembered that neither coming to hold a we-attitude nor holding a we-attitude need be intentional action in all cases (although when it is not it still conceptually could have been intentional action). Thus, an agent can acquire a belief, also a we-belief, without his reflection and intentional action as a kind of pattern-governed activity, based on for example teaching (recall chapter 3). In general, an agent can come to accept something as correct without having intentionally arrived at this kind of dispositional acceptance state. An example of such nonintentional acceptance is an agent's (e.g., child's) acceptance of many of its basic values, preferences, views, and skills on the basis of environmental influences (teaching and exposure to others' relevant behaviors).

While nonintentional acceptance thus is possible, intentional activity may yet seem to be involved in a broader sense, assuming that human beings at any moment are doing something intentionally except when sleeping or having somehow lost their consciousness. The acceptance would then in the above kind of example be based on the child's intentional acceptance "under some description" and is thus only unintentional but not fully nonintentional acceptance (e.g. in the sense of being causally produced without any intentional control). Pattern-governed behaviors in the sense of chapter 3 can lead to such acceptance. For instance, collective perceptual takings that there is a UFO over there can be regarded as acceptances in this sense. Here the state of acceptance is based on a perceptual taking, an essentially nonintentional *pgb*.

When speaking of beliefs in the context of the Collective Acceptance account, I will concentrate on acceptance beliefs, which are above kinds of states of acceptance of a content (sentence, proposition) as correct (or true), while mere believing is a state in which the agent experiences something as true or real (cf. Cohen, 1992; Tuomela, 1995 and 2000c). Such a state of acceptance is in general (but not always) produced by the mental action of acceptance and involves judging that its content is true or correctly assertable. When rational, it is based on the agent's reflection of what is being accepted and often also on relevant evidential considerations – for example, his view of the other group members' acceptances. An acceptance state is a disposition to act intentionally in accordance with the content of that state, the content serving as a motivating and guiding reason for those actions. Whatever else (e.g., wants, emotions, etc.) those reasons may include, intentions and beliefs of a relevant kind must always be involved in the standard case of intentional action and also in the case of unintentional action that is "based" on intentional action in the embeddedness sense of the previous paragraph.

Acceptance may in part be based on incorrect beliefs and involve personal ignorance (but not complete collective ignorance) concerning the accepted item. To take an example, acceptance of squirrel fur as money or of the earth being flat may be based on incorrect ideas about the items involved without the activity losing its character as acceptance. The person in question may, for instance, accept that squirrel fur is something one can exchange for flour and meat in the market, and so forth, without having a fuller understanding of the concept of money. In general, I argue that the question of how much intentionality and of which kind (cf. I-mode versus we-mode intentionality, correctness versus falsity of relevant beliefs) there must be in each particular case is to be decided in part on the basis of the collective outcome – what kinds of activities result from collective acceptance and from the maintenance of what has thus been accepted. Trivially, people must be able to do with money roughly what we full-fledged members of society generally do with it, and the same goes for schools, churches, governments, and so on. (Cf. chapter 6 for further reasons.)

One question that needs a comment in the case of the CA model, based in part on teaching and learning, is: who teaches the teachers? There may be, but need not be, a first teacher. In any case the first teacher may be the inventor of an idea or practice, which then spreads out in the group and the following, obeying or maintaining of which becomes a social practice, perhaps even a normative one. In general, a practice may arise rather spontaneously and involve "self-learning" and "self-training," if needed. Some suitable spreading or diffusion mechanism, such as imitation, may serve to make the practice or habit of a single individual or a few individuals into a social custom that is, and must be, collectively accepted. Thus, even if a social practice can be initiated by a single individual, it needs to be collectively accepted.

In my stylized account, in the case of I-mode acceptance each member individually accepts the same sentence s (e.g. s = Squirrel fur is money or, rather, the dot-quoted version .Squirrel fur is money.), perhaps believing (or perhaps there being even mutual belief in the group) that also the others have accepted s. This, however, is not enough for my

Collective Acceptance account. It requires we-mode acceptance if not for the creation of a collective construct at least for its fully satisfactory maintenance. The we-mode in its core sense entails thinking and acting as a group member in a full-blown sense, and thus that the group members collectively taken are committed to seeing to it that what is collectively accepted is correctly assertable – and usable – for the group members (recall the appendix to chapter 2). When rationally accepting something for the group, the participants are in effect functionally collectively committed to a system of norms which in general *requires* that the members, when acting as group members, perform certain actions (e.g., inferences using the accepted sentences – be they objectively true or not – as premises) and *permits* and *enables* the performance of some other actions (cf. section 5.3 for examples). In general there will be social sanctions (approval, disapproval) to control the group members' activities governed by their normative collective commitment.[4] Forgroupness entails that the group members are prima facie mutually aware (or at least can become aware) of what has been accepted for the group. Furthermore, if an item is rationally accepted for the group, it must accord with the group's interests and should serve the group's goals and interests. This is important especially in the case of more permanent social structures such as social institutions typically are. (See below section 6.3, for further arguments for the requirement of we-modeness.)

Collective acceptance in the sense of the participants' actively holding – and being committed to hold – an idea for the use of the group is a disposition to collective social action in the we-mode. The actualization of this disposition is a collective social action with the purpose of realizing the accepted sentence, making it true (or correctly assertable), or acting on it, depending on the case. Furthermore, the participants' collective commitment indicates the steering function, with respect to the group, of collective acceptance and its we-mode character.

Consider the following example of a collective action performed with some (even if perhaps not full) collective intentionality, viz., collective social action performed for the same shared social reason. In a group there might be a (weak) we-goal to oppose a tax increase; viz., this is the group members' goal, and they believe that the others share this goal and believe that this is mutually believed among them. Collective acceptance in this kind of situation can be construed as acceptance either in the sense of conative commitment to a sentence or proposition s (intention to make s true or to uphold s, e.g., s = We will prevent the tax increase) or doxastic commitment to s (the "acceptance" belief that s is true, e.g., s = The earth is flat). Collective acceptance here may be just (weak) "we-acceptance," viz., each person comes to accept s, believes that the others accept s, and also believes that there is a mutual belief about the participants' acceptance of s. This we-acceptance in general involves awareness not only concerning what one oneself accepts, but also of what the others accept.

In the case of belief (or acceptance belief, to be more precise) what is accepted is a descriptive or descriptively used sentence. In the case of intention the sentence is an intention expression such as "We will do X," where "will" is conatively used and in the case of acceptance belief the sentence can typically be expressed by "Our group's view is that p." In the I-mode case we have private commitment to the sentence and in the we-mode case the group's collective commitment to it.

Stronger forms of collective acceptance "for the group" than in the above tax example are norm-based, institutional acceptance and plan-based or agreement-based collective acceptance. An example of the former is the collective acceptance that drunk driving is wrong and punishable, that anniversaries in a marriage ought to be celebrated, and perhaps also in some collective that squirrel fur counts as money. The last example is based on the social norm that everyone in the collective ought to treat squirrel fur as money. An example of plan-based or agreement-based collective acceptance is the group members' joint decision to elect a certain person as their leader. In general, the agreement (and shared intention) to accept a sentence s results in the acceptance of s – indeed, there is no conceptual room here for agreeing to accept s and not accepting s. Acceptance of s thus is the conceptually in-built "result event" of the agreement making in question. The participants' continued acceptance of the agreement entails that they will have the intention to continue to hold on to s. The intentions to enter agreement making, to accept s, and to continue to hold on to s need not be joint intentions (cf. Tuomela, 2002d on this problem).

Once a sentence, s, has been collectively accepted, collective acceptance (CA) can be regarded as a disposition to perform relevant collective social actions (viz., actions, including inferences, performed for the same social reason) concerning the accepted content, say s. The social reason here will be (of a kind that has an object fitting the general description of) satisfying or upholding, as the case may be, the (content of the) sentence in question. At least when the group is an "egalitarian" and unstructured one, they must mutually believe that they have collectively accepted s and understand what such collective acceptance is (and thus that they are committed to s). As their social reason involves not only the idea of satisfying or upholding s but also the idea of doing this in part because the others also do it, we can see that intentionally performed collective acceptance involves taking into account social expectations. The participants, if rational, must believe or be disposed to believe, not only that they themselves have accepted s, but also that the others have similarly accepted s and in fact that the others also believe similarly of the others (and so on higher up in the belief hierarchy; cf. above, section 2.6). The fuller cases thus must involve at least loop beliefs: each person should believe something not only about the others' beliefs but also about their beliefs concerning his belief.

I will below concentrate on cases where the persons involved in collective acceptance are the same as the target persons, viz., those for whom the proposition s is accepted, so to speak. An example in which this is not the case would be one where a parliament passes a law concerning young people. Here the target persons would be different from those involved in collective acceptance. It has been argued that in such cases (supposing, for simplicity, that laws are not plainly forced upon the target) the decision-making or "operative" persons must be suitably "authorized" by the target persons. For simplicity's sake, my explicit formulations will primarily concern groups (collectives) that do not have the kind of normative structure which essentially affects collective acceptance. Accordingly, groups in the present context (and in my later discussion of social institutions) are to be taken merely as – typically intensionally characterized – collections of people, of which nothing more needs to be antecedently assumed except perhaps that if some persons belong to a group they must at least think that they do. (The group could be an informal group, an organization, or a society, and so on.) There are other, important cases of collective acceptance in which structured social groups are involved. In such cases we speak of a social group's acceptance of a proposition and the members' acceptances must also be somehow involved. However, in typical cases only the operative members (viz., those members in virtue of whose activities attitudes and/or actions can be attributed to groups) will jointly accept the proposition in question, while the others in some weak sense ought to tacitly accept it or go along with the operative members' collective acceptance of the proposition. All this concerns only the we-mode attitudes and activities of the members; their I-mode attitudes and activities may differ and in the extreme case even be opposite. The case of structured groups is central and is covered by the Collective Acceptance account.[5]

As seen, while collective acceptance as coming to hold a thought in common is collective activity which may sometimes be we-mode social action, collective acceptance as mere collective holding of a thought, being dispositional, is not yet literally collective social action (viz., collective social action of the acceptance kind, and of course not causal collective social action such as jointly building a house); but when accompanied by full-blown collective commitment it can be regarded as the action of "seeing to it" that the accepted content will come about or, as the case may be, remain "correctly assertable" (see Tuomela, 1995, chapter 3 for such necessarily intentional "stit" action). When collective commitment is satisfied, we get collective action on (viz., because of) the collectively accepted thought (reason). This is full-blown collective social action (also in the sense of chapter 4).

The following general thesis of primary, nonderived collective sociality in our constructivist, acceptance-related sense will be defended, where s may be an arbitrarily complex sentence (or proposition, a dot-quoted sentence in my explication).

(*CAT*) A sentence s is *collective-social* in a primary constructivist sense in a group g if and only if it is true for group g that (a) the members of g collectively accept s, and that (b) they collectively accept s if and only if s is correctly assertable (or true) (*collective acceptance thesis*).

In the analysans, (a) is the assumption of the categorical collective acceptance of s while (b) is a partial characterization of the kind of collective acceptance which is needed here. Clauses (a) and (b) of course entail that s is correctly assertable in the group, in the spirit of our model. The conjunction of these two clauses can be referred to as the CAT formula.

In logical terms,

(*CAT**) s is *collective-social* in a primary constructivist sense in g if and only if $FG(CA(g,s)$ & $(CA(g,s) \leftrightarrow s))$

Here the "operator" CA represents the collective acceptance of s as true or as correctly assertable by g for g. CA must be a performative achievement-expressing notion and "acceptance" is general enough to cover both the creation and upholding of s and has achievement conceptually built into it. Thus, the equivalence in (*CAT**) expresses a kind of conceptually necessary connection.[6] In standard cases collective acceptance involving (at least a substantive amount of) collective commitment to what has been accepted can be required (cf. section 5.4). When speaking of the CA model in this book, I will assume such collective commitment and accordingly take collective acceptance, and action based on it, to be in the we-mode.

Forgroup (g,s) (or FG(g,s) for short) can be interpreted as "group g takes s to be correctly assertable in g-contexts" (correct assertability from a group's perspective) or even doxastically as "g treats or holds s as correctly assertable in g-contexts," where g-contexts are contexts related to the activities of the group members of g when they act in a full sense *as group members* as opposed to privately. What has been collectively accepted for a group is, more generally, taken to be for the use of the group, and to further the group's basic purposes. Furthermore, forgroupness here also involves that s is available as correctly assertable in the sense that the group members are enabled and permitted to use s (or, even more generally, the thought that s) qua functioning as group members, and on some occasions they may be obligated to use s as correctly assertable, be s "objectively" true or not (e.g., the members of the Flat Earth Society are obligated to assert s = The earth is flat , or its truth-equivalent, when asked about the shape of the earth). Acceptance for the group in the case of intentional collective acceptance in normal cases entails mutual belief concerning the acceptance (this follows in part from the standard awareness feature related to intentional action).

Some further clarifying points are now due. First, consider what the sentence s in typical cases can be like. In the case of intended collective goals (and intentions) the surface form of s could be "We will achieve G," where "will" expresses intending and G is a goal state. In the case of collective beliefs (which strictly speaking will be acceptances and may be called "acceptance beliefs"), the formula s may take the form "We believe that p" or "It is our view that p." In the case of collective wishes s may be "We wish that p," and so on. Also normative statements can be involved. Thus s may be "Everyone in g ought to do X when in C." As said, I propose that s in a finer analysis be understood to be a dot-quoted sentence in Sellars' terms, and thus also allowed to be a "mental sentence" or a thought in "Mentalese" (cf., above, chapter 3 and Sellars, 1969 and 1981). Recall that a dot-quoted sentence .s. is one which plays the same role in a given language or representational system as s plays in our base language, here English.

The group members are collectively committed to using .s. not only in their overt theoretical and practical inferences and overt actions appropriately based on such inferences, but also in their thinking, so that we can employ either .s. or its counterpart in "Mentalese" in the present context or indeed take .s. also to cover the mental uses. The contexts in which the commitment becomes manifested in action are – in my quasi-Sellarsian system – in part based on various world-to-mind, mind-to-mind, mind-to-world rules of thinking (conceptual activities) in the covert case and on world-language, language-language, language-world rules of "languaging" (conceptual activities) in the overt case. (The "direction of fit" terminology could to some extent alternatively be applied here; cf. below.)

Let me clarify correct assertability a little further for the case of full-blown and "normally" rational group members. First note that we can derive from (*CAT*) and some logical assumptions concerning FG that FG(g,s), and it entails "s is collectively available or *premisible* in g-contexts." Premisibility is the idea of taking s to be correct or to be assumable in the context in question. But a group member does not really have to *believe* it is true. (Nevertheless, premisibility in g can be viewed as a notion in the belief family, construed in a wide sense of having mind-to-world direction of fit.) To accept something as correctly assertable entails that one has the right to use the sentence as a premise and, as seen, sometimes the person ought to use it. In our above example, s was "The earth is flat." Using it as a premise means accepting it as a premise in one's practical inference or using it as the basis of one's action. We can now ask whether one can accept s and −s. The answer is that a rational group member cannot do it. Note, however, that one can to some extent rationally accept s *qua a member* of g and but not accept s (or even accept −s) *as a private person*. My present account does not rely on the notion of correspondence truth as an analytical notion. The basic notion here is the normative notion of a group's treating something as correctly assertable. In the case of *descriptive* sentences, correct assertability is simply truth, and then we are speaking of the group's taking s to be true in the present context. (Cf. Sellars, 1968; Tuomela, 1985, for viewpoint-dependent picturing truth.)

There is also a kind of "shadowy side" in collective acceptance in our present sense. A group can *collectively reject* (CR) ideas. For instance, let s = Human beings are a product of natural evolution. A group might reject s. I submit that this entails not only that it does not accept s, but that it accepts the negation of s, viz., −s. In other words, I claim that collective rejection is a subspecies of nonacceptance by which the group is able conceptually to construct notions. We do not, however, need to adopt a special technical notion of collective rejection for this job, for my present thesis reduces the task to collective acceptance, viz., CR(g,s) amounts to CA(g,−s). It can be mentioned here that there is also another way of dealing with "negative items," although these two ways are complementary and do not compete. Briefly, a group may (and here must, if rational) accept also that it rejects s and accepts −s. Thus, in symbols, $CA(g,CR(g,s))$ and $CA(g,CA(g,-s))$ would be true in this case. For instance, a group may accept, for example, that the thought that human beings are a product of natural evolution is to be rejected (this is of the kind $CA(CR(g,s))$). In my account collective acceptance has as one of its intuitive source ideas that it concerns what the group members are licensed to write down and use as premises. In my example, $CR(g,s)$ is accordingly taken to entail that they may use −s as a premise, and ought to use it in our example when the genesis of the human race is the object of inquiry.

While acknowledging that it is a contingent question what a group collectively accepts, I will now present some examples, tokens of which are normally rendered as collective-social by the Collective Acceptance account, and correctly so: (a) Tom and Jane love each other. (b) Tom and John are friends. (c) Jim is our leader. (d) It is our collective goal to get our lake cleaned up. (e) Squirrel furs are money for us. (f) Marriage obligates the spouses to take care of their children. (g) The policeman shows his badge to give impetus to his order. (h) The Deutsche Bank is a bank. Examples (a) and (b) are here assumed to be based on a shared we-belief so that, respectively, love and friendship are mutually recognized by the participants. This we-belief serves to account for the collective acceptability by the participants of the relevant sentences involving these predicates. Sentence (c) is social in view of collective, belief-based acceptance. While one could be a leader based on, for example the law, in our present informal example mutual belief is supposed to do the work. Thus, contrary to (a) and (b), the basic predicate (here "leader") does not by itself entail the we-belief. Case (e) is a standard institutional case entailing the creation of obligations and rights. Case (f) gives part of the legal and moral notions of marriage, collectively accepted in the agreement-making sense by the suitably authorized members of the society passing the law and, at least in a well-functioning society, by the members of society in a different, we-belief-based sense. Case (g) involves the badge as a social symbol for the socially constructed powers of a policeman. Case (h) is complex. The sentence itself can be assumed to be collectively accepted in the mutual belief sense. It involves the institutional notion of bank, assumed to have been previously constructed by the acceptance of the society of a legal-social account of what a bank is, so to speak, viz., by the various laws, rules, and collective expectations characterizing the predicate "bank." Collective-social notions in the present sense are not necessarily institutional, although they come close to that (cf. chapter 6).

We can say roughly that a sentence is collective-social in a *derived* sense if it is not "constructively" social in the above primary sense but *presupposes* for its truth (for the group) that there are some relevant true (for the group) sentences, which are collective-social in the primary sense. For instance, sentences using "power," "unemployment," or "wealth" are at least in some cases candidates for constructively social sentences in the derived sense. Latent or unilateral social influence are social features of the social world that would not – and correctly so – be cases of even derivatively social features in the constructivist sense (not even when many agents are concerned). The same holds for "naturally" social emotions such as envy often is (cf. Tom envies John for the latter's new car). Furthermore, many shared we-attitudes are not socially constructed either (for instance, shared fear may be a "natural" or "non-constructed" social phenomenon). Next, "Jane uses lipstick in order to attract men" is weakly social but not collective-social and is by the CA account. Sentences about social strata, correctly enough, are not counted as collective-social (cf. "People walking briskly at least three kilometers a day live longer than people on average"). Nor is a sociologist's characterization "This group is socially cohesive" even derivatively collective-social, understanding cohesiveness here to be based on interaction frequency. Furthermore, invisible hand phenomena are social features of the social world that would not either be derivatively collective-social features.

The above testing of (*CAT*) concerning different kinds of examples shows that it works correctly with respect to positive and negative cases. This defense of the Collective Acceptance model gives an important and central argument for the correctness of the wide program of social constructivism as understood in this book (see chapter 6 for the case of social institutions).

5.3 THE COLLECTIVE ACCEPTANCE ACCOUNT MADE PRECISE

The Collective Acceptance model (CA model) of sociality concerns the collective acceptance of sentences (propositions, dot-quoted sentences) for the use of the group. It says that the very acceptance of a sentence creates its correct assertability (or truth) for the group in question. If a social sentence s in group g is collectively accepted by the members of g, I write CA(g,s). From a formal point of view CA is an operator which, in the case of a group g and a sentence s, says that in g s is collectively accepted. As argued, collective acceptance must in the present context be acceptance *for the group* in question, so that also objectively false sentences can be allowed to be correctly assertable in the group. I also claim that the Collective Acceptance account covers not only central collective-social properties and entities (including collective attitudes) but also all social institutions (cf. chapter 6).

To see better what is involved in the Collective Acceptance model, we start by considering the performativity aspect of the model incorporated in collective acceptance. This aspect is largely supposed to account for the creation and maintenance of the collective features of the social world. The operator CA in part expresses the group members' (qua group members') shared scope of concern, their "intentional horizon" (recall the appendix to chapter 2). It can consist of the "things" (entities, properties, facts, etc.) in the world they are (at least in a dispositional sense of "when the question arises") intentionally concerned with in their thoughts and intentional actions, briefly the class of things intentionally represented in the group members' attitudes qua group members. Presently we will consider the part of the group's intentional horizon that consists of the content of such social sentences collectively accepted for the use of the group in the we-mode.

The group members collectively accept goals (thus intention contents) and joint goals (joint intention contents) as well as views (belief or acceptance contents) for the group. This kind of collective acceptance is entirely relative to the group's intentional horizon: the group members collectively accept sentences for the group, at least in a weak sense, and our account also requires that they thereby collectively commit themselves to regarding the accepted sentences as correctly assertable (or true) for the group. As argued, this collective acceptance can be weaker than intentionally performed joint action performed with the intention to accept something for the group. It is nevertheless assumed that in this context the participants think that they are behaving in a group context with we-mode thought contents.

I mark the fact that a sentence has been thus accepted for the group by attaching the intensional FG-operator to that accepted sentence to express forgroupness. Collective acceptance in the strong sense under discussion is assumed to entail forgroupness and collective commitment to the accepted sentence (see section 5.4 for collective commitment). The accepted sentence needs to be in the group's "acceptance box," so to speak, and this is marked by FG(g,s). The group members are collectively committed to regarding the sentences in the acceptance box as correctly assertable (or true). This acceptance box has two subboxes, the intention subbox (related to intentions and assertability) and the belief subbox (related to beliefs and truth). All the elements in the group's acceptance box can be used by the group members qua group members in their relevant reasoning, in all the "moves" related to correct assertability or truth the members make within the intentional horizon of the group. The correct assertability of a sentence is viewed from the group's point of view (technically, the sentence is within the scope of FG).

Following the treatment in Tuomela and Balzer (1999), let me now introduce a "performative implication" or "group-implication" ($\rightarrow_g$) expressing the outcome of collective acceptance for the group, viz., an implication as viewed by the group. It can be taken to represent and spread the performative aspect of collective acceptance, viz., that by collective acceptance a proposition gains a certain epistemic status entitling the group members in their reasoning to use this proposition as a categorical assumption, as something being or counting as "true for the group" or "assertable for the group."[7]

In logical terms, we can define group-implication, or g-implication $\rightarrow_g$, as follows:

$$s \rightarrow_g s' \text{ if and only if } FG(g, s \rightarrow s')$$

This implication is what the collective acceptance thesis (*CAT*) of section 5.2 in effect uses. Next, I assume that FG distributes over material implication, viz.:

(1) $FG(g, s \rightarrow s')$ implies $FG(g,s) \rightarrow FG(g,s')$

Formally, we start with the following central assumption expressed informally in (*CAT*):

(2) $FG(g,CA(g,s) \leftrightarrow s)$

Assuming (1) and (2) we get

(3) $FG(g,CA(g,s)) \leftrightarrow FG(g,s)$

which our informal discussion also has employed. FG is also assumed to distribute over conjunction, that is, $FG(g,s \text{ and } s') \leftrightarrow (FG(g,s) \text{ and } FG(g,s'))$.

The set of all sentences s such that $FG(g,CA(g,s))$ can be taken to represent the intentional horizon of group g. There is thus an obvious connection between group g's accepting a sentence s in the performative sense and s's being in g's intentional horizon. In the spirit of the CA model we could say that by accepting a sentence s to belong to the group's intentional horizon, the members of g have made it available for their group-specific deductions and practical inferences. They may use it in their local system of inference (deduction, practical inference, and what have you), which is obtained from the standard logical system of inference by adding precisely those sentences which the members have accepted plus (at least a "perspicuous" subset of) their deductive and "practical" consequences. Indeed, qua group members, they are collectively committed to so using them, and only them, in appropriate circumstances (e.g. when a view concerning a certain matter is required), and are committed to refraining from using sentences incompatible with the accepted ones (see the examples below).

As claimed, in general the truth of FG(g,s) is compatible with the "objective" falsity of s. For instance, it might be the case that FG(g, Stars determine our fate), while it is not true that stars determine our fate.

To discuss and justify the present approach in more detail, we consider the left-to-right implication in our central formula (2):

(*PERF*) $CA(g,s) \rightarrow_g s$

Verbally, it is true for the group g that if they collectively accept s, then s (for the group). (*PERF*) is true simply on the basis of the notion of collective acceptance, which is an achievement notion relative to the group's "intentional horizon." From an outsider's perspective only FG(g,s) is true.

Here are some simple, idealized examples of the practical inferences that are licensed for the members of g when inferring and acting qua members of g (**MB** stands for mutual belief and p,q are sentences; we do not here attempt to give a logically rigorous analysis of them):[8]

(I) (i) FG(g,p); (ii) MB(g,p $\rightarrow$ q); (iii) therefore, FG(g,q).

(II) (i) FG(g,p) (where p = We will achieve goal P); (ii) therefore, I, qua a member of g, will contribute to our achieving goal P.

(III) (i) FG(g,p) (where p = The earth is flat); (ii) qua a member of g, I am to avoid big falls (such as falling down from the brink of the earth); (iii) therefore, I, qua a member of g, will avoid traveling to (what I believe to be) the brink of the earth.

Consider now (2) and the implication from left to right in it. This implication captures the performative side of s's being collective-social: by being collectively accepted, s becomes (or is performatively made) true for the group.

The right-to-left implication in (2) can be said to express reflexivity. Generally speaking, social concepts and sentences are reflexive in the following sense. A collective-social sentence using a putatively social predicate (e.g. "money," "leader," or "marriage") does not apply to real things (such as certain pieces of paper or squirrel furs in the case of "money") unless collectively accepted and, so to speak, validated for that task by the attachability of the FG-operator to it.

Let us consider money as an example. The predicate "money" does not refer to itself, but rather to coins, dollar notes, squirrel furs, and so on. The reference here means that "money" correctly applies to those things. The loose talk about reflexivity in this context therefore should be understood as being about presupposition-stating or constitutive sentences, such as in the colloquial expression "Money is not money unless collectively accepted to be money." This is not a matter of what phrase to use, but what the concept of money is. (Recall, however, that the members accepting that, say, squirrel fur is money, can do it under another description, and need not possess the full, circular concept of money.) This concept is expressed by what the user of the predicate "money" in English is entitled to say and, especially, extralinguistically do (and what he may be obligated to do). The concept of money thus also connects with some deontic powers and obligations collectively bestowed upon those who use the predicate "money" and who belong to the collective in question. By deontic powers collectively bestowed upon a person we mean things such as his being normatively permitted or required to perform certain actions. The discussed presupposition (viz. that money is not money unless collectively accepted to be money) is central precisely because of the following assumed fact: it is up to the members of the collective – and nobody else – to bestow those extralinguistic deontic powers upon its members. This contrasts with sentences involving only physical predicates like "tree" or "mass." In their case it is not up to the members of the collective to do more than stipulate how to use certain linguistic phrases and, for example, what word to use for trees.[9]

Using the above notation we may say generally that for a social sentence s the group-relative implication "s $\rightarrow_g$ CA(g,s)" is true. Thus CA(g,s) is a necessary condition for s or, in this sense, a presupposition of s. As indicated, this implication expresses that the social sentence s is reflexive, and we say that s satisfies the condition of reflexivity relative to the collective acceptance if and only if

(*REFL*) s $\rightarrow_g$ CA(g,s)

This principle gives a central and often emphasized "mark of the social": for s to be correctly assertable for the members g it must be collectively accepted by them and for them. (See the appendix of chapter 6 for reflexivity in the case of institutional concepts.)

That a collective-social sentence satisfies a collectivity condition with respect to truth (or correct assertability) in a group entails that necessarily (due to collective acceptance) whenever some member of the group finds this sentence to be true then the same holds for any other member in the group, provided that the group has collectively accepted s. Accordingly, we have here a close analogue of the Collectivity Condition (*CC*) for goals discussed in chapter 2. Using the abbreviations CA(g,s) as above and ASC(i,s) for "s is correctly assertable for person i," we formulate the matter technically and say that CA satisfies the Collective Ascribability Condition if and only if on "quasiconceptual" grounds (resembling (*CC**) of chapter 2) it is true for g that

$$(\textit{COLASC}) \ \mathrm{CA(g,s)} \rightarrow_g (\mathrm{i}) \ (\mathrm{ASC(i,s)})$$

This condition can be taken to be entailed by the full notion of collective acceptance for a group, viz., the Collective Acceptance model. It represents the "individualization" of group acceptance for all group members. Putting the matter in slightly looser terms, it can be taken to say that (a) whatever is accepted and acceptable for a group in this kind of context is assertable for any member and that (b) what is acceptable for a group member qua a group member is assertable for any other group member qua a group member.

Combining (*PERF*) and (*REFL*) and remembering the relativization to the group (viz. forgroupness) allover in our treatment we arrive at (*CAT**) of section 5.2. I have also accepted (*COLASC*) as an underlying conceptual condition for CA. As to the derivative sense ("basedness" sense) of collective sociality, the reader should recall the brief discussion in section 5.2.

5.4 COLLECTIVE COMMITMENT

I have above required of collective acceptance, in the context of (*CAT*), that it be for the group and that it involve collective commitment concerning what has been collectively accepted. I will now consider collective commitment in more detail starting with its weak, we-attitude sense. While one might call aggregated I-mode commitments collective, I will here understand the notion of collective commitment to entail commitment qua a group member and thus commitment to further the group's constitutive goals, standards, and norms, briefly its "ethos." This is (weak) we-mode collective commitment (cf. the criterion of we-modeness in the appendix of chapter 2). To illustrate the case of the dyad with you and me as its members, if we are collectively committed to a proposition s, the following must be true: I am committed to s qua a group member and will act accordingly, in part because I believe – and use as my premise – that I ought to do what it takes to make (or keep) s correctly assertable for the group ("us"); and I believe that you are also similarly committed to s and will act accordingly, in part because of your similar personal (not necessarily social) normative thoughts; furthermore, we both believe that all this is mutually believed by us. Here s could be "The earth is flat," and we are talking about your and my commitment to premising it and acting on its presumed truth (or correctness). It can also be said that each of us is collectively committed, or "we-committed," and not only that we collectively taken are collectively committed. In the present weak sense of collective commitment my account goes in terms of shared we-belief only and collective commitment is thus analyzed in terms of attitudes concerned with binding oneself normatively to an item qua a group member. Hence communication is not required and still less is explicit agreement making at stake.

The normativity involved in the above weak case need only be relative and instrumental in the following sense. Suppose we have formed the plan-based joint intention to paint the house. We must here understand what a joint intention involves and especially understand that its satisfaction conditions are of the kind that we must jointly perform its content action. The end result, that the house has been painted by us, accordingly is what we are collectively committed to by our joint intention. We will be disposed to think that in order to arrive at this end result we not only ought to perform the joint action in question, but each of us ought to perform his part of it. This "ought" involves only an instrumental, means–end type of normative relationship. However, if there was an agreement to perform the joint action, there is also a noninstrumental, intrinsic "ought," due to the very notion of agreement, to paint the house together and to perform one's part.

The present "attitudinal," weak notion of collective commitment can be strengthened, on the one hand, by requiring the normative aspect to rely on a personal norm (e.g. a personal norm one has accepted for governing his interaction with others) or on an intersubjectively shared norm or normative belief towards s (instead of only a personal normative belief). The next possibility is that commitment is grounded in an objective norm "in the public space." Such a norm may be sanctioned by objective sanctions (e.g. fines). State laws are an obvious example of this type of case.

On the other hand, this strengthening will lead to increased *social responsibility* towards others in the sense that one is socially committed to others to see to it "that something is thus and so." Thus it can be required that the participants normatively expect that the others perform their "parts" of the collective commitment to uphold s. In its full form – present in the case of agreement-based joint intention, for instance – this social aspect will concern rights and obligations of the participants. In our example, I would then be entitled (have the right) to expect that you will be committed to me to do your part, and I am by symmetry obligated to you to perform my part. One central feature that has been emphasized in the literature is that collective commitment requires that the participants intuitively speaking "stand or fall together" and cannot without criticism from others alone give up their commitment (cf. Gilbert, 1989; Conte and Castelfranchi, 1995). This is correct when social commitment is involved. However, when it is not involved there are only prudential (and perhaps psychological) reasons against unilateral rescinding, e.g., the content of the commitment may not be realizable and one's aim goal will not be satisfied. (When speaking of collective commitment without qualifications I will below assume that social commitment is involved.)

It can be said that a group is in a full sense committed to an item if and only if its members are collectively committed to that item in the present strong sense involving social commitment. In such a case the members can accordingly be said to be collectively committed as a group and each of them can be taken to be collectively committed as a group member, thus collectively committed in the we-mode (cf. above remarks). Thus, each member is entitled to say "We are collectively committed to s" and make the appropriate practical inferences, acceptable to all group members. Such more personal (although not private) inferences may concern the member's particular personal commitments in the situation at hand (think, for example, of the different tasks that may be involved in joint action).[10]

So in all, collective commitment qua a group member may be based on *subjective commitment* (involving only personal normative thoughts) and beliefs about others, or it can in addition involve *intersubjective commitment* (involving appropriate intersubjective norms or normative thoughts).

Finally, it can be *objective commitment* (viz., commitment in the public space based on objective norms, epistemically available to anyone), and this objective commitment can involve – and will below be taken to involve – also *social commitment* to others. Note that the norms and normative thoughts will concern actions supporting the content s, and here also linguistic norms will find a place (recall the discussion in chapter 3, which was also about linguistic norms). In most cases the normative collective commitments are *relative* to the intentions and goals that people have. Social practices may, however, involve absolute commitments, for example, when based on moral considerations.[11]

5.5 QUALIFICATIONS AND ADDITIONS

I will now elaborate further on some aspects of the Collective Acceptance model. (CAT) and its technical counterpart (CAT^*) of section 5.2 are grand theses saying that collective-social sentences consist precisely of the collectively accepted sentences satisfying the central CAT formula FG(CA(g,s) & CA(g,s) ↔ s) for collective acceptance, and those which are based on it (derivative collectivity). I assume – and this seems to suffice – that s is a descriptively used sentence, although it may contain normative predicates or presuppose for its truth that certain normatively specified circumstances or conditions obtain. For instance, the members of g may accept that a group member i is their leader, and by accepting this they also come to accept the entailed fact that i has the power to order them to do various things.

The central concept of collective acceptance in (CAT) must be understood broadly enough so that agreement making, authority, and power find their place in the account – for example, those who collectively make things true in the sense of (CAT) may be authorized "operative" members in some cases. In cases like that of a parliament creating a new law, we are thus dealing with agreement making by an authorized body of persons (the "operative" persons) who – acting with the power they have been given – create the laws when acting in their right positions and in the right circumstances (recall note 5 and cf. Tuomela, 1995, chapters 5–7, for discussion).

However, the laws and other created social entities are basically upheld by the target people. Accordingly, while the fact of the creation of a social entity (e.g. an institution such as leadership) by collective acceptance is generally a *contingently* true matter (perhaps a Cartesian demon could in principle have created it as well!), the main point in our present discussion still is that it is *constituted and sustained* by the group members' collective activities based on their we-attitudes (cf. also chapter 6).

Underlying my Collective Acceptance model is the assumption that in each context of application one can distinguish between sentences whose objective correct assertability – collectively taken – in principle is *entirely* up to the members of the group (or up to their conceptual activities, especially what they on metaphysical grounds can accept as true) and sentences whose truth is at least in part up to nature, to the way the world is, and thus in part dependent on the causal processes occurring in the external world. The sentence "Squirrel fur is money" belongs to the first class of sentences and "Stars determine our fate" to the second. Thus, the first sentence will be correctly assertable for the group due to collective acceptance and no external, objective truth standard applies to it. The second sentence can only be correctly assertable for the group as a kind of stereotypical belief. It cannot be true in the standard objective sense, because it is not up to the group members to determine whether stars indeed determine our fate (cf. Tuomela, 1985, chapter 6, for two mind-independence principles clarifying this). The present point gives an argument for the employment of the forgroupness concept.

Both class one and class two sentences can be collectively accepted as correctly assertable for a group, but only in the case of the latter kinds of sentences can the question of full objective truth and of objective error meaningfully be raised. Sentences collectively accepted for the group can be called "groupjective" (to invent a term for the present kind of social objectivity) if they do not express objective truths, viz., if they are sentences in our first class. A groupjective sentence is epistemically objective for each group member, viz., he can epistemically treat what the sentence expresses as ontologically real (even when it is not). What a collectively accepted sentence such as "Squirrel fur is money" expresses thus is epistemically objective but ontologically groupjective (subjective for the group), precisely because the truth of the sentence depends on collective acceptance (cf. Barnes, 1983; Searle, 1995; Tuomela and Balzer, 1997; Tuomela, 2003).

Let me comment on the present dichotomy (or actually the underlying situation) in terms of some examples. We distinguish between a physical concept such as that of a tree and a social concept such as that of a leader. We can regard both concepts as collectively constructed, although in the former case not without the real world strongly constraining the construction (cf. chapter 3). In the physical case, the tree exists in a causal sense independently of whether it is conceptualized and known or not, but we cannot say the same of leaders. Leaders cannot exist without people (viz. the group members) taking them to be leaders. Thus, the group members must have thoughts amounting to leader-thoughts and leader-obeying-thoughts for there to be leaders at all. So there cannot be leaders without people having thoughts about leaders and hence without their having some kind of concept of a leader. The next example is that when we speak of a person as a leader or of something as money, the relevant predicate in question is already being assumed as a presupposed background notion. Thus, when people take Tom to be their leader or a certain kind of piece of metal to be money, they must already understand the concept of leader and the concept of money. Here we are talking about people applying the concept to a particular item to create an instance of the concept and more importantly to give a new social status to it. The CAT formula applies to this case, and we will see in more detail how it can be applied to institutions in chapter 6.

There are intermediate cases between purely social notions like that of a leader and strongly physically constrained notions such as that of a tree. Consider, for instance, action concepts and actions – compare opening the window or insulting someone. The actions in question – what really happens in the world – are conceptualized in a mind-dependent, intensional way. What conceptually amounts to an act of insult, for instance, requires a specific, culture-dependent way of conceptualizing action. We can say that it depends on one's (cultural and social) point of view or conceptual-epistemic framework what these activities are (cf. the viewpoint-dependent realism advocated in Tuomela, 1985). Nevertheless, it is not at least *entirely* up to us to make a piece of behavior – to cite cases involving an increasing amount of construction – a case raising one's hand, opening the window, or an act of insulting someone. This of course contrasts with the case of institutions such as squirrel fur as money. In the action case the matter always constitutively depends on something happening in "out there."[12] As the CA model accepts only social constructions of the full kind – those which are entirely up to us – actions and reasons and related things will not qualify as socially constructed items in our full sense.

Let me still consider the further issue of people believing that such and such a view or idea (something expressible by means of a that-clause) has been collectively accepted for the group. If all the members at a certain point of time collectively are the agents of the acceptance, they normally (with the qualifications current action philosophy has stated) will have the belief in question when collective acceptance is *intentionally* performed activity. But in other cases, for example when the collective acceptance concerns the maintenance of a social institution and not all group members take part in the collective acceptance (e.g. in the structured case), there may well be people who do not have the belief in question. Furthermore, in the case of institutions that have existed for a long time, some people may have forgotten what they are all about. Thus, in the case of leadership, guilt, responsibility, and other similar social concepts we generally have $CA(s) \leftrightarrow s$ for the group in question, but there may be group members who do not have the belief that s. There is in any case a conceptual distinction between s and the belief that s to be made also in the CAT case (viz., in the case of strongly social concepts) and there may be constraints for correct collective acceptance (e.g. a leader must accept the collectively offered position of being a leader). Thus somebody could be a leader or be guilty of something even in the strong social sense of these notions without the fact of somebody's being the leader (or being guilty, etc.) and the belief in the fact amounting to the same thing. It is only when the collective acceptance is correctly performed in accordance with the imposed constraints (if any) and when all group members take part in collective acceptance that there is equivalence, but even in these cases the analytic distinction between collective acceptance and its content can be made.

Furthermore, as collective acceptance is group-relative, there may be cultural and social differences between different groups. Thus somebody might be a leader (guilty of a crime) in the sense of one group (e.g. society or smaller community) but not in the sense of another group. All this has to be distinguished from the epistemic problem of how the applicability of the concept in question is epistemically judged in the case of each of these different concepts (of, say, guilt). Such epistemic assessments may be based on different criteria in different groups even in the case of objective constraints such as the law (cf. the importance of the selection of the members of the jury in the Anglo-American legal system).

While what is (entirely) up to us to decide in the meant sense is an ontically determinate fact, it is still difficult to thus tell what precisely the scope of the Collective Acceptance account is in an informative way. In chapter 6 I argue that what is thus up to us clearly includes social institutions (in formal, informal, and belief-based senses). Here, for example, various kinds of social positions and roles are included and so are social rules and norms. Accordingly, law is included here, and a case can be made for morality to be included as well.[13] Mathematics is another area to which the Collective Acceptance account seems basically applicable.

I cannot here try to argue for these kinds of broad claims, but rather present them as conjectures. I wish to emphasize that the Collective Acceptance account in no way entails that the propositions or sentences to which it applies are arbitrarily made correctly assertable by the whims of the members of a collective. Thus, for instance, in the case of law (justice), morality (moral goodness), and aesthetics (beauty) surely some more or less objective standards, or "excellence criteria," depending on prior collective acceptance, can come to play a role somewhat analogously to the case of truth (I am of course assuming here that a consensus account of material truth does not work). The final say in these matters, however, is the collective's acceptance of the view in question as correctly assertable, perhaps given a number of highly restrictive objective and (other) rationality constraints.[14]

There are some further points to be made about the notion of collective acceptance and (*CAT*).

1. It may first be noted that in (*CAT*) s could be about a rather "global" entity such as a natural language. For instance, s = Our language is French. Indeed, although I will not here argue this, natural language is in part collectively constructed (but recall above section 3.6). This may be the most general entity (collective good) that is collectively created. The collective creation of a natural language may be called "first-order" in comparison with the "second-order" creation of social institution predicates within such a natural language.

2. We can compare the performative operation of collective acceptance with Tarski's well-known Convention T: True(p) $\leftrightarrow$ p. From a formal point of view Convention T is a fixed-point formula as is (*CAT*), and thus both involve conceptual reflexivity (the latter, however, only within the scope of the Forgroup-operator). (*CAT**) contains the formula CA(g,s) $\leftrightarrow_g$ s, which is quite similar to Convention T. The only difference lies in the relativization to the group g of our formula. Then we may say that the account of collective-sociality given by the Collective Acceptance model is a fixed-point account at least in spirit if not quite in letter (viz., formally).

A correspondence account of material truth is often based on Tarski's theory. Assuming such an account, we can say that while according to Convention T the truth of a sentence (left-hand side) is brought about or made to depend on conditions in the world (supposedly expressed by the right-hand side), the direction of fit, so to speak, is opposite in the case of (*CAT*). The latter formula, furthermore, expresses only the group's point of view. Briefly, while in a correspondence account the truth of a sentence depends on the way the world is, in the Collective Acceptance model the relevant parts of the world are made to correspond to what we collectively intend or are kept in line with what we collectively believe it to be like. In the case of (*CAT*), we collectively mold or maintain or "renew" the world to fit our ideas rather than vice versa. We do not only collectively create meanings (viz., give some words uses), which task is assumed to have been completed here, but we also in part bring it about that the world fits these created concepts. There is no conflict here, but rather a division of labor. Correspondence truth can account for descriptive truth that is not up to us, while the Collective Acceptance model accounts for the rest – the part having to do with language, rules, and norms, and indeed all collective-social things – and does so possibly differently in the case of different groups.

3. In the case of (*CAT*) we have a *self-validating* aspect of collective production: if squirrel fur is money then people are collectively committed to behave in the right way concerning the collectively accepted norms regulating money, and when the right action comes about, this will support the present application of (*CAT*). Note that squirrel fur is money even if all individuals do not succeed in such *norm-obeying* action, as long as it is true that they collectively take squirrel fur to be money in the sense of (*CAT*).

4. How about collectively accepted collective skills and the like (such as Kuhnian "paradigms" in a scientific community)? Speaking of the collective acceptance of sentences or propositions may seem criticizable in the case of skills (cf. the skill involved in riding a bicycle or removing a brain tumor). However, it seems that the matter can be handled through speaking of the acceptance of sentences that serve to describe (and "name") the skills or practices in question. For instance, it can be collectively accepted that at a festive dinner the meat has to be carved in a special, skill-requiring way.

5. Thesis (*CAT*) has *ontic* import in the sense of connecting with the mind-independent causal order. This is because it serves to give the participating group members rights and duties in a sense having naturalistic content, their having rights and duties entailing their being (conditionally) disposed to act in certain specific ways. To be more specific, according to the Collective Acceptance account social institutions in the full-blown sense, qua some kind of collections of position-involving normative structures, can be causally effective ultimately only via the group members' minds and actions (not always consciously, though). As to the ontic nature of social institutions, it will be argued in chapter 6 that social

institutions amount to normatively governed social practices with a special conceptual and social status. Such "entity-looking" items as money, marriage, property right (etc.) get an "adverbial" analysis in terms the such social practices, viz., the social activities here have such and such special "adverbial" features (e.g. in the case of money, they may involve uses of special kinds of metal pieces in suitable exchange activities).

Physical social artifacts such as church buildings, cars, chairs, books, and generally much of at least a city-dweller's environment and "public social space" and "social geography" should be mentioned here. All these exist as causally effective entities. They have causal features and intentional, mind-dependent features. The latter relate to their purported use or function. Accordingly, both their physical and their intentional mental features are causally relevant. We can thus speak of their causal properties qua their having suitable physical features but also, and especially, qua their being artifacts expressing normative or nonnormative collective practices. (See Tuomela and Balzer, 1997, for further discussion.)

6. I will next answer a couple of general questions that have been asked. First, given that collective sociality and especially institutions depend on collective acceptance, are for example institution-expressing sentences (cf. (*CAT*)) analytic or synthetic? The matter depends on one's idea of analyticity. My basic answer is this.

(1) (a) If a sentence s is collectively accepted by a group g, then it does not follow that it is analytic, where "analytic" means true by virtue of the meanings of the words in s. (b) If a sentence s is collectively accepted by a group g, then it is "group-analytic," where "group-analytic" means necessarily true on conceptual grounds, viz., no alternative is conceptually possible, relative to the fact of the acceptance of s. (The group could of course have accepted something else.)

Notice that if s = squirrel fur is money then CA(s) does not make it an analytically true sentence, but still, considering the linguistic institution of promising, in CA(Promising entails the obligation to satisfy what has been promised) the accepted sentence is analytically true but I would say that this fact is due to our conceptual system that is reflected by our natural language. (There is also a moral dimension to promising, and that is something additional to the present conceptual dimension.) Supposing that our language is a collectively accepted thing, we can say this. That the term "promising" entails an obligation that is part of the collectively accepted meaning of the word. In general:

(2) (a) All semantic sentences (viz., sentences concerning meanings of linguistic items) are collectively accepted by the linguistic community

that is using the language (in the past, now, and in the future). (b) If a semantic sentence s is collectively accepted by a group g, then it does follow that s is analytic.

The second basic question is this: does collective acceptance of an institution (or other collective-social item) entail that the acceptors also endorse the institution (or item)? My brief answer is this:

(3) (a) If a sentence s is collectively accepted by a group g, then s is endorsed by g in "technical" sense, viz., in the sense that it is right for the members of g to use s in their theoretical and practical inferences and to act on its truth also in a nonlinguistic sense. (b) If a sentence s is collectively accepted by a group g, then it does not follow that s is endorsed as morally right (assuming that the criteria of morality come at least in part "from outside" g and concern in principle "all rational human beings," or something like that).

5.6 COLLECTIVE ACCEPTANCE AS SHARED WE-ATTITUDE

As noted earlier, collective acceptance may take various forms extending from an established, rule-based system to reach formal agreement at the one extreme and a rather unstructured build-up of shared we-belief or we-intention at the other. What is common to all these forms is that the participants come to hold a we-attitude – this is what the "construction" or "creation" of a collective idea or thought amounts to. Accordingly, collective acceptance always results in and involves that the members of the collective come to hold either a conative we-attitude (one with the world-to-mind direction of fit) or a doxastic we-attitude (one with the mind-to-world direction of fit or the world-to-mind direction of fit – the latter when the belief is a constitutions institutional one) and in general also maintain, and act (or at least are disposed to act) on the basis of, the we-attitude in question. As argued, in the context of the formula (*CAT*) the we-attitude must be in the we-mode (at least for a substantial number of group members). We can then say that collective acceptance in a sense is constituted by the corresponding we-attitude (or, more precisely, by coming to hold and holding it). It is the "jointness" of this attitude that yields collective acceptance and that involves the group and is for the group.

Accordingly, my central claim here is that collective acceptance for the group as required by genuine collectivity such as that involved in social institutions can be explicated in terms of we-mode collective attitudes: collective acceptance amounts to coming to hold and holding the right kind of achievement-oriented collective attitudes or shared we-attitudes involving a substantial amount of collective commitment towards the sentences (or propositions) accepted for the group. The commitment involved in the we-mode we-attitude can be either conative or doxastic, in accordance with the nature of the attitude at stake. Genuine holding of an attitude obviously also requires appropriately acting on the attitude in question. A shared we-attitude (viz., the content of the attitude being shared in the we-mode) is the social reason why the participants act collectively. (While I here emphasize we-mode shared we-attitudes, I showed in chapter 4 that also I-mode we-attitudes are important in the case of core social practices.)

We recall that the members of g share a we-attitude A if and only if (a) the members of g have the attitude A, (b) the members of g believe that the members of g have A, and (c) they also believe (or are disposed to believe) that it is mutually believed in g that the members of g have A. Of these, the somewhat idealized *genuineness* clause (a) is required because there cannot of course be a truly shared attitude without basically all the members participating in that attitude. The *conformity* clause (b) gives a conformative social reason for adopting and having the attitude A, and the *social awareness* clause (c) strengthens the reason by making it intersubjective.

The notion of we-attitude by itself is social in a central sense, and an action performed on the basis of a we-attitude accordingly is social, too; let me note in passing that an action is performed in the I-mode (respectively in the we-mode) if and only if it is performed because of an attitude had in the I-mode (respectively we-mode). In this chapter the focus is on collective sociality and on we-mode attitudes (and actions). Note that in simple cases of I-mode we-attitudes there is no group-level involved beyond aggregated individual attitudes, contrary to what our (*CAT*) requires.

Let us once more consider the reasons for thinking that collective acceptance of a content as true or correctly assertable involves coming to hold a we-attitude. Firstly, on the basis of the general idea that what is accepted as true must in some relevant circumstances be capable of serving as a basis of action, it is assumed here that what is collectively accepted as true or as correctly assertable is a thought that can – and in suitable circumstances will – serve as a reason for relevant (intentional) collective action. Note that this only makes intentional collective action the basic case, but allows also nonintentional collective acceptance (with the restriction that the acceptance could have taken place intentionally, although it did not). Next it is assumed that the collective action in question can be explicated as collective social action, viz., action based on a shared we-attitude (recall the discussion in section 4.2 supporting this). Now we arrive at the view that a collectively accepted and held thought is a we-attitude content and that collective acceptance indeed amounts to coming to hold and holding a we-attitude.

Furthermore, in the case of collective sociality, and therefore in the case of social institutions, the we-attitude must be held in the we-mode. This is basically because the participants must be taken to act as group members in these contexts, which clearly involve group phenomena. For instance, if certain pieces of metal are to count as money in the group, there must be social belief – we-mode we-belief – to this effect, viz., that those items indeed are money for their group. (This contrasts with the situation where the members only we-believe individually that they can use the pieces of metal in their everyday commerce). Thus a relevant collectivity condition explicating forgroupness must be satisfied and the group in question must be collectively committed to the collectively accepted and "we-attituded" thought. (To avoid circularity, we-mode explicate (a2) of chapter 2, requiring forgroupness and collective commitment but not collective acceptance, is to be used in the present context; see chapter 6 for detailed arguments for the we-modeness requirement.)

Next, the central we-attitude in the case of collectively acting on a collectively accepted thought must be either a we-intention (or, more broadly, a we-attitude in the intention family of concepts with a world-to-mind direction of fit) or a we-belief (or, more broadly, a we-attitude in the belief family of concepts with the mind-to-world direction of fit except in the case of constitutive beliefs). This is basically because collectively accepted thoughts must be capable of leading to collective social action and because such action requires such we-attitudes. The conclusion of the argument is that collective acceptance is coextensive with holding either a we-intention or a we-belief in the we-mode (in the weak sense of (a2)). Other we-attitudes can but need not be present.

I have earlier given some examples of the we-attitudes that (a token of) collective acceptance can uniquely extensionally amount to. Thus, I have claimed that a joint or collective intention to accept a goal (e.g., to collectively build a bridge or reduce the atmospheric ozone hole) will qualify and that so will a mutual belief (e.g., the mutual normative belief that Independence Day is to be celebrated by lighting candles or that one should give Christmas gifts to one's close friends and relatives). To mention some other examples, explicit contracts between people having the right authority, for example members of the parliament, are one type of collective decision making (passing a law) binding the whole collective (which has vested the parliament with its authority).

In accordance with what has been said earlier and above, it is my thesis that the family of intention concepts (including intentions, commitments, and agreements) and acceptance beliefs (doxastic takings) is all that the acceptable set ATT of attitudes needs to contain. Thus we can write ATT = {I,B}, taking I = intention and B = belief, both in the we-mode. We arrive at the following idealized "we-attitude thesis":

$$(\textit{WA})\ CA(g,s) \leftrightarrow (\text{for all i in g})\ (WI_i(s))\ \text{or (for all i in g)}\ (WB_i(s))$$

To make this formula work syntactically we must here "nonstandardly" assume that WI marks the fact that s expresses a we-intention in the we-mode and WB marks that s expresses a we-belief in the we-mode. Given this, (*WA*) comes to say that collectively accepting that s is noncontingently equivalent to the following fact: we, the members of group g, share a relevant we-attitude – indeed an acceptance-involving attitude – about s in the we-mode (more specifically an attitude in the intention family, WI or an acceptance belief WB) and – as attitudes involve action dispositions – are disposed to collectively act on the basis of this shared we-attitude.

5.7 CONCLUSION

This chapter has presented the Collective Acceptance model, which clarifies the conceptually and philosophically central features involved in the (typically objectively and rationally constrained) social construction and constitution of the social world and thus forms a central cornerstone in this book's arguments, both for the narrow and the wide construction theses or programs. Some central features are collective acceptance (expressing the creation and maintenance of collective social constructions), the reflexivity of collectively constructed notions, and the I-mode–we-mode distinction, of which the we-mode aspect was argued to be the more central in the present context.

I have accordingly made a case for the truth of the thesis that (*CAT*) is a central principle for understanding and making philosophical sense of at least the linguistically codifiable aspects of the nature of collectivity, sociality, and the social world. Very many topics have been discussed in this chapter, and I will not here make an attempt to summarize them. Let me, however, state some results or supported theses that are highly central for the chapter: considering a sentence s, it holds that s is a collective-social sentence, viz., a (dot-quoted) sentence expressing collective-social intentionality (aboutness), in a primary constructivist sense if and only if the members of g collectively accept s for themselves, being collectively committed to it, and they collectively accept s if and only if s (for them). Formally, this account amounts to the conjunction of the following theses rendered in our previous symbolism:

(a) $FG(g,CA(g,s))$ (Acceptance)

(b) $FG(g,CA(g,s) \rightarrow s)$ (Performativity)

(c) $FG(g,s \rightarrow CA(g,s))$ (Reflexivity)

Here $CA(g,s)$ is understood to entail g's being collectively committed to s – and not only achieving the correct assertability of s for the group. Collective-social sentences in a derived sense are sentences relevantly based on collective-social sentences in the primary sense.

Secondly, collective acceptance amounts to sharing a "right" kind of we-attitude about s, viz., either a we-intention or a we-belief (broadly understood). Thirdly, the right kind of we-attitude here is one in the we-mode and it is based either on an agreement to make s true (this includes plan-based joint intention) or on mutually believing (accepting as true) that s, depending on the case in question.

As a core social practice is based on a shared we-attitude as its reason and as at least a we-intention or a we-belief must be involved, every exercised core social practice is *collectively accepted* by its participants. Nevertheless, this acceptance need only be in the I-mode and thus need not satisfy the CAT formula. However, the kind of collective acceptance that our construction of collective sociality and social institutions requires must satisfy this formula and be in the we-mode.

CHAPTER 6

Social institutions

6.1 SOCIAL INSTITUTIONS INTRODUCED

In this chapter I will consider social institutions (or, as I would like to say, "collective-social" institutions) but mainly in a broad sense. They form the most important class of collective-social entities. Roughly speaking, by a social institution in the broad sense (e.g. money, language) I mean a specific type of norm-based – and possibly also aim-based – social practice. Roughly speaking, social institutions give or "define" the ground rules for how to act or for what counts as a collective item with a signified symbolic or social status in a society (or other collective). In this sense they are a kind of collective good available to all (cf. the forgroupness requirement). One can also say in more technical terms that institutions are special kinds of ordered pairs of social practices and norms (or systems of norms). This way of speaking emphasizes that there are two key elements in an institution – norms and collective activity, and the norms must confer a special symbolic or social status to the activity (or an item involved in the activity).

The notion of a social institution is used in several different senses in the literature. In different disciplines there are various ingrained usages and theorists often have different things in mind when speaking of institutions; and even when they have the same thing in mind they often emphasize different features of their shared analysandum. Although I will not give a survey of the social science literature here, let me briefly comment on the present embarrassment of riches. Some of the aspects or ideas are as follows. First, according to the aforementioned broad notion, a social institution is often regarded as a kind of recurrent, norm-based collective activity. A "constitutive" version of this view says that institutions define "the rules of the game in society" (cf. North, 1998). A second, more narrow idea restricts social institutions to those collective activities in which the normative frame is given by a hierarchically structured system of positions and roles, along with the accompanying exertion of power or influence.[1] This is the organization sense of institution. A third notion, adopted by game theorists, is both more general and more specific than the first one. According to this approach, a social institution is an equilibrium point in a repeated game. On the one hand, this characterization is more general in that it does not involve normative features; on the other hand, it is restricted in that it applies only to activities that can be modeled as a game in the sense of game theory. Furthermore, it is idealized in requiring equilibrium behavior. However, many extant social institutions seem not to be in equilibrium in the "self-policing" sense normally required by game theorists. Thus, the requirement of equilibrium behavior, if informatively specified, often is false in actual life, or else it tends to be a tautological requirement if left fuzzy and vague.[2]

Furthermore, social institutions (be they patterns of activity or whatever related) may be characterized by their social functions (cf. section 6.4). This approach can also include accounts in terms of invisible hand processes and the like (cf. chapter 7). Social functions will be involved in my account to some extent, even if it need not be assumed here that all social institutions are functional.

I will not try to give a more detailed survey here (but cf. section 6.4 and the notes to this chapter). Instead, let me try to say what I think is important of *typical* social institutions, even if all the things to be said are not perhaps strictly conceptual truths applying to *all* social institutions. Rather, my comments reflect possibly contingent features generally accepted for social institutions in different fields such as sociology, economics, and social science, and more generally in common-sense thinking about them. Later in the chapter I will be concerned with some highly general features of institutions that are constitutive of all social institutions.

Basically I take social institutions to be collectively – but not necessarily intentionally – made devices for creating order in a human community, typically society, and helping people to satisfy their basic needs, such as needs related to food and shelter, sexual relations and reproduction, sociality and social power. Whatever the exact list of the underlying needs is and whatever their precise nature is, we have here a strong underlying reason for the coming about of social institutions. As a result, institutions in different areas of social life arise: familial, educational, religious, political, and economic institutions.

To go into some detail, institutions, involving sanctioned norms (ought-norms and, to some extent, also may-norms), serve to give cooperative, public-good friendly solutions to collective problems and especially problems in which individual interests or preferences conflict with collective ones. Here we have such game-theoretically characterized collective action problems as (a) coordination dilemmas (e.g. on which side of the road should people drive), (b) collective action dilemmas in such as expressed by the Prisoner's Dilemma and Chicken, in which there is partial conflict between collective and individual interests and preferences, and, (c) situations of full conflict (zero-sum situations in game-theoretic terms). The institutional solution to these situations is to create sanctioned norms that guide people to behave in one way rather than another way such that freeriderism is avoided and order both in a collective and an individual sense is increased (for detailed discussion of collective action dilemmas in terms of a "we-ness" approach, see e.g. Tuomela, 2000a, chapters 10–13). The order aspect obviously involves that people will act in the direction the norms specify, and the norms at least typically are supposed to serve basic human needs and interests.

There will often be side effects of the order thus created. One such effect is that people behaving in accordance with the institutional norms will achieve psychological economy in their thinking and in the resulting action. They do not need to engage in decision making each particular time when a norm-governed situation is at hand and this makes it possible that the resulting actions become routine actions. So both thinking and acting tend to get more routine, we can say, and this leaves room for new innovative activities. (The other side of the coin is that routines may psychologically restrict the new avenues available.)

As will be seen later, all social institutions can be assumed to involve a new social status for some social practice or some object involved in such practice. Institutions also may be conceptually (or "symbolically") innovative. Indeed, I will emphasize both of these aspects below. Not surprisingly, I will apply the Collective Acceptance model to the case of social institutions and claim that its central CAT formula will clarify the situation and helps to distinguish those normative practices that are institutional and involve a special social and conceptual status from those that are not (cf. also section 6.4 on Searle's view). My project is a somewhat stylized philosophical (conceptual, metaphysical, and "design-theoretic") one, purporting to analyze the notion of a social institution and related notions. I am basically analyzing institutional notions meant to deal with social institutions as we ordinarily conceive them – and will mainly but not exclusively concentrate on society-wide institutions providing services, viz., public goods, to everyone.

As in chapter 5, I start from the platitude that social institutions and other related notions are collectively man-made. This is explicated in terms of performative collective acceptance for the group. It can be noted that in modern western societies the collective acceptance related to social institutions has typically been codified and we are mainly dealing with the continued collective acceptance of, say, greenbacks as money, due to the government of the US (cf. the performative print "This note is legal tender for all debts, public and private" on a dollar note). But this kind of codification does not work socially unless there is some amount of informal or "uncodified" acceptance of the official regulations.

As collective acceptance is a very general and vague notion in colloquial use, it is in my analysis contextually connected to – indeed argued to be coextensive with – relevant shared we-attitudes (basically in the we-mode). For me, social institutions are essentially group phenomena and this is in part accounted for by my we-modeness requirement. Collective acceptance involves not only the possibility that institutions are formed by external *decree* or by the members' *agreement making*, but also gradually in some kind of involuntary *evolutionary* or *invisible hand* process (cf. the remarks in chapter 7). There is also the issue of the *legitimacy* of social institutions. It concerns the justification and the bindingness of the institutional norms. The justification will vary depending on the institution at hand. I will largely bypass the broad question of legitimacy below. My relevant interest will be the functioning of an institution. If an institution is grossly unfair, for instance, and thus lacks legitimacy, the target people may not act as the institutional norms require; and so on. Thus, my analysis concerning institutions in force will implicitly take into account the motivational impact of the legitimacy of social institutions.

Let me next consider some general principles for classifying social institutions. Firstly, there is the generality aspect, which, however, is relative to particular societies. Social institutions may be classified according to their generality in a certain presuppositional sense. (1) Language can be regarded as the most fundamental, underlying social institution (recall section 5.5). People must rely on the correct use of concepts in all their other institutional and conceptual activities. Concepts can be regarded as rules to be mastered by people as skills, even if they need to have explicit knowledge of the rules, for example in the sense formulated in chapter 3. The skill is that they are able to classify things correctly, for example apply "red" correctly in the sense that red objects are included and nonred things are excluded (cf. section 6.2). Such institutional linguistic abilities and skills are presupposed in institutional acting of the kind that, for instance, using money involves. (2) Money, marriage and property are examples of institutional social objects and social institutions that typically are general, viz., society-wide. Thus, they are not specific to any "within-society" institutions such as some organizations are. (2) presupposes (1). (3) Organizations involve specific positions and "task-right systems." They typically presuppose the existence of various political, economic, and other (perhaps cultural and religious, etc.) institutions, and of course they presuppose language. Thus (3) presupposes (2) and (1).

For an organization to be a social institution it must satisfy the CAT formula of chapter 5 – or so I will argue. According to this formula, the organization-expressing sentence or account must be collectively accepted for the use of the group such that the collective acceptance of the sentence entails that it is correctly assertable (or true), and conversely. This entails that the FG (forgroupness) and CoCom (collective commitment) aspects, based on CA (collective acceptance), must be involved. What then are the organizations that qualify? An important (but possibly nonexhaustive) class of them consists of "public-good" organizations that have been constituted to serve some relevant goals (needs, interests, what have you) of the members of the collective and the collective in question for the members in a public-good fashion (based on forgroupness). The collective need not quite be a society, but it seems that it must be a community that can relatively independently satisfy its relevant goals and interests (e.g., it could be a minority group in a society which has instituted special kinds of food services or burial services in the form of an organization for its members). Accordingly, a (public or private) postal service established for a community will at least typically satisfy FG, CoCom, and CA and thus be the meant kind of social institution. But a business company need not satisfy FG and the CAT formula (equating truth-functionally the proposition expressing the organization with its collective acceptance) and thus may not be an institution even for its employees (and still less for the larger community within which it operates). On the other hand, some business firms aiming at profit making may yet satisfy the analysis to be given, and in that case I will count them as social institutions. (Admittedly, in ordinary parlance all organizations may be called institutions, and I do not want to legislate about the use of words, but rather to make a central conceptual distinction and suggest a verbal usage to go with it.)

Secondly, there is the fact that there are many kinds of collective acceptance relevant to social institutions. There are stronger and weaker kinds of collective acceptance based on stronger and weaker kinds of collective intentions and shared beliefs. What is central, too, is that collective acceptance can be either in the we-mode or in the I-mode, or these modes may be mixed so that some people act and obey norms in the we-mode, while some others do these things in the I-mode. As a rule of thumb, let us keep in mind, anyhow, that collective acceptance amounts to holding either a we-intention or a we-belief, and at least in the full-blown institutional case it must be in the we-mode. In structured collectives in which special operative members have the authority to collectively accept institutions for the collective and who perhaps also have the power to coerce and pressure the other members to accept what has been instituted, the other members need only accept the institution in a tacit sense involving the possibility of at least some degree of dissent and opposition (at least if the collective is based on nonvoluntary membership, such as are societies).

Thirdly, we have to distinguish between institutional cases in which there is no socially constituted object from the stronger cases like money or property. This connects to the more general question of the ontology of institutions. In colloquial talk a social institution can be of various ontological kinds. As examples from literature and common parlance witness, there are at least the following possibilities for what ontological kind of entity a social institution prima facie is: (a) social practice – for example the old practice of sauna bathing on Saturdays in Finland; (b) object – money (as notes, coins, etc.); (c) property of an individual – for example being an owner; (d) linguistic entity – for example natural language; (e) interpersonal state – for example marriage; (f) social organization – for example the national postal system, a university.

Note that of these, (a)–(e) are often general, society-wide, although they do not have to be so, while (f) is typically not (however, society can also be seen as a kind of social organization). I will accept that social institutions can be conceptualized in these various ways, but I emphasize that they are all related to *norm-governed social practices* and signify some elements in them. Indeed, one can say even that a social institution ultimately amounts to a special kind of norm-governed social practice (or set of practices). Some degree of social "functionality" is necessary for an institution. For instance, when we take money to be a social institution, we imply that the use of money (e.g. in contexts of exchange) is an institutional social practice. Similarly, what married people qua being married do and are disposed to do can be regarded as norm-governed social practices. A person who owns a house, for instance, can engage in the social practice of selling and buying and in the social practice of prosecuting people who violate his rights by trying to damage his house. The other cases are analogous. Thus there are linguistic practices (case (d)) and business practices, teaching practices, religious practices, and so forth that are related to business companies, the school, and the church, respectively. The social practice often is not joint plan-based action but, rather, individual action performed partly in view of what the others involved in the practice do.

Several authors (e.g. Barnes, 1983; Searle, 1995; Bloor, 1997) have suggested that social institution concepts are reflexive (self-referential).[3] However, I have not seen any detailed logical treatments of the question. It is therefore appropriate to try to say clearly and precisely what is at stake and to consider whether indeed the claim for reflexivity is true. I have already shown in chapter 5 that collective-social notions are reflexive. Because standard institutions as understood in this chapter will also be collective-social notions, their reflexivity is entailed by the reflexivity of the latter. A detailed and somewhat technical clarification of reflexivity is to found in the appendix to this chapter.

6.2 THE BASIC IDEAS

This book has already argued that there are many kinds of institutions and that the word "institution" is often used rather vaguely. In this section I not only want to bring more clarity to the conceptual and philosophical issues related to institutions, but also to present and advocate my own views. I will start by discussing what unites the different kinds of social institutions and then proceed to a discussion of what distinguishes different kinds of institutions from each other. One of my central theses will be that every "standard" kind of social institution requires for its maintenance the presence of some we-mode we-attitudes (at least in the case of a substantial number of participants) and activities based on them.

As seen, the notion of a social institution in force presupposes some kind of normatively regulated repeated collective acting in a group context, where both the normative structure and the social practices that it governs are based on a suitable kind of collective acceptance. Thus institutions fundamentally relate to social collectives or groups (here "group" and "collective" are initially used synonymously in the liberal sense of chapter 5). The practices are assumed to solve relevant collective action dilemmas and, as a result, produce goods (such as material and informational infrastructure, security, justice, etc.) for the use of the collective in question. In the present general case institutionalization involves the creation (or at least the collective acceptance of the creation by someone) and maintenance by the group members via their collective acceptance, of specific repeatable ways of acting and of "symbolic" (conceptual) statuses relative to group tasks and functions. (I am here speaking only of internally controlled groups.) For instance, in some tribes certain ritualized activities (e.g. rain dance) and certain roles (e.g. hunter) are institutional in this sense. I claim that in its most general and basic sense, institutional acting involves acting and functioning in a normatively governed way as a group member (as opposed to acting as a private person). In the present context this involves that the member in question functions in a certain group position or role (be the positions differentiated and specific or not), where these notions are understood in their broadest sense. Acting as a group member accordingly necessarily involves a group context, viz., acting for the group as related to some group task, purpose, or function (cf. the appendix to chapter 2). In the group's view there is a right and a wrong way of acting, and thus we have a weak element of normativity here.

In the case of groups with structure in the sense of division of labor and tasks, we must be concerned with different kinds of group positions and roles and also with a distinction between operative and nonoperative members for deciding and acting. In such cases acting as a group member amounts to acting in a certain norm-governed position or role. Acting as a group member typically entails that one acts in a position and is thus in principle replaceable by some other individual (group member) of the right kind. Thus the relevant notion of group member has been abstracted from the specific individual features of persons and this makes possible the change of members without transforming the group.

In the full institutional case we should assume extensive collective commitment to the instituted item. Given that, we can here equivalently speak of full-blown institutional acting in a group as acting in the we-mode. However, institutional acting without collective commitment and thus acting in the I-mode of course can occur in actual social life, given the existence of an institutional context and a substantial amount of collective commitment to it by the group (collective). In the case of structured collectives such as a modern state, there is the "state machinery" (government, parliament, and what have you) to collectively accept institutions for the state, and this machinery contains the institutionalized possibility to coerce people to act as required by the institutional norms. This often yields I-mode conforming activities.

Social institutions can be primarily dependent on (we-mode) we-beliefs or (we-mode) we-goals. Most of the examples to be discussed below rely centrally on such group-constitutive we-beliefs, but there are also goal- or aim-based institutions (e.g. the school system). (Institutions based centrally on we-goals also must involve we-beliefs of course, as their basic principles must be socially understood and believed.) Let me here give an explicit analysis of we-mode we-beliefs in their core sense (recall (a2) of the appendix to chapter 2).

(*WMB*) Agent x's belief (more precisely, acceptance belief) that p is in the we-mode relative to group g if and only if x believes (accepts) that p qua a member of g and at least in part for (the use of) g and is collectively committed to (relying on and using) p.

As to the relevant notion of we-mode collective commitment applying to an individual, recall section 5.4. A more specific explicate is as follows:

(*WMB**) Agent x's (acceptance) belief that p is in the we-mode relative to group g if and only if p is collectively accepted by the members of g as a belief content for g (x's position, if there is clear-cut positional structure) and they are collectively committed to p for (the use of) the group.

The fullest, or core, notion of a we-belief in the we-mode now comes out as follows, recalling from chapter 5 that we-mode we-beliefs are acceptances ("acceptance beliefs"):

(*WMWB*) Agent x has the we-mode we-belief that p if and only if x believes that p in the we-mode and believes that the agents in g believe that p in the we-mode and also believes that there is a mutual belief in g that all the members share the we-belief in the we-mode that p.

In the full-blown or, as I say, "standard" case, covering, for example the general institutions of money, language, and law, as well as such specific (or "narrow") institutions as the school and the banking system, institutional acting is a social practice governed by a social norm accompanied by sanctions (cf. note 1 for this widely accepted view). This serves to create the collective outcome that the group as a whole operates "as intended," viz., so that it tends to fulfil its basic tasks and functions and to provide public goods for the group.

Elsewhere I have discussed social norms and also sketched a simple account of social institutions which emphasizes the normative character of social institutions and the reflexive nature of the institutional notions created. This account relies on two kinds of collectively "made" and accepted social norms: (i) formal or informal authority-based norms ("rule-norms" or "r-norms," as I have called them), which are grounded, directly or indirectly, on group-authorized agreement making (resulting in, e.g., laws, charters, informal rules) and (ii) proper social norms ("s-norms"), which are either society-wide or group-specific norms based on normative collective expectations and which require action in response to them (cf. the norm of mutual gift-giving).[4]

Authority-based norms ("r-norms") are basically norms that an authority, such as a government or governing board, imposes on the members of the collective in question (e.g. a professor must teach a certain amount of classes in his field during each academic year). These norms are explicitly stated, as in the paradigmatic cases of state laws, and they can "exist" in a weak sense even if people do not pay much attention to them, although they in many cases ought to know them. (If they come into conflict with the norms, and are consequently rebuked, they cannot defend themselves in those cases by saying that they did not know the law.) The other category of norms is based on mutual normative behavior expectations in the collective in question (e.g., the members of the press are to sit on the left side of the hall during a political meeting). These norms are the proper social norms (s-norms). They may be traditional and transmitted in connection with habits: people just learn to obey the norms during socialization. Often they are not codified and perhaps not even verbalized.

Sanctions are generally associated with social norms; they are respectively either "official" authority-imposed sanctions ("r-sanctions") or social sanctions ("s-sanctions" consisting of social approval and disapproval). The more legitimate (right and just, etc.) the target persons find the norms in question, the more inclined they of course are to obey them.

In the case of general institutions like language, money, and private property, society-wide norms are involved. In the case of institutions in the organization sense (e.g. a university), the norms generate "task-right systems" (TR systems) for the positions involved (see section 6.5). There can be task-right systems utilizing either kind of norm. Typically, in an organization there is a task-right system based on r-norms and another one based on s-norms, and there may be tension and even explicit conflict between these two task-right systems. The resulting social institution of this organizational kind can be represented as a pair <SP,TR>, where SP is a social practice or a class of social practices involving recurrent collective social action governed by and "carrying out" a general, relatively enduring task-right system TR. When TR is based on r-norms, I will speak of an r-institution and in the case of an s-norm-based institution of an s-institution. (Mixed cases can also occur.)

We can also say that a social institution amounts to collective norm-following or collective normative social practices that, at least in some cases, involve a collective good and purport to solve a collective action dilemma. As the norms are collectively created, we have reason to think that the CA account and its CAT formula expressing "attitudinal reflexivity" applies to institutions in the present organizational sense (see section 6.5 for further discussion of this problem and the appendix for attitudinal reflexivity).

As said, general institutions include money, property rights, and language. (More precisely speaking, it is the social practices involving these things that are social institutions.) The first two as we currently have them are best construed as r-institutions, while language seems to represent a mixed case. Mutual gift-giving is an example of a pure s-institution.

Our classifications do not end here. There is yet another central type of social institution that I will now start discussing in terms of an example. Consider a village in which a social practice of playing soccer on Sunday afternoons has arisen. A social norm may (but need not) develop to govern this practice. For instance, its content could be that all young boys in the village ought to (or are normatively expected to) participate. The next step would be that this institutional practice is conceptualized for instance as the "Sunday Match," and it may gain some new special features involving social activities related to the game. Then the Sunday Match will become an ingrained concept that the group members use in their thinking and action. The notion of Sunday Match so conceived involves special group activities grouped together by the label "Sunday Match" (or, more precisely, its dot-quoted version .Sunday Match.). In other words, those activities get a new conceptual and social status by being subsumed under this new label. The Sunday Match thus has acquired a special conceptual and social status for the group members. This status can be expressed by the constitutive norm "The Sunday Match is our football game" (cf. Searle, 1995, and section 6.4 below for constitutive rules). It refers not only to a match being played on Sundays, but to a specific kind of match played in a certain way in this and possibly other villages. This constitutive rule makes the use of the concept Sunday Match normatively governed: this concept, and the label "Sunday Match" that goes with it, is to be used for the football game activities in question.

The notion of Sunday Match is a self-referential notion, for its content is socially construed and involves that the people collectively take it to be the Sunday Match in their group. We have a social institution here, and it is a type of institution in the sense of being capable of having instances. This Sunday Match institution may also begin spreading to other villages, as it is not tied to particularities like certain specific participants.

What I have just said about the Sunday Match also applies to other analogous activities like going to the sauna on Saturday afternoons (the Finnish Saturday sauna practice; cf. chapter 7). Even when this practice was fully in force (some generations ago) no social norms concerning the "internal structure" of it exist at least allover in Finland. Furthermore, there is (or was) no social norm demanding that people ought to participate in the social practice. Still there is the social notion of Saturday sauna, viz., people use and in some context need to use this notion to be able to describe correctly what a certain collective activity amounts to. It would seem right to say that there is a normative collective commitment to the "social existence" of the concept of Saturday sauna.

There are also object-related institutions. Thus, Citroen 2CV owners have adopted certain institutionalized practices, and it can even be said in view of them and of their (and others') attitudes that this car is an institution. An important point in the process where a weaker social institution develops into a strong one is whether the participants and possibly other members of the collective in question have conceptualized the practices by means of a concept that they also then use in their own thinking (especially belief contents) and collectively take the practices in question to fall under that concept.

6.3 THE FINAL ACCOUNT

6.3.1 Social institutions in the "standard" sense

To recall some general points from section 6.1 related to social institutions pertaining to a collective or group (primarily society or community), we may speak of a group's goals and assume that the group, if acting rationally, takes care of its members' needs (typically conceived as something objective) and wants (subjective items) to a suitable degree. The group members' goals and perhaps also needs may be in conflict with each other – there are coordination problems and more serious collective action dilemmas (e.g., problems with the Prisoner's Dilemma or Chicken structure). An institution is meant to solve such problems. Note, furthermore, that a group may have its own nonaggregative and irreducible goals – as in the case of *compromise-based* goals determined by the operative members when designing or revising an institution.

What was just said applies only to (organized) groups that can act and plan their actions. In the case of the evolution of language and rudimentary economic exchange, there can hardly be irreducible group goals or group-binding goals, but only something like aggregated individual goals (or shared we-goals).

By forming institutions a group then typically purports to solve collective action dilemmas and thus tries to help its members satisfy their needs and goals – especially in ways that are compatible with the group's own goals and views. On the other hand, the group also tries to prevent its members from getting involved in irrational behavior and to safeguard people from physical and mental damage. We may here speak of the group's controlling and monitoring its members. Both individual level order (rational behavior) and collective, macro level order is thereby created. A collective makes its members' need and want satisfaction more economical (e.g. by reducing transaction costs) and thus helps people to save time and energy for innovative activities. In the case of collective action dilemmas, it may even be impossible in practice to provide collective goods, as is well known. Furthermore, institutions socialize people and thereby create homogeneity, which helps to maintain both individual and collective level order in the long run. (See section 6.3.2 for the group control aspect.)

Proceeding to a more detailed account, I will concentrate on primary social institutions, viz., institutions that do not themselves consist of institutions. The following classification of increasingly stronger social institutions can now be usefully proposed in view of our discussion:

(a) institution as norm-governed social practice or as a "regularity in behavior"
(b) institution as conferring a new conceptual and social status to some entity (e.g. person, object, or activity)
(c) institution as conferring a new deontic status (and status functions to go with it) to the members of the collective in question (Searlean institution)
(d) institution as an organization involving social positions and a task-right system

In view of what will be said below, (a)–(d) can be taken to represent increasingly stronger kinds of social institutions, and norms of some kind will be involved in all of them. The strongest case (d) has already been commented on. Case (c) is the case which fits for example money, marriage, and property. (Searle, 1995 seems to take (c) to cover all social institutions; see section 6.4 for discussion.) However, I take (b) to be an equally important notion, because it involves the emergence of a special conceptual and social status (but perhaps not deontic status) of something conferred by collective acceptance. This case has been considered in section 6.3.1 (recall the "Sunday Match") and will be discussed further below.

Reflexivity applies to cases (b), (c), and (d), but need not apply to (a); see the appendix and thesis (*R*) below for a discussion of reflexivity. In case (a), which I accept as a case of institution because of common academic usage of the term, there need not be the kind of new conceptual status based on collective acceptance that entails reflexivity, whence reflexivity might fail in the case of (a). For instance, if institutions are viewed as regularities in behavior in equilibrium as many economists and game theoreticians do (recall note 2), there need be no collective acceptance involving we-intentions or we-beliefs. Thus the meant kind of attitudinal reflexivity is missing (cf. the appendix).

What I have called the "standard" cases of social institutions, then, are cases belonging to (b), (c), or (d). I will now proceed to give a kind of explanatory theory or account of the standard cases. My analysis will go in terms of the CA model (and its CAT formula). I will assume that the correct analysis of them will have to account for reflexivity on the basis of arguments for the presence of this feature that have already been given (recall the money case and the Sunday Match case as examples). As to case (d), accordingly only those cases of organizations that do satisfy the CAT formula qualify as institutions in my "standard" sense.

As argued in chapter 5, collective acceptance in the case of social institutions basically amounts to holding either a we-intention or a we-belief ("acceptance-belief"). As also argued, it must be for the use of the group and involve collective commitment. There are institutions based on a strong kind of collective acceptance. Thus property rights, for instance, and other r-institutions understood as modern law-based notions seem to require group-authorized agreement making. But agreement making, and, derivatively, authority and power, can be fitted into my account. Roughly speaking, agreement making amounts to the shared acceptance of a norm-entailing, nonsingular sentence (content), say s, accompanied by the joint intention and commitment to carry out (or, as the case may be, maintain) what s says (cf. also chapter 2, end of section 2.4).

In reference to (*CAT*), the collectively accepted institution-expressing sentence s expresses an ought-to-do, ought-to-be, a may-do, or a may-be norm – or a system of such interrelated norms typically specifying positions and functions. Mutual belief, at least in a dispositional sense concerning the acquisition of a flat-out mutual belief, must also be required, and it is taken care of by the requirement that the members share a we-attitude towards the content expressed by sentence s.

Power is involved also in other ways, and this is especially relevant in the case of structured collectives. The point is simply the well-known one that for the agreed-upon norms to be in force a system of sanctioning and control is needed and that this system may result in some amount of coercion of members to behave in accordance with the norms. In heterogeneous structured groups the nonoperative members may have to be coerced so to behave. My account basically requires of the nonoperative members that they tacitly accept what has been decided for them and this can be so weak as to allow for substantial disagreement in thought, although less in action. (See section 6.3.2 for related discussion.)

We recall from section 6.1 the various ideas that have been constitutively connected to social institutions in different academic fields. I will now abstract from "area-specific" notions and venture to give a rather general summary account or theory of standard social institutions. The account relies strongly on the analysis (*CAT*) discussed in chapter 5 and assumes, for the sake of simplifying the formulations, that the collective in question is an unstructured one and that it is the same one that collectively accepts the institution-expressing sentence. This sentence, s, can be a complex and compound one, and it is assumed to include a constitutive norm (r-norm or s-norm), such as is "Squirrel fur is money," among the norms it expresses.

(*SI*) Sentence s expresses a *social institution (in the "standard" sense)* for collective g if and only if

(1) s expresses or entails the existence of a social practice (or a system of interconnected social practices) and a norm or a system of interconnected norms (including a constitutive one) for g, such that the social practice generally is performed at least in part because of the norm

(2) the members of g rationally collectively accept s for g with collective commitment; here it is assumed that collective acceptance for the group entails and is entailed by the correct assertability of s.

In this analysis I take an institution at bottom to be a system of social practices governed by a system of norms. The institution is one *for* the group, viz., for the benefit and use of the group in question. We may also speak of institutions *in* a broader collective (say in the sense in which a corporation might be an institution in, although not perhaps for, a society). Furthermore, in a more general analysis than that given by (*SI*), it may be necessary to deal with two groups, say g and g', such that the institution creates a collective good for g' and g is the group maintaining the institution. The institution could be a nonprofit organization that, as collectively accepted by g, provides goods for g' (say poor people in a certain corner of the globe, although here we may consider the possibility that g = g' = mankind).

The institution, viz., the norm-governed social practice or some specially focused-on aspect of it in some cases, need not yet be functionally successful when it satisfies (*SI*). While it can be said to function to create order and solve one or more collective action dilemmas (which need not be more than coordination dilemmas), whether it succeeds in that is a different matter. But we can require this:

(*FSI*) Suppose that sentence s expresses a social institution for group g. Then the social institution in question is *functionally successful* if it solves a collective action dilemma (the dilemma it intuitively "purports" to solve).

To comment on the clauses of (*SI*), (1) is not by itself rich enough to capture a standard social institution as can be seen from trivial examples of norms that are "arbitrary" from the group's point of view. A system of norms seems more likely to give a basis for an institution than does a single norm. Even if that were given, (1) would not suffice. There might, for instance, be externally imposed and strongly sanctioned norms imposed on a group (by some kind of dictator). The norm might then be in force but only in a sense involving I-mode acceptance, and this might be an institution in sense (a). Thus forgroupness and collective commitment would be lacking. A standard social institution, here assumed to be at least collectively rational, must thus involve (rational) forgroupness, which entails serving the satisfaction of the group's goals. Thus clause (2) gets a partial justification from this angle.

I understand clause (2) to entail that a standard social institution concept is reflexive because of the facts of collective acceptance, as collective acceptance in the above sense (making true the CAT formula of chapter 5 and formula (11) in the appendix below) entails that the concept in question must appear in the members' belief contents. As will be shown in the appendix to this chapter, this suffices to make the institution concept reflexive. Suppose, for simplicity, that sentence s above is of the simple monadic kind "For all x, if x is P then x is S," where x can be a practice, an object, or a state, as the case may be (recall section 6.1). As the institution is assumed to be a primary or nonderived one, P is not an institutional concept by itself. But here it gets a new conceptual and social status because P-things now become institutional S-things, on the basis of collective acceptance. Accordingly, it can be assumed that clause (2) of the above analysis (*SI*) entails this:

(*R*) The fact expressed by sentence s, viz., that P-things are S-things, is reflexive in the attitudinal sense that the members of the collective g collectively accept s, and hence the concept S will occur in their belief contents when they use s to express the mentioned fact for them.

I would like to emphasize that when I speak of the special social and conceptual status that institutions get in the present account, the basic idea is simply that an institution is created (with the qualifications mentioned earlier in chapter 5) and, especially, maintained by our collective acceptance and that this, via the idea formalized by the CAT formula, gives a new status to the institutional structure or aspect that the collectively accepted sentence s expresses relative to the case where there was no such structure. Thus, it is the performative intersubjectivity, so to speak, involved in CA that gives the new status. In simplified cases like "Squirrel fur is money" (= s), we give squirrel fur the status of money, and this new social and symbolic status obviously also has consequences for action – for example for exchange activities and other relevant interactions between people. As squirrel fur gets its new status, in (*R*) S gets its new status from the collective acceptance of the sentence of s involving the base property P. The base property can be institutional, but it can also be noninstitutional (as in the squirrel fur case). Notice that the new status may also be related to a norm to use certain concepts for certain practices – this is what happens in case (b) of institutions.

The notion of a special social and conceptual status is somewhat vague, but the basic idea is clear enough and is given by the requirement that the institution-expressing sentence s must include as its component a *constitutive* r-norm or s-norm (or more broadly an expression of a *constitutive ethos* in the sense of section 6.3.2). It could be, for example, "The Sunday Match is our football event" or "Squirrel fur is our money." The fact that, according to clause (2) of (*SI*), it is collectively accepted, indeed we-believed, in the we-mode entails that there is a new social concept in and for group g. Our football game gets this new conceptual status that it and the rituals involved can be fully captured only by the definite description "Sunday Match." It is also entailed that the football game then gets a special social status (based on the aforementioned we-belief), even if there need not be a participation norm. But there will be a norm requiring the conceptualization of the football event as the Sunday Match. Similar remarks can be made of other institutional cases. Even a simple example like a certain group of young people having the normative practice of wearing red jeans can under some circumstances be a social institution, if there is a collectively accepted norm of participation and if there is a constitutive norm saying something to the effect that red jeans is their special dress. In all, given the present view of a conceptual and social status, we can say that the fulfillment of the CAT formula entails the existence of a special conceptual and social status, as the mentioned constitutive norm was assumed to be a conjunct in s.

Let us now consider our various cases (a)–(d) in light of (*SI*). As seen, case (a) need assume only recurrent I-mode action, such as aggregated behavior based on instrumental rationality (cf. "Members of group g ought to have lunch at Alfredo's because it is the cheapest nearby restaurant"), and the CAT formula clearly need not be satisfied (e.g. forgroupness and collective commitment are missing). In contrast to (a), an institution in (b) and in the stronger cases involves a special social status and typically a "concept" for the group in question.[5] This entails that the institutional structure expressed by s is accepted and maintained at least to some extent in the we-mode rather than in the I-mode (see 6.3.2 for arguments).

As all social institutions – including the weak case (a) – are based on social practices, and as social practices (at least in their core sense discussed in chapter 4) arguably are based on we-attitudes, at least this much collective intentionality will be present in all social institutions. What is more, indeed *we-mode* we-attitudes need to be present in cases (b)–(d), as will be shown below.

All institutions are normative in some sense, although not in all cases in one and the same sense. The b-case, the "concept" sense of an institution, is interesting. First we notice that it does clearly satisfy the CAT formula, which makes it attitudinally reflexive and expresses that an institution must be collectively accepted for the use of the group. Roughly, the collective acceptance in the group for the group of the constitutive norm "Our practice of playing football on the village lawn on Sundays is the 'Sunday Match'" (= s) makes s correctly assertable for the members, and conversely. Here the social practices that the institution involves and that the institution concept presupposes or entails may be normative in that it involves obligations and rights for the members participating in the social practices involved. Nevertheless, it need not be normative in this strong sense (which sense would indeed make it a case of (c)). Neither need it involve a social norm (which would typically be an obligation norm) to participate in the social practice (or practices) in question. But there will be a normative collective commitment to the "social" existence in the group of the concept in question – let us say the concept of the Sunday Match or the concept of the Saturday sauna. This collective commitment need not yet concern the practice in question. It concerns the social existence and use of the concept in suitable circumstances.

Recall from chapter 5 that my core notion of commitment is, roughly, the notion of a normative binding oneself to a propositional content. If all group members are entitled to the same practical inference (within the group's realm of concern) and if they also believe that the others are, we can speak of a shared norm in a rudimentary sense; and we speak of an interpersonal norm when there is a mutual belief among the group members that the members share the norm in question. If, furthermore, the norm is "in the public domain" (e.g., it is a public, mutually known fact that there is this kind of norm that the members accept or are supposed to accept), we can speak of an objective norm and consequently of an objective collective commitment. In the case of a "concept" institution (b-case), we are dealing with the use of a certain concept in one's descriptions and inferences. Let us consider the case of squirrel fur as money. Speaking in terms of the Collective Acceptance model, in the CAT formula we now have s = Squirrel fur is money, and "money" here is a predicate applying to squirrel furs. Thus "money" expresses the central concept that the institution involves (we can even say that the concept of money is the institutional concept in question), and s gives the central assumption underlying the use of the concept and the nonlinguistic activities related to it. It simply says to what kind of items the predicate "money" in the context of collective g can be applied.

I wish to emphasize that even if the participants (the members of g) are collectively committed to the existence in the group of the central institution concept and to its use in both linguistic and nonlinguistic activities under suitable circumstances (cf. the discussion of ought-to-be and ought-to-do rules in chapter 3), they are not yet thereby collectively committed to participating in the social practice expressed by the concept. Thus, even if one is committed to the fact that the Saturday sauna is an institutional notion in parts of Finland, and to using this concept in one's descriptions and inferences in suitable contexts (e.g., when asked about some special bathing ritual engaged on Saturdays), one is not thereby committed to participating in the sauna practice. Notice that if there is a participation norm but not yet a concept, we arrive at a social institution of kind (a) rather than kind (b) or something stronger (recall note 5).

When applied to institutions of kind (d), viz. social organizations, (*SI*) should actually be formulated so that it makes the operative–nonoperative member distinction, because organizations do involve such a distinction (both for decision making and for carrying out what has been jointly decided).[6] In any case, (*SI*) captures the view that a social institution in this sense involves one or more recurrently performed social practices, SP, and a task-right system, TR. Thus sentence s is supposed to express the pair (SP, TR), in colloquial terms that there is a (typically position-involving) social practice or system of interconnected social practices governed by interconnected and interlocking social norms (either authority-based norms or proper social norms). Clause (2) entails that the social norms in question must be in force. Roughly, they are in force if they are obeyed to a suitable extent and are also suitably sanctioned. Due to the assumption of collective acceptance for the group, we get the result that a social institution is for the use of the social group in question and is, indeed, a we-mode concept (see the discussion of we-modeness below).

An organization internal to a community, g, such as a business company, in general is not a social institution, because it fails to be constituted for the community and thus for the use of community members and thus fails to satisfy the CAT formula involved in (*SI*): a truly full-blown social institution is assumed to deliver services and goods available to the members of g. A business firm such as Shell, aiming at maximizing its profit, is not designed to be essentially for the group g in contrast to, say, the schools system, the health system or the postal system of g (if it has one). However, it is compatible with my account that Shell still is an institution relative to the group consisting of its employees and shareowners – this depends on whether it satisfies (*SI*) for this group.

The present account of social institutions is highly general and synchronic. It is, however, possible to give more content to it and to make it dynamic (see chapter 7). The result is a detailed mathematical model that I have called a "social mill." It shows on a general level how social institutions can be initiated, maintained, and revised via the agents' collective practices.

6.3.2 Institutional activities as we-mode activities

Does the kind of collective intentionality needed in institutions have to be we-mode intentionality rather than merely I-mode intentionality? One of my theses in this chapter has been that we-mode we-attitudes are required by institutional action (recall (*SI*)). The requirement of the presence of we-mode intentionality involves two aspects, the we-attitude aspect and the we-mode aspect. First, social institutions that exist and are in force in a collective must involve sociality operating on the level of individual group members, for the group members are the ultimate movers and agents here. However, they can only create, maintain, and revise their institutions via their social awareness of the situation. This leads to the requirement of the presence of we-beliefs and, when creation and change is at stake, to the requirement of the presence of we-intentions. The second aspect is that also relevant *we-mode* we-attitudes must be present (initially at least in sense (a2) of we-modeness, which requires forgroupness and collective commitment). The creation and maintenance of a social institution is a group affair. The institution exists in the group, so to speak, and for the group. Accordingly, it is concerned with acting fully as a group member (viz., in the we-mode) rather than as acting as a private person (viz., in the I-mode), and the group is (normatively) committed to its institutions. To the extent it succeeds in carrying out its commitment, which requires by and large that its members or a substantial amount of them obey and hold on to the commitment, to that extent the institution is functional in the meant, "right" sense. Thus, my central argument for we-modeness assumes that a social institution is a group thing and says that a functionally successful social institution must involve we-mode we-attitudes.

I will now present a more concrete argument for the required presence of we-mode we-attitudes. Let us start with the elementary case of a group that has started to use money as a medium of exchange. As seen, in my account the essential ingredients or constituents, if you like, of social institutions are relevant social practices (or systems of them, in advanced cases) which are based on the collective acceptance of certain ideas, e.g. that certain pieces of metal (called "Coins") are money in the group. In my account the institution-expressing proposition (s in (*SI*)) will be "Coins are money in our group" (or its functional equivalent).

Let me show in concrete terms that the institution-expressing proposition "Coins are money in our group" must, on pain of the institution not being functional, be believed by any rational institution user and that it must be regarded as a we-mode we-belief. Suppose that two members, x and y, use Coins as a medium of exchange, believing that Coins are used as an exchange medium in this kind of transaction. Thus x and y have a belief to the effect that it is (normatively) correct to use Coins as money in their collective. However, their exchange clearly requires more. Each agent must believe that the other also believes this, for otherwise, for example, he would hardly dare to sell his house without being paid cash. Even more is needed. Suppose x lacks the belief that y believes that x believes that Coins are correct exchange money for the group in question. Here x thus believes that it is not (fully) rational for y to engage in the exchange, because y, in accordance with what has been assumed, might not believe that x has a belief to the effect that s, viz. that Coins are correct exchange money. In such a case an important reason-element for y to act rationally would be missing (cf. y selling his house to x). This in turn makes it rational for x not to engage in exchange with y. My argument so far indicates that we-attitudes (here we-beliefs) are to be required in the kind of institutional activities at stake, given that the participants are believed to be "moderately" rational and require good reasons for putting their money into play.

The whole argument is in fact driven by the idea that the institution-expressing proposition, which is for the group, must be socially believed. This is because an institution is a group phenomenon operated by the group members. Accordingly, the (continued) institutional use of Coins as money requires that the group members share, and are committed to, the social belief that Coins are money ($= s$, in (SI)) for their group. When using Coins as money, people must of course understand that they are money for the group, that they not only can be used as money but in many cases must be used as the only kind of valid money. The social belief that Coins are money in the group, when spelled out, turns out to be a we-belief, indeed one for the use of the group to which the group by its collective acceptance of Coins as money has committed itself. The group's commitment involves that both x and y stick to s on the basis of their thinking that they ought to do so and mutually know that they are so committed and that Coins are money for the use of group members. The sanctions for failing to be so committed might well be that the uncommitted person loses a considerable amount of money in our example and, furthermore, that the others begin to regard this person as an unworthy exchange partner. This indicates that there is also social commitment involved – recall the discussion in chapter 5. So all in all, there is belief as a group member and action on this basis, and also collective commitment as a group member. Thus, we are dealing with *we-mode* we-beliefs here. (Let me note in passing that in the case of the institution of language, one can argue analogously with the case of money that communication, e.g. truthful informing, must involve we-mode we-attitudes.)

I will speak in more general terms and give a deeper reason for the we-attitudes having to be in the we-mode in all institutional cases. Assume that a group, g, has and is committed to certain constitutive goals, values, beliefs, standards, and norms. Let us say that they form its ethos, and we will call it E. We can assume that E is constitutive for the group (entailing forgroupness in my sense) in the sense that unless the group strives for its satisfaction and/or maintenance it will tend to disintegrate and lose its identity.

As seen, forgroupness concerns what is taken by the group members to be in the interest of the group in the sense of serving the group's and its members' central goals or interests (viz., rational or objective ends) to the extent that they are compatible (which is not always the case). Forgroupness – when truly adopted by the group members – is bound to lead to a view of social relations based on group membership, thus on group perspective, and on sociality, viz., the view that people typically seek the company of others and take into account in their thinking and acting what those other members of the group think of them. The group – regarded as some kind of unity – becomes central in people's activities. This in general normatively requires that the resulting we-mode action, governed by the group's goals and interests, not be strategic action *vis-à-vis* the internal affairs taking place in the group (although it of course may be strategic concerning other groups). Thus, instead of dealing with other agents with which they are in dependency relationships as rationally acting (potential or actual) enemies they, at least to begin with, regard them as members of the same group, which involves the idea of cooperativeness (or "harmony") based on the group's shared ethos. This also leads to the selection of cooperative action alternatives (especially in collective dilemma situations) and shared we-mode goals leading to the performance of those alternatives conducive to the group's ethos. Helping and altruism thus naturally get a place here instead of, for example, enmity.

In the we-mode case things are being put in the public domain (or rather the group domain) precisely in the sense that forgroupness does it: forgroupness licenses the use of collectively accepted ideas in practical inference and action related to the group domain. In principle, everybody is assumed to contribute to the group good, to do his fair share, but is also allowed to have his piece of the common group cake (products of the joint enterprise), so to speak.

After these general remarks, I will proceed to a more concrete argument for we-modeness. My account proceeds in terms of ought-to-be and ought-to-do norms such that the ought-to-be norms relevant here are taken to require the ethos E to be fulfilled in the group. This idea, viz. that there is some such collectively accepted E which is to be upheld, gives the rock bottom of my analysis in the sense that the "justification buck" stops there. This is compatible with there being deeper explanations (e.g. psychological and/or evolutionary) as to why precisely a particular ethos E has been chosen and indeed why the members are disposed to stick to it. Consider now the following informal sketch of an argument relying on the group ethos idea.

(1) It ought to be the case in g (and for g) that E is fulfilled (viz., satisfied and/or maintained by the group members' activities conducive to E).

(2) The group (and group members collectively), perhaps via their operative members, ought to see to it that the ought-to-be norm expressed by (1) is satisfied.

(3) The group members ought to commit themselves to (possibly recurrently, as the case may be) intentionally performing actions conducive to E.

(4) The group members are collectively committed to E in view of (1)–(3), and they act purporting to fulfil this commitment.

(5) Intentionally performed actions purporting to fulfil E are actions qua a group member.

(6) The group members' (intentional) actions conducive to E here are we-mode actions.

(7) The institutions of g must not contradict E and must in general be conducive to E.

(8) An institution of g must involve we-mode action, which by definition (recall chapter 2) must be based on we-mode beliefs or we-mode we-intentions and possibly on other we-attitudes, purporting to uphold E.

Premise (1) expresses the group ethos in terms of a constitutive ought-to-be norm that has been (perhaps not at least fully intentionally) collectively accepted for the group. The basic idea has been discussed above. While (1) is a crucial premise, (2) also plays an important role. Recall the comments in chapter 3 concerning ought-to-be versus ought-to-do rules and the claim that in the present context the ought-to-be rule can be taken to entail a corresponding ought-to-do rule. Here this amounts to the entailment of (2) by (1). As to (2), the group – or its operative members – ought to inform and educate people accordingly and they ought to apply sanctions for deviating behavior; thus a system for monitoring, controlling, and sanctioning group members' activities may have to be established. This premise does a lot of work, but it is hard to see how to weaken it if one really wants to have institutions at least in a full-blown sense requiring the idea that the group can act and acts. Premise (3) gives the intentional means or specification for making the obligation in (2) satisfied (note that (1) also allows nonintentional activities conducive to E).

We must of course assume that g can intentionally act or at least that the members of g can intentionally act, perhaps jointly, qua group members, and indeed act so as to fulfil E. The problem here is why this action needs to be, at least in many cases, we-mode action rather than I-mode action. Premise (3) explicitly requires intentional action and thus at least private commitment to it, viz., at least a private intention to perform something X which the person in question believes to be conducive to E or some aspect of E, perhaps under his own private description of this aspect. The central premise (4) is strong, as it gives collective commitment and action realizing it. Its truth is based on the idea that the group members indeed have internalized the group ethos and its normative force upon them, and that they also are able to turn the resulting commitment into action. Let me say here in support of (4) that the social identity (or partial identity) of the participants involves the group and its ethos. We-mode thinking and acting is generally required to avoid alienation from the group. The participants must refer to this fact as one of their reasons for acting. (Other considerations favoring (4) have already been presented above, and further reasons supporting it will be presented later in this section.)

Premise (5) is true by definition – as defined in the appendix to chapter 2 – and the same remark applies to (6). Premise (7) may seem somewhat idealized, but actually a rather minimal view of the functionality of the institutions of g for g will justify it. So, we have come to the promised end result expressed by (8), that institutions require we-mode we-attitudes.

A possible objection to the requirement of we-modeness might have to do with the "psychological burden" it allegedly places on institution users (cf. the similar argument in the case of the assumption of mutual belief in social contexts). Let me counter that "fear" by the following points, to some extent familiar from chapter 4.

(i) The we-attitude contents can be "presuppositional," constitutive reasons (cf. section 6.5 or chapter 4) for action and interaction, as opposed to being (purely) motivational reasons. The we-attitudes need to be respected in the various institutional activities undertaken in the institution, but, being dispositional states, they need not be occurrent nor be reflected upon in normal circumstances, but only in cases of institutional breakdown (or something analogous). Without essentially affecting the functioning of the institution, the talk about we-attitudes (e.g. we-beliefs) might in the limiting case be revised to be taken to involve only dispositions to acquire the we-attitudes (which themselves are dispositions), the release condition being, for example, the observed "demand of the situation" (cf. Audi, 1994, for an account of the case of single-agent belief).

(ii) The we-attitudes here are also weak we-attitudes in the sense that the third, social awareness clause is either omitted or taken to involve only shared first-order belief (recall chapters 2 and 4).

(iii) Recall that my explicit formulations have only concerned the case of unstructured groups (or groups in which the structure does not effect the situation). However, modern societies are highly structured, and this assumption does not hold true of their basic institutions such as money, law, or education. In such collectives (societies or smaller collectives) it is the operative members who decide about what will be money, for instance. In these realistic cases the other, nonoperative members only need to tacitly accept what the operative members have decided (cf. note 5 of chapter 5). Thus, we-mode we-beliefs are not required on the part of the nonoperative members, but something weaker, such as that "m is money in this society," will suffice for the rational use of money. (And this suffices to exclude activities performed without sufficient understanding, like small children or chimpanzees "buying" candy from slot machines with suitable pieces of metal.) Thus, in such a case the collective can be committed to m being money without most of its members being committed in the we-mode. It seems that here the institution of money can rationally function even with this rather minimal assumption.

(iv) The view of we-attitudes as presuppositional reasons allows for institutional acting which has become routine and skill-like (cf. chapter 4).

As seen, we-attitudes are needed, firstly, because they create the social reality needed as a basis of institutional action (institutions affect the world only via the individuals' minds). Secondly, institutions are group things, and they basically require that the agents act qua members of the group (society, organization, task group, etc.) in a committed way. This is precisely the requirement that some thinking and acting in the we-mode is needed in the institutional context. These two facts are central both for the understanding and the functionality of institutions. Indeed, the better the group succeeds in acting as a group the more functional it and its institutions will be in the long run.

The following "change argument" for we-modeness still strengthens my point. Suppose that there is strong disturbance concerning monetary exchange activities and that in our example gold somehow becomes unavailable for coin making. Then perhaps silver would be used. This kind of change presupposes that there is suitable understanding available in the group concerning the nature of the institution (here money), and this understanding requires seeing the special status given by the group to some item, here for example pieces of silver, and the exclusion of other equally valuable materials as counterfeit or incorrect materials. While the reason-giving we-attitudes normally are only dispositional and need not be manifested, the well-functioning institutional group – roughly, a group acting satisfactorily to achieve its main goals (cf. section 6.5) – must in principle have the conceptual and factual resources at any time to change and revise its institutions, and it must be prepared to act accordingly. This entails that each phase t_i, $i = 1, \ldots, i, \ldots$, is basically equal from the point of view of the disputed we-modeness question. This kind of control and monitoring can take place smoothly if there is we-mode collective commitment including social commitment, for then the members will be disposed and have reason to act so as to further the group's goals, thus to help to switch from gold coins to silver coins. Furthermore, the revision process is made much easier if group- (or we-mode-) level negotiation, communication, and spreading of information (all in the we-mode) are available. The change argument does not quite entail the presence of we-mode we-attitudes at each stage, but it makes it plausible to require that the relevant participants must have the disposition to acquire suitable we-mode we-attitudes, the disposition being manifested when the meant kind of disturbance occurs. By point (i) above this supports my thesis.

I would like to mention some other considerations that speak for the we-modeness thesis to some extent, although it seems hard to show that they have a bite in all cases. First, functionally best institutions must involve we-mode intentionality, while in everyday life I-mode intentionality will sometimes suffice for the functionality of social institutions (see Tuomela, 2000a, chapter 6, for the argument). A further point is that, as social institutions can be taken to purport to solve collective action dilemmas (cf. the Prisoner's Dilemma type of case), cooperative solutions cannot rationally be arrived at without substantial amounts of we-mode action towards shared collective goals (cf. Tuomela, 2000a, for various arguments). Every institution, when successful, provides order compatible with the ethos of the institution, and thus solves a coordination problem (recall (*FSI*)).[7]

6.4 SEARLE ON SOCIAL INSTITUTIONS

In this section I will discuss some aspects of Searle's (1995) account of social institutions, especially features that are concerned with the role of collective intentionality in the creation and maintenance of social institutions. His account is interesting, rich, and important. Even so, some critical points against it need to be made. The theory seems too narrow on two counts. First, it leaves out a central class of social institutions. This is the class consisting of social institutions relying on expectation-based social norms or, as I have called them, proper social norms. Secondly, Searle's emphasis on deontic status and status functions seems to be too demanding in general. While it works well for some cases (e.g. money), it does not apply to all those institutional cases where a new "conceptual and social status" in the sense of my account is involved. Thus it does not, or does not seem to, apply to concept institutions.

According to Searle, part of society – including at least institutional facts – is conceptually created by us and via our collective intentionality in a language-dependent way. The following three basic ingredients are the cornerstones in his creation of institutional facts (Searle, 1995, p. 28): the imposition of a new function on an entity, collective intentionality, and the distinction between constitutive and regulative rules.(Actually, there is also the demand of new deontic status and status function, but it is assumed to be entailed by the above, mainly collective intentionality; cf. below.) Constitutive rules do not merely regulate but, according to Searle they also create the very possibility of certain activities (p. 28). A constitutive rule typically has the form "X counts as Y in C," where "the 'counts as' locution names a feature of the imposition of a status to which a function is attached by way of collective intentionality, where the status and its accompanying function go beyond the sheer brute physical functions that can be assigned to physical objects" (p. 44). "So the application of the constitutive rule introduces the following features: the Y term has to assign new status that the object does not already have just in virtue of satisfying the X term; and there has to be collective agreement, or at least acceptance, both in the imposition of that status on the stuff referred to by the X term and about the function that goes with that status" (p. 44).

Searle's account of social institutions goes in terms of "status functions" involving deontic powers conferred on the agents through collective intentionality (in a sense to be discussed below). Furthermore, a constitutive rule of the kind "X counts as Y in C" must be present. The requirement of the emergence of deontic powers is introduced later in the book (cf. p. 110). In this account the first basic idea, then, is that the members of a collective, so to speak, collectively construct a social institution by conceptually giving something a new deontic status and a function to accompany it, and this is always expressible in terms of constitutive rules that are paradigmatically of the form "X counts as Y in C" (p. 40). Considering the case of money as an example, X could here be a certain kind of piece of paper with a status and functions that have nothing to do with money. The collectively accepted constitutive rule "This kind of piece of paper (X) counts as money (Y) in our community at the present time" gives X the new status Y with a new function (something like a quantitative, transferable unit of value for use in certain kinds of exchange) to go with this status. According to Searle's account, money is not money unless collectively believed to be money – this is the self-referentiality (reflexivity) of social institution concepts he stresses (cf. the appendix to this chapter).[8] Accordingly, collective acceptance must be taken to entail shared belief in this sense. It can still be noted that in the final analysis the thing (object, fact, etc.) to which the new status is given is a physical or material thing (or in any case a noninstitutional thing). The use of "X counts as Y in C" can be iterated, and matters related to this are discussed at length in his book.

Let me now discuss Searle's deontic power account in more detail. The deontic powers collectively conferred on people are enablements and requirements. Searle's basic hypothesis here is this (p. 111): "There is exactly one primitive logical operation by which institutional reality is created and constituted. It has this form: "We collectively accept, acknowledge, recognize, go along with, etc., that (S has power (S does A))." Searle thus takes many different kinds of activities to be power-creating (or power-maintaining, as the case may be). For convenience, I will below mostly use only the first term, viz., "collective acceptance." Searle does not say much about the applicability and interconnection of the aforementioned different acceptance-related notions, and this leaves the theory somewhat vague. For one thing, the theory is supposed to account for the rise and maintenance of social institutions, but it seems that, for example, "going along with" will not suffice for the first of these tasks and perhaps not always for the maintenance aspect either.

The presence of shared belief seems to be a minimum requirement. Thus, on page 32 we find: "If everybody always thinks that this sort of thing is money, and they use it as money and treat it as money, then it is money. If nobody ever thinks this sort of thing is money, then it is not money. And what goes for money goes for elections, private property, wars, voting, promises, marriages, buying and selling, political offices, and so on." Searle seems to be saying here that it is a sufficient and necessary condition for the existence of social institutions that they are collectively "taken" to exist. Actually Searle should require something like mutual belief, at least second-order beliefs. For instance, a person believing (in a sense involving acceptance) that a piece of metal is money cannot rationally use it for exchange unless he also believes that the others believe it is money (cf. section 6.3).

I see several critical weaknesses in Searle's theory. Firstly, there is the account that goes in terms of the collective acceptance conferring deontic powers on some agents. For instance, the first story has it that "This kind of piece of paper (X) is money (Y)." The second story says that people are collectively given powers to use certain pieces of paper as money. The function account and the deontic power account are of course meant to represent different aspects of a phenomenon. Nevertheless, Searle does not make it very clear what a status really is.

In fact I claim that Searle's basic requirement of the presence of deontic power is wrong, for – as already said in so many words – there are institutional cases involving reflexive institutional notions that create new conceptual and social statuses but no deontic powers interrelating the members of the group.[9] (Recall section 6.3 for my account of the notions of conceptual and social status.)

Secondly, consider constitutive rules. Searle's account is given by means of constitutive rules of the form "X counts as Y." Here statuses and functions are imposed on whatever the X-term denotes, and that is a rather mixed bunch of objects (such as pieces of paper, houses, persons, and activities). The distinction between constitutive rules, the distinction between them and regulative rules is not very clear in the case of normal real-life examples of institutional social practices. While it makes sense in the case of chess – Searle's favorite example – it is far from clear that in the case of everyday social practices like engaging in conversation, gardening, sauna bathing, and so forth, a strict distinction of this kind (any more than an analytic–synthetic distinction in the case of descriptive statements) can be made.

Waiving this problem, I find it problematic that in his account institutional facts exist only within systems of constitutive rules (p. 28), whereas in my account proper social norms, including normative conventions, are also capable of normatively characterizing social institutions and as a result we may speak of both constitutive r-norms and s-norms (recall section 6.3). But according to Searle, in chess checkmate rules and legal pawn moves count as constitutive rules. "It is important to emphasize that I am discussing rules and not conventions. It is a rule of chess that we win the game by checkmating the king. It is a convention of chess that the king is larger than a pawn. 'Convention' implies arbitrariness, but constitutive rules in general are not in that sense arbitrary." Rules need not be encoded in Searle's account. However, over and above that liberalization, a viable account of social institutions clearly needs to allow for proper social norms (expectation-based norms) to play an important role (recall for instance the Sunday Match and the red jeans cases). Nevertheless, they seem to be excluded in Searle's theory. This is because he excludes conventions and because conventions – when specifying a normative practice – correspond more or less closely to proper social norms. However, perhaps Searle means that the "arbitrariness" of conventions entails that they are only nonnormative customs. Even if that were the case, it still seems that proper social norms are excluded, as they are not considered in his book. (See Tuomela, 2002b, for further discussion.)

Thirdly, while Searle takes language and money to be social institutions, a clear formulation of the notion of institution is missing in his book. He is mainly concerned with institutional facts, but does not give a conceptually precise account of social institutions. For instance, what is the ontological status of social institutions such as money (which Searle calls an institution)? Is it an object, a collective action, or a deontic power (or set of powers), or some kind of combination of these?

Fourthly, Searle's account does not clearly distinguish between the different kinds of collective intentionality relevant here, nor does he specify the roles of these different kinds of collective intentionality. He concentrates on "we-intentions," but there are we-intentions of various kinds.[10] Furthermore, doxastic collective intentionality can in some cases also perform the task of institution maintenance and in some cases even the task of institution creation.[11]

6.5 SOCIAL ORGANIZATIONS AND INSTITUTIONAL SOCIAL PRACTICES

In this section I will return to social institutions in the sense of organizations (assuming that those to be regarded as social institutions satisfy also clause (2) of (*SI*)). I will present a sketch of a conceptual-logical framework within which one can discuss all kinds of social practices (recurrent collective social actions), but there will be a special emphasis on institutional social practices. The sketch to be presented prepares for the presentation in chapter 7 of a more formal account of social institutions and serves to give its philosophical basis.

The following basic notions for my present discussion of social institutions in the organization sense will be needed – among others – in our conceptual framework: (1) agents (position holders) $x_1, \ldots, x_v$, $x_{v+1}, \ldots, x_m$; (2) actions $X_1, \ldots, X_m$ by single agents; (3) joint actions $X, Y, \ldots$ (viz., various kinds of acting together); (4) $\mathrm{Part}(X_i, X)$ part relation for joint action; (5) social practices $SP_1, \ldots, SP_k$; (6) r-practices (viz., practices dependent on authority-based norms, viz., r-norms); (7) s-practices (viz., practices dependent on proper social norms); (8) times $T_1, \ldots, T_n$; (9) contexts (settings) $C_1, \ldots, C_p$; (10) the central goal or goals G of the organization; (11) task-right system "defining" the organization in question TR; (12) positional task-right systems $TR_1, \ldots, TR_m$ corresponding to the position holders $x_1, \ldots, x_m$; (13) we-attitudes $WA_1, \ldots, WA_k$ partially "defining" $SP_1, \ldots SP_k$; (14) dependence $\mathrm{Dep}(X, Y)$ between actions X and Y.

Let me now explain how this conceptual framework can be applied to organizations and the accompanying institutionalized social practices. In the next chapter these ideas will be embedded in a mathematical account of social practices and institutions. Although the symbolism there will be somewhat different (due to the use of mathematical formulas), the ideas of the present section will underlie that treatment.

To discuss a social institution in the organization sense, I will make some rather uncontroversial, although perhaps idealized assumptions. First I assume that we are dealing with a collective g whose normative structure is defined by a task-right system TR. What is a task-right system here? It is basically a collection of ought-to-norms and may-norms serving to define an institution (such as an organization) or an institutional position. A TR system need not be only a conjunction of such norms. It may also contain some norms (metanorms, norms of interpretation, etc.) characterizing the organization as a whole and also specifying the positional action-regulating norms.

Over and above the central TR system we must also assume that the collective has a set of basic goals G. More broadly, in a more general treatment we would operate with the notion of ethos (recall section 6.3) and take G to be a part of the ethos. The latter notion covers not only the constitutive or central goals of the organization, but also its central values, standards, norms, and underlying beliefs. I will speak here as if G were a single goal or a conjunction of several basic goals. We can take G to be governed by an ought-to-be rule: it ought to be the case that G obtains. G gives the basic task of the organization. In a sense, g then amounts to (TR,G). This is an idealization, of course, for there are many background assumptions that need to be operative here. From the participating members' point of view they may be presuppositional and other beliefs. I will, however, ignore them below to keep my account simple and perspicuous.

Let me now comment on social positions and task-right systems in some detail (cf. Tuomela, 1995, chapter 1). A person's social position in a specific interactional field, say one existing in a collective, is connected to his social task or tasks and his social rights and hence to the roles, offices, and informal social functions attached to these. Thus a person's position as a husband or as a teacher can be taken to be characterized by certain formally or informally characterized tasks, rights, and roles, including tasks based on proper social norms (s-tasks) and s-rights. Accordingly, a position will be connected to norms of various kinds (r-norms and s-norms).

A social position is regarded as a social person category (or a collection of such person categories) to which relatively permanent norm-based tasks and rights of the kinds mentioned pertain. Examples of positions are the category of professor (to which a professor's official duties and "role duties" relate) and the category of "mother figure" in a group (this would only have a role attached); a holder of an office post, say a bookkeeper, could also be the group's mother figure, and then to his full personal position in the group would be connected all the formal duties and the role tasks attached to the category of bookkeeper, as well as the role tasks in the role of mother figure.

For our present purposes we can accordingly regard a position in a collective as a person category of the aforementioned kind (or a collection of such categories). Power relationships will be involved in the task-right network. For instance, a leader's positional tasks may presuppose that he can order his subordinates to act in certain ways and can influence their thinking in this regard, and this reflects his power (both "agreement-based" power and "belief-based" power) related to our distinction between r-norms and s-norms. A person typically has many positions, presumably at least one for every social collective of which he is a member. His total position in the society in question is a conjunction of all his positions in the collectives included in his society. The following, somewhat idealized, consensus-flavored picture of the network of tasks and rights now emerges. In a group there will be positions, and a position holder will or may have r-norm-based tasks (he ought to do X in C, for example) that he is assumed to be carrying out – typically without negative interference from others. There will also generally be rights (viz., he may do something X, without the others interfering). A position holder may also have tasks and rights based on proper social norms, and his social roles will be built out of them (see Tuomela, 1995, chapter 8, for further discussion).

To continue the development of the present conceptual system, assume that we have several sets of agents, possibly overlapping sets. I will nevertheless assume, to keep things simple, that there are only two disjoint sets, the first consisting of $x_1, \ldots, x_v$ and the other of $x_{v+1}, \ldots, x_m$. These agents are position holders in g. The agents are assumed to perform their positional activities, X_i, in the same or different contexts (including locations) $C_1, \ldots C_p$ and at the same or different times. Furthermore, their position-defining task-right systems $TR_1, \ldots, TR_m$ are (or at least can be) different. A task-right system for a position holder x_i will consist of suitable ought-norms and may-norms that say what x_i is supposed to do in various circumstances relevant to the functions of the organization.

Note that TR and G in our present set-up are macro notions, and X,Y are intermediate level or "meso" notions, while for example X_i is a micro notion. A task-right system is a kind of system of behavior restrictions and behavior enablements. If for example TR_i contain the task-norm "x_i ought to do X_i in C_i" his action alternatives are normatively restricted to one action in this situation. What about right-defining norms or permissions, then? Suppose our agent is permitted to do X_1 or X_2 in C_i, say. In the previous ought-case there was only one permitted action, but here he may choose between two actions or tasks. Note that permissions also restrict, for the space of all possible actions in g is normally larger than the space consisting only of, say, X_1 and X_2.

The activities performed by the subgroups are social practices when viewed over time. Suppose in the first group only one social practice is made up of the agents' positional activities, and similarly for the second group. Thus, we have two separate social practices, SP_1 and SP_2. So, in all we have highly disjoint subgroups and corresponding activities to deal with here. The basic elements G_i (individual x_i's positional goals), TR_i, and SP_i, can all be different, and they can be performed in different contexts at different times. (On the other hand, they can of course also be highly similar or even the same.) The only required overarching thing, anyhow, is (TR,G). This is the case from the macro point of view. As to the acting agents, they can, nevertheless, be assumed to believe that they are carrying out the same general g-defining goal and acting in view of the g-defining task-right system, even if they do not know that that goal is G and that that task-right system is TR. Each agent (member) is performing his positional activities governed by his task-right system and believes that the other members are doing similarly, and they also believe that this (viz., that every member is performing his positional activities) is mutually believed by the members. (This is the first shared we-attitude we have here.) Accordingly, we have the following kind of particularized indexical thoughts, for each x_i thinks: I am performing activities, X_i, related to my subgoals, G_i, in view of my position-defining task-right system, TR_i, and I believe that the others are acting similarly, *mutatis mutandis*, and that this is mutually believed in the collective g. This indexical we-attitude presupposes that the agents believe that their goals are subgoals of the total goal G and that their task-right systems are embedded in the full task-right system, TR, and that this is mutual belief in g. (This is an underlying, presuppositional shared we-belief in g.) We also have the indexical versions of this we-belief: x_i believes that his goal is a subgoal of the total goal G and his task-right system is a part of TR and he also believes that the same holds for the other agents beliefs' concerning their goals and task-right systems and that all this is mutually believed in g.

A further point is that in the case of customs there is in a sense no power structure. The sense in question is that there is no authority imposing such a power structure – that might turn the custom (s-item, often s-norm) into an r-item. The introduction of a TR system often also introduces power and may sometimes supersede over a custom (with about the same content), which then becomes a practice based on an authority-based norm (r-norm). In the s-case, the introduction or, rather, emergence of a TR system may also sometimes define power or, better, a mutual view that some persons have power concerning the introduction and revision of practices. (Cf. Tuomela and Bonnevier-Tuomela, 1998; Nee and Ingram, 1998; and Mantzavinos, 2001; for the conflict between r-norms and s-norms.[12])

What is it for x_i to perform his positional activities, X_i, related to (G_i, TR_i)? There are several possibilities, and it is difficult to be informative on this topic on a priori grounds. On a general level, there may be activities that are actionally independent of others' actions, there may be actionally dependent activities $(Dep(X_i, X_j);$ e.g. linked activities), and there may be joint actions or acting together (X), thus acting positionally in the we-mode between certain agents. We can say that the positional pairs (G_i, TR_i) are related in view of the part–whole relation to (G, TR). In this sense there is an in-built similarity between all the pairs (G_i, TR_i) and consequently also a similarity between our two groups and the social practices SP_1 and SP_2. The similarities have psychological reality precisely in view of the two different kinds of we-attitudes (one related to the participants' positional activities and the other related to the believed relationship between (G_i, TR_i) and (G, TR)).

We may generalize this account to connect the social practices performed between different collectives, say C_1 and C_2 in the dyadic case. If their social practices are close enough, we may want to speak of identical or similar social practices (think of for example farming practices or religious practices).

Note a couple of obvious things. The TR systems can be grounded either on authority-based norms or on proper social norms or on mixtures of these. In the case of collectives with no normative structure, the TRs cancel out and we are left with goals (and underlying beliefs).

The above construct is primarily that of a theoretician, who infers what G and TR are. However, every position holder must know approximately what he himself is doing, thus under some description he must act functionally right. The basic criterion is that an institution should work about right and that the participants must know enough for this to be possible.

Given this discussion we could in a straightforward fashion formulate a more detailed version of (SI) or, better, of (SI^*) in note 6, for the case of organizations in terms of positional task-right systems such that now the task-right system of g would replace the earlier formulation in terms of systems of norms (cf. chapter 7).

What can we then say about the kind of collective acceptance (CA) that is used for their creation and maintenance of an institution in the organization sense. While they can be initiated by one person, a collective – at least in some codified form – must be involved in order to complete the process of creation. Accordingly, collective acceptance at least in the sense of the right kinds of action dispositions must be present (some of them must be or relate to we-mode we-attitudes; cf. section 6.3).

Consider for example the postal system created for a nation to serve the needs of people in a community g. Such an organization consists of norm-governed social practices or, rather, systems of practices. The norms form a task-right system for the organization. These norms must originally have been *collectively* accepted (cf. above). Consequently, we must require that the operative members (the members having the authority to decide for the group) collectively accept a proposition s, which may be a long conjunction of propositions – including normative ones – for the company. The complex organization-defining proposition s forms, or at any rate contains, the constitutive rule(s) for the organization in question. The creation of the organization may have taken place a long time ago. Today the situation might be very different and the original position holders may not be there, although the positions must at least largely be there. It would, however, seem that at least in a properly functioning organization at least the operative members who are responsible for taking decisions and action must collectively accept s (recall note 6). However, it is compatible with this that ordinary employees might not care about what s expresses and might not even accept it, but in some sense – falling short of outright rejection – disagree with it.

Clause (2) of (*SI*) thus is required to be satisfied in the case of those organizations that are institutions in my standard sense. This seems plausible for organizations designed for communities. The entailed forgroupness assumption must then be satisfied. This excludes for example business companies operating within the host community g from being institutions for g, although they in a contrived sense may be institutions for the personnel and shareowners of the company (recall the discussion in section 6.3). Why business firms do not qualify concerning the wider host community is because it is not constitutive of them that they serve the goals of group g and are thus in this strong sense for the group g (although they contingently might do it). However, the postal system serving a community is an organization created for the community, and it is a social institution not only in an intuitive sense but also in the sense of (*SI*).

Let me note that there is the conceptually interesting limiting case that an organization might be "dormant" for some period of time. By this I mean that the content s would exist on the books and could be for example legally valid without there being any activity in the company and perhaps no actual position holders. This is a limiting case which our analysis accepts but which of course does not constitute a functionally successful organization during that period.

6.6 CONCLUSION

In this chapter a variety of social institutions have been discussed from a philosophical point of view. Abstracting from contingent features of social institutions one can arrive at a simple account in terms of the Collective Acceptance model. This account captures an interesting and important class of social institutions consisting of institutions in the concept sense, institutions involving a new deontic status, and institutions as organizations. It is argued that social institutions of the three kinds give the instituted item a new conceptual and social status. (The requirement of a new deontic status that Searle, 1995, demands of institutions does not apply to institutions in the concept sense.) The Collective Acceptance account also shows in what sense institutions are reflexive. My second central point in this chapter has been that proper social norms, viz., norms based on mutual expectations, can ground social institutions as well (this apparently contradicts Searle's account).

Institutions are based on collective acceptance and hence collective intentionality. The general type of collective intentionality pertinent here is shared we-attitude, basically we-intention and/or we-belief. It is argued at length that the we-attitudes have to be in the we-mode, at least in the full-blown cases.

Collective acceptance (thus collective intentionality in the form of shared we-mode we-attitudes) and the special social and conceptual status constitutively created by collective acceptance are central elements for the present study of the conceptual, epistemic, normative, ontological, and functional nature of social institutions. We-mode and other group-level concepts are needed in a serious study of the social world – partly simply because people have we-attitudes. These concepts seem not to be reducible to individualistic notions. Such social institutions as the educational system in a modern society involve an interconnected system of social goals and beliefs (in my system: we-goals and we-beliefs), and I do not see much hope for an individualistic "bottom up" approach starting with a simpler conceptual basis than I have used. However, from an ontological point of view it can be said that my account does not require more than meso-level (or jointness level) elements, thus in the last analysis dependent and interacting individuals. Group concepts are needed by the participating agents, but that only gives groups "intentional existence," viz., existence in the sense of being elements in the contents of the participants' thoughts (cf. Tuomela, 1995, chapter 4).

My basic explications have usually been given only for the simple case of unstructured collectives, but I have also indicated how to proceed in the more realistic case of structured collectives, where power considerations become more important.

APPENDIX: INSTITUTION CONCEPTS AS REFLEXIVE
CONCEPTS

I will here mainly consider general social institutions related to such social entities as money, marriage, property, or (even) language. These institutional social objects can be represented by (meaningful) predicates, viz., predicates with established uses. Such predicates (or rather their synonymy classes defined by means of Sellars' dot-quotes) can be called concepts. Assume now that S is such a predicate. S can be "money," "marriage," "ownership," and so forth. These predicates, or their appropriate linguistic modifications, occur in institution-expressing or institution-entailing sentences. Here are some invented examples of such sentences, all of which are preceded by a necessity operator (based on collective acceptance according to my view): (a) "For all x, if x is a squirrel fur, then x is money" (institution-expressing sentence), "For all x and y, if x is an item of money and y is a member of g, then y is entitled to use x as money in his commercial affairs" (entailed sentence); (b) "For all persons x and y in collective g, if x and y are married to each other, then x and y are committed to fidelity towards each other" (entailed by marriage institution); or (c) "For all persons x in g, if for some y, x owns y, then no person z can legally use y without x's permission" (entailed by the property institution).

Let me now discuss reflexivity and use money as my prime example. The fact that money is assumed to be a social entity means that it is socially constructed. In my explication this means in part that we have for the group g (recall the Forgroup-operator of chapter 5):

(1) CA(g, p)

where p is an institution-expressing sentence or proposition, for example p = Squirrel fur is money, or more precisely, p = For all x, if x is a squirrel fur, then x is money. Given (1), we can say that according to p, squirrel furs express or symbolize money.

But (1) is a necessary condition for something being a social entity or – which here amounts to the same thing – a social institution (assuming that an object can be called a social institution and not only the activities which maintain its existence). As said, some philosophers have argued that also reflexivity is a necessary feature of such institutional concepts as money. What does this mean? Let us assume that meanings can be analyzed as possible uses. The inferential use of concepts certainly is central (recall the brief discussions in chapters 3 and 5). However, I will here simplify things and consider the central referential use to be the only kind of use that counts for the purpose of discussing and illustrating the circularity problem. I will keep the pragmatic referential use aspect as the central feature of the analysis, but in order to capture a certain central element of reflexivity, I start with a "semantifying" abstraction from use. Consider thus the following analysis of reference, in analogy with a possible worlds' analysis of the meaning of predicates:

(2) $S: W \longrightarrow E$

Here W is a set of contexts to which the concept or predicate S can be potentially applied. S is a function that maps W into E, a set of sets, say E_i, of entities falling into the extension of the predicate in each possible context W_i. Each such context consists (at least) of a set of (actual or possible) objects, and the meaning function simply specifies how to classify them into those to which the predicate S correctly applies and those to which it does not. We may call the sets E_i the reference sets of S. In our example reference set E_i is a set (possibly a singleton set) of squirrel furs. Not to completely neglect the pragmatics of the situation, we give a referential use reading to (2) and say that it shows how S is correctly applied to (or is true of) the members of the subsets of E in various contexts. According to (2), for every context W_i in W there exists a set E_i such that $S(W_i) = E_i$. Not to make an untenable metaphysical idealization, we may alternatively allow that the use function (2) is gappy either in the sense that for some contexts it is not associated with any reference set (viz., E_i) at all. Let me emphasize that as our meaning function serves to define correct use, it is (implicitly) normative.

Who are the users of predicates such as S in (2)? They are the group members. We may accordingly suggest that the pragmatic use reading of (2) be cashed out in terms of collective acceptance, which involves the group members' dispositions to use the linguistic expressions in various circumstances. Keeping in mind that (2) is also, and indeed very centrally, concerned with potential use, the assumption that the CA-operator, incorporating both potential and actual use, be employed here seems right. Furthermore, it must be noted that from an objective, group-external point of view, any singular use of the predicate S means that it is applied to an object, say x, such that the sentence $S(x)$ will be true in the particular context. But as a description of what is taking place, we say that the group members here collectively take $S(x)$ to be true. Combining the above points, the suggestion is that our full theoretical description of the language-use situation would include the employment of the following formula, taken to be true for the group:

(2_g) CA(g, The referential meaning of the predicate S is given by the (function S: W $\longrightarrow$ E)

(2_g) is a kind of pragmatic version of (2), and in it the arrow $\longrightarrow$ can now be understood simply in the formal mathematical sense of a function but without the use connotation, as the use aspect has now been built into the collective acceptance part.

Corresponding to (2_g) we have rules of language, for instance ought-to-be and ought-to-do rules of the following kind:

(3) It ought to be the case that any full-fledged member of the community g uses the predicate S nonaccidentally in accordance with (2), or better, obeys (2).

(4) Every full-fledged member of community g ought to obey (2) when using S.

We must allow that a full-fledged member of g, even in ideal circumstances, fails to apply S fully as (2) says. This is because of "meaning finitism" (to use Bloor's phrase of 1997). I would like to express this by saying that as each member of g must necessarily learn his concepts on the basis of a finite number of examples and because the context set W must in principle be taken to be an open, indefinitely large set, (2) will in general be only a partial function. Such a partial function codifies the referential use of a predicate in a group g, and it represents what is being taught to children and other novices. S could accordingly be regarded as a kind of socially shared standard which is needed for successful communication and for a commonable language.

Actually, what the members of g learn when being taught the concept S may differ even if they learn correctly the exemplars used in teaching S. Thus even the assumption of a single social "dictionary" use is somewhat idealized. In any case, it can be said that the members of g may extrapolate differently into unfamiliar and previously unknown contexts (viz., contexts not incorporated in the partial function (2)). In this sense, (2) could be taken to be a kind of approximation not only of the members' uses of S, but of the fuller, open meaning of S (which has the feature of remaining forever open in principle).

Returning to the case of social institutions and institutional social objects, the claim that they are reflexive can be analyzed as follows:

(5) The concept S (e.g. the concept of money or .money. in the Sellarsian framework) is reflexive if and only if the (members in the) sets in E

can on conceptual grounds be correctly characterized by S, whereas this is not true, at least on conceptual grounds, if (2_g) is false.

In (5) correct characterization of a set in E means simply that for any reference set E_i it is true that unless its members satisfy S, formula (2_g) will not be true. This relation expressed by "unless" can be regarded as the relation of presupposition. In the case of money, we have that for S to correctly apply to (the members of) the reference sets E_i in E, the squirrel furs (elements of E_i) must be items of money, and the sets E_i must be sets consisting of items of money. The "must" here is the must of presupposed conceptual necessity. Because of this necessity element, we can write, in obvious notation, our assumption as $E_i = E_{i,s}$ and stipulate that $E_s = \{E_i\}$, $i = 1,2,\ldots$

Thus, when (5) is true of S, we can use the following strengthened, reflexive version of (2) in its analysans part:

$$(2^*)\ S: W \longrightarrow E_S$$

and use (2_g^*) CA(g, The (referential) meaning of the predicate S is given by the function S: W $\longrightarrow$ E$_S$) as the collective-pragmatic counterpart of the reflexivity formula (2^*).

As seen from (2_g^*), the group members in our example are assumed to take or accept squirrel fur to be money, viz., E$_S$ involves the idea that squirrel furs are money. Because of the attitudes involved in CA we can also speak of *attitudinal reflexivity* – to correspond to *reflexivity simpliciter*, referred to in (5). Thus, basically, (5) clarifies not only concept reflexivity but also, because of the collective acceptance assumption it involves, reflexivity in an attitudinal sense (or, if you prefer, pragmatic or collective acceptance sense). At bottom, (5) then is seen to be based on attitudinal reflexivity.

We can assume for the present context, satisfying (2_g^*):

(6) If squirrel fur is money then it must be (collectively) accepted in g to be money.

Philosophers who have written about social institutions typically argue that money and similar examples satisfy (6) or, most typically its analogue, which says that the candidate item must be believed to be money (cf. Bloor, 1997, p. 35). The belief is to be regarded as an acceptance belief (cf. chapter 5). We are often dealing with codified, norm-based acceptance in this kind of situation. Should the society (or the group g, more generally) cease to take squirrel fur to be money, the relevant activities (e.g. exchange activities using squirrel furs) related to (6) would become irrational and pointless. Furthermore, it can be said that here squirrel fur is collectively taken to represent and symbolize money, and unless that is the case the collective construction has failed. But if indeed squirrel fur is (stands for) money, then (6) must be true. Thus (6) is crucial for (attitudinal) reflexivity and it also seems clearly to be true. Its truth supports the idea that social institutions at least in many standard cases (e.g., money, marriage, property) involve reflexive institutional social objects.

On the other hand, we also have the performative truth that

(7) Squirrel fur is money if it is (collectively) accepted to be money.

The truth of (7) relates to the feature that money and similar objects are "made by us," viz., collectively constructed by the members of group g. Thus, whether or not squirrel fur is money is totally up to the members of g to decide. There are no laws of nature that are relevant here, nor is there anything outside the collective g that is ultimately relevant to this matter of creation and maintenance of an institutional social object and social institution.

Let us now generalize (6) and (7) and use the above symbolism and, to take a simple monadic example, p = For all x, if x is P then x is S, where, for example, P = squirrel fur and S = money. We also make use of the obvious fact that the instituted object is instituted precisely for the group in question (rather than for another group). The instituted object is not ontologically and conceptually fully objective and group-independent (although it can be epistemically objective). This is because the built-in conceptual content – for example that squirrel fur counts as money – is already a group-relative matter, as it is based on the acceptance of the content by group g.

We get (making now explicit use of the "forgroupness" operator FG):

(8) $FG(p \rightarrow CA(g,p))$

and

(9) $FG(CA(g,p) \rightarrow p)$

We also assumed

(10) $FG(CA(g,p)$

Combining (8), (9), and (10) we have

(11) $FG(CA(g,p) \& (CA(g,p) \leftrightarrow p))$

viz., the CAT formula of chapter 5. Here proposition p expresses a kind of "constitutive norm" (in a kind of analogy with Searle's notion of a constitutive rule; cf. section 6.4). Thus we have normative content in (11), at least in the sense the members of g ought to uphold p. Accordingly, (11) can be regarded as a kind of constitutive expression or formula for reflexive social institutions. It makes p reflexive within the group's "horizon" (viz., within the possible worlds compatible with what is meant for the use of the group, FG). Here p may be an institution-expressing sentence in the sense that it attributes a new conceptual and social status (the status of money in our example) to an antecedent and here noninstitutional thing (squirrel fur). The connection between the concepts of money and squirrel fur is conceptual or, better, social-conceptual. This is the connection expressed by (2*), and thus we can also say that the concept of money is also attitudinally reflexive and collectively taken to be reflexive simpliciter – rather than only say that the proposition that squirrel fur is money is attitudinally reflexive.

We can also say that our concept-constituting (2*) is collectively accepted as the concept of S or as what S amounts to (in the reflexive case). To accept a concept here amounts to the collective acceptance of a semantical statement concerning the meaning of S or what the concept S amounts to when viewed as a rule:

FG(CA(2*) is an analysis of the concept S)

As (11) contains a constitutive norm, it also gives a social-normative (as opposed to a merely linguistic-normative) status to the concept S. Assuming as above that something P is S in g, the predicate S obtains a kind of normative status due to the group members' objective commitment to p (viz., collective commitment "in the public space," epistemically available to anyone). Its truth or, rather, its being collectively taken as true guarantees for many standard cases (such as money, marriage, and property) that each person in g comes to have certain rights and certain duties relative to the other members of g (e.g., in contexts of exchange to which p applies, one is entitled to use squirrel fur as a medium of exchange).

Consider the case with an object that is not a social construction. We have the linguistic social institution of calling trees by the predicate "tree" in English. Applying (2) to this case we get

(2') "tree": $W \longrightarrow E$

where E is a set of sets of trees. There is overt circularity here after all, for the word (predicate) "tree" is taken to refer to trees; and I emphasize that it seems possible to give a fully acceptable characterization of trees without using the notion of tree and it is at least possible to characterize trees without invoking people's attitudes. In contrast, in the case of the predicate "marriage" one cannot (at least not always) specify the set of relationships in E without using the concept of marriage, at least in an intensional context (e.g., in specifying a belief content).

The above considerations seem to apply also to specific organizations like schools and churches. For instance, a school is not *that* school unless collectively accepted to be *that* school in the group (or at least among its operative members; cf. section 6.5). Sufficiently liberally understood, this statement, requiring the correct applicability of (11) to this case, seems right. However, it must be emphasized that in the case of developed societies there is division of labor also with respect to collective acceptance. Thus not all members of the community actually need to know all the details and may not even have heard of the organization in question.

This investigation has given support to the following thesis: all or at least all "standard" social institutions are reflexive, be they institutions concerning only linguistic matters or other kinds of institutions. (Both fact-reflexivity in the sense explicated by (11) and the attitudinal concept reflexivity in the sense of (2*) are involved in this thesis.)

CHAPTER 7

Social practices and institutions in a dynamic context: a mathematical analysis*

7.1 INTRODUCTION

The aim of this chapter is to study social practices and the dynamics of their maintenance in precise mathematical and logical terms, relying on the theoretical developments of the earlier chapters. While the present chapter does not much advance the philosophical arguments presented earlier in this book except for the dynamic account it offers, it shows that the views espoused in the book are practical in the sense of being implementable in formal mathematical terms. This also serves the interests of research in distributed artificial intelligence (DAI), and the system can, furthermore, be used for computer simulations of social processes. While chapter 6 was concerned with social institutions in a synchronic sense, the present chapter creates a mathematical account of the diachronic case, which in principle applies to all (core) social practices, including all the institutional ones discussed in chapter 6.

The chapter will concentrate on the function of collective attitudes in this dynamics, and on the macroscopic level. Social practices will be regarded as core social practices, viz., recurrent collective activities based on collective attitudes, more precisely shared we-attitudes. They are maintained (upheld, renewed, and changed) on the basis of their (believed) success. The success of an action within a social practice depends on the content of the collective attitude (especially intention) that causes the action. This content may concern not only the mere performance of a collective action but also its performance in a certain manner or as meeting certain normative standards.

A collective attitude, such as a shared we-attitude, can be distinguished from a proper group attitude, one attributed to a group. The former is attributed to the members of a group or collective while the latter applies to the group. For instance, we may attribute an intention to perform something X to a group, and this entails – in the case of groups with no structure – that the group members jointly intend to perform X (or at least something resulting in X). The group intention is thus a "macro level" notion while the collective or joint intention is a "meso level" notion applying collectively to the group members. In this case, every group member is also assumed to have an intention (equivalently, goal) to contribute to X. This intention, which is a we-intention in our terminology, is ontically (although not conceptually) a "micro level" notion.

In this chapter we will in general ascribe *distributive* attitudes to collectives, especially *unstructured* collectives. Thus, it is true for the attitudes considered here that an attitude correctly applies to an extensionally characterized group, say I, if and only if it collectively applies to the group members. (The distributivity assumption is not true for all social predicates; cf. "cohesion.") For instance, if I consists of i and j (we write I = {i,j}), then I has a goal X if and only if i and j collectively have the goal X. Furthermore, both i and j then have the goal X or at least the goal to contribute to X.

For reasons of simplicity, we focus on the macro level, putting to one side the details of the micro level as well as a formal treatment of the kinds of inconsistencies that should reasonably be allowed.[1] In section 7.8 we briefly describe the main topics related to the individual level. Up to that section, we will discuss collective attitudes without explicating them as shared we-attitudes. This chapter concentrates on the basic case where collective action is neither plan-based nor formally coordinated (cf. customs), and only in section 7.9 do we discuss the special features of those important social practices that are based on institutions or norms.

As the general conceptual and philosophical importance of collective attitudes and social practices as the basic building blocks of society has been discussed and emphasized earlier in this book, we will not here discuss the matter but proceed directly to detailed work.[2] Operating with technical mathematical tools, we will below discuss the dynamics of social practices, especially their maintenance, on the basis of the collective attitudes underlying them. Our analysis sheds light on how and why recurrent social goals are maintained, a question of primary importance for multiagent action theory.[3] Although our treatment may still be lacking in realism, it gives an approach which future research can make more complex and more realistic.

The focus of the treatment is on intentionally performed activities, but the system to be created still leaves plenty of room for unintended activities and results generated by either unintended activities or merely I-mode intentional activities, as will be shown in section 7.6.

7.2 PRECONDITIONS OF SOCIAL PRACTICES

The participants in social practices must of course have lots of (background and other) abilities and knowledge, and the circumstances of action must satisfy certain normality conditions.[4] Among the general ability conditions are obviously mental, social, and physical conditions. Roughly speaking, the participants must thus have the right kind of knowledge and beliefs and react in the right way to circumstantial conditions, and they must be sufficiently rational and emotionally balanced for the required actions to come about. They must also have largely right beliefs about their social surroundings, and especially about their fellow participants' relevant thoughts and actions (such beliefs obviously are pertinent to the circumstances at hand), and in many contexts, such as cooperation, their attitudes must be sufficiently "pro-social" and "groupish." Furthermore, the participants must of course have learned to perform the actions that the social practices require. Equally obviously, "nature" (the physical circumstances) must be sufficiently "cooperative" for the social practices to be successful even over a longer time span. Below we will not further analyze the kinds of preconditions that are related to standing abilities. What we wish to draw the reader's attention to are those kinds of circumstantial conditions that relate to the generation of the relevant attitudes and actions. All these circumstantial conditions are required for the causal generation of action. We call them *trigger conditions* (or *evoking conditions*) for action. If metaphysical determinism were true, these conditions would be not only necessary but also sufficient. As, however, indeterminism rather seems correct, they cannot in principle be sufficient causes, and thus probabilistic or other "indeterminizing" considerations are needed in a finer account. (For simplicity, we will nevertheless later use a postulate that makes causes sufficient for their effects.) The problem of the weakness of the will, viz., *akrasia*, can here be handled either in the trivial sense of requiring the kind of normal conditions which exclude it, or by speaking only of successful action, or action *ex post actu*.

We can distinguish between two kinds of trigger conditions for action. First there are conditions which definitely have to obtain, and which are brought about by a change of the environment, like for example the right time. Trigger conditions of the second class state the absence of obstacles. When all the trigger conditions for action obtain, the actors will, or at least are likely to, perform the intended action. This collective (indeed, joint) action may be more or less successful for each of the participants.

Its success depends on the content of their collective attitude, and on their beliefs (expectations) concerning the activities themselves (e.g. the ways and manners in which they are performed) and concerning how well the results of the activity satisfy the standards and criteria they have for the kind of case at hand. The actors have their criteria for determining the success of the action. If these criteria are met, the collective action is classified as a success, and a "success account" of an actor is increased by a positive amount. If the action was not a success, the success account is decreased. We here assume that the overall success of the collective action can be determined on the basis of the success of the individual part performances. Note, however, that as in the we-mode case the parts are parts of a collective action (in some cases a joint action), the success of the collective action gets a rather holistic analysis, too. In the I-mode case obviously a more individualistic analysis of the success of collective action will do, as there only private individual actions, goals, beliefs, and other mental attitudes are involved.

Successful action will be repeated. Suppose the joint action was two neighbors riding together in a car to town to work. Suppose that the initial ride was a success for both of them. Then, the actors agree to repeat the action the next day, and so on. They may come to form the joint intention to ride together every morning during the week. Here a social practice is getting formed.

In this kind of context we will speak of individual "*attitude trigger conditions.*" What the trigger conditions amount to in the case of intentional actions and intentions leading to them are *reasons*. We can thus speak of *reasons for intention* and *reasons for action* in this case. (As the well-known "toxin puzzle" indicates, there may be reasons for intention that are not reasons for the action that the intention concerns. Thus, if there is a "reward" for forming the intention to perform something X but a "punishment" for performing X, there may be reasons for intending but not reasons for action.) To keep the full realm of activities within our scope, we will below nevertheless speak of trigger conditions rather than reasons.

If the joint or, more generally, collective action proves to be successful, this is rewarding for the participants and will make it more likely that they will continue with the practice. In the case of failure, the opposite of course is the case. Realistically, this reward factor should be evaluated on the basis of viable learning theories, but as a simple alternative in the present context we may just look at the actors' experiences with such performances in the past. There was at least one such experience, and when things go well, at future evaluation points there will be many. The actor checks whether the past performances on average were successful, which is the case if and only if the success account is above the initial level, the level immediately before the first joint ride.

If the trigger conditions are all realized, the joint intention is highly likely to be present the next morning, and the above story is repeated with minor changes (cf. the comments in section 7.3). If on average the rides are successful for both actors, a social practice of taking the neighbor to work will develop.

The main ingredients needed to account for such a practice are the collective intention, the corresponding collective action, the trigger conditions, and the levels of success of the actions. If we add a causal mechanism that relates all these states and events, we obtain a small, self-contained system, viz., a social practice.

7.3 STATES AND SENTENCES

Social practices occur in social systems that develop over time. Such systems can be modeled by sequences of states, where states are characterized by sets of sentences. These sets must be rich enough to contain sentences expressing individual and collective attitudes as well as the performance of actions. Actions are here characterized as pairs of states, that is, as state transitions. (This is a slight simplification, but does not distort our present purposes; cf. Sandu and Tuomela, 1996, on this.) This requires a recursive definition of the set of sentences.

The basis of the definition is given by a set T of points of time, a set J of individuals, a set of "ordinary" objects (which will not be explicitly used here), and a set ATT of *attitude-kinds* (like belief, intention, fear). In some contexts J can include position holders in a collective. However, in this chapter we shall not mathematically take into account the additional features of social practices that are due to their possibly relying on social institutions (but see section 7.9).

We begin with a set S_f of *nonattitude* sentences, sentences which do not express (individual or collective) attitudes. S_f is the smallest set which (a) contains a given, suitable *basis*, a set of first-order sentences S_0 containing nonsocial, psychological and material predicates and variables for time, individuals, and objects, and (b) with any a,b also contains: a and b (viz., a & b), a or b (viz., a v b), a → b, a ↔ b, and −a (viz., non-a). The choice of the basis S_0 is left open.

Actions are represented as pairs (C,E) of sets of sentences such that members of C describe the *conditions* which have to obtain so that the action (C,E) will be performed, and E is a description of the action's "relevant" *results* – in the case of intentional action results as intended by the actor or actors. Our formal approach is open to different views about action and of carving up the action situation. Let us mention two possibilities. Trigger conditions could be regarded as *objective, nonmental* conditions which serve to trigger or evoke or lead to the formation of the agent's mental states relevant for action. Here C would consist of the mental states thus evoked, and E would at least contain the in-built result event of the action. Consider an agent i's opening the window as an example. He is prompted to act because it is too hot in the room and the window is closed. These belong to the nonmental trigger conditions. C now includes sentences like "i knows that the window is closed," "i knows that he is in the room," "i believes that if he opens the window the room temperature will be lowered," "i intends to open the window," and other trigger conditions (that we need not here specify); and E would contain "The window is open." Supposing that E indeed occurs, the triggering conditions and the conditions C caused it. The second interpretation that is possible here is that the triggering or onset conditions are also mental, for example the agent's perception that the window is closed, and so forth. The conditions C would here be objective and typically standing conditions (relative to the onset events) like that the agent is in the room and that the room is warm, and that the agent knows these things.

Among the actions there are – and should be – collective actions, that is actions whose characterizing sentences refer to more than one individual. The actor or actors performing an action are not made explicit, they are represented implicitly by their names, which occur in the sentences of C and E. The actors are explicitly referred to only in the representation of the performance of an action; see the *act*-predicate and axiom (A3) in section 7.4.

We assume that a set of *basic* actions $\{(C_1,E_1), (C_2,E_2),...\}$ is initially specified such that C_i, $E_i \subseteq S_f$. The sets C_i and E_i can be regarded as partial descriptions of states.

In order to define the full set of sentences, three predicates are used: (1) $act(t,I,C,E)$, to be read "at time t the set of individuals $I \subseteq J$ performs action (C,E) collectively"; (2) $catt(I,att,p,t)$, "at t, the individuals in the set $I \subseteq J$ share the collective attitude of kind *att* with content p" (which amounts to the group I's having that attitude here); and (3) $iatt(i,att,p,t)$, "at t, individual i in J has the individual counterpart attitude, also denoted by *att*, with content p" (recall the remarks in section 7.1). *att* may be for example *belief* or *intention*, and p is a sentence expressing the content of the attitude (e.g. what is believed or intended). In the most important case, when *att* = *int*, catt(I,*att*,p,t) says that, at time t, the members of I jointly intend to do p (which can be written as $jint_t(I,p)$). Here the individual counterpart attitude *int* related to *jint* is either (i) an intention to bring about p, or (ii) the intention to perform one's part in bringing about p. Case (i) concerns weak kinds of joint intentions (shared we-intentions in the sense of chapter 2), whereas in the case of plan-based, we-mode attitudes (ii) must be used.[5]

It may be recalled from the appendix to chapter 2 that a collective attitude in the we-mode implies a collective commitment of the people concerned towards realizing or upholding what is expressed in the attitude's content while in the individual mode such a commitment need not obtain. Collective commitment, in turn, implies that the individuals sanction and/or help each other, and they may use deontic vocabulary concerning rights and obligations in the context of their activities.

Referring to the above items, a set S of sentences is defined as the smallest set with the following properties. (a) $S_f \subseteq S$, (b) if $I \subseteq J$, t ε T and C,E ⊆ S then *act*(t,I,C,E) ε S, (c) if *att* ε ATT, t ε T, $I \subseteq J$, i ε J, and p ε S then *catt*(I,*att*,p,t) ε S and *iatt*(i,*att*,p,t) ε S. The recursion over members of S in (b) and (c) is needed because attitudes may themselves become the objects of actions, for instance, when an action aims at the creation of, or change in, a collective attitude.

In the following, we will informally identify a collective attitude with its kind *att* and content p, that is, with the pair (*att*,p). As the collective attitude will below be either a collective intention (viz., shared we-intention in the sense of chapter 2) or a we-belief, we are dealing with a version of collective acceptance of the proposition p here, viz., CA(p) (recall the discussion in chapter 5). Accordingly, p can express a view (e.g. p = The earth is flat) or an intention (e.g. p = We will make a revolution). The content p can also express a norm, for example, p = Everyone ought to do X when in circumstances C; this is a highly relevant possibility in the case of normative social practices and social institutions.

In our presentation below we will, for simplicity's sake, identify an action with the pair (C,E) of its conditions and relevant effects. (These results must minimally include the result event of the action in question – or, more generally, it must include an event or state satisfying the success criterion of the action.)

7.4 FRAMES

A frame contains those items that below are used in order to define social practices.

(1) A set S of sentences satisfying the above conditions. Po(S) is called the *state space*.

(2) A set $T = \{1,2,3,...\}$ of points of time.

(3) On T we introduce an infinite sequence $P = (z^1, z^2, z^3, ...)$ of periods. Each period $z^i = (z^i_1, ..., z^i_4)$ is such that, for some t in T, $z^i_1 = t$, $z^i_2 = t + 1$, $z^i_3 = t + 2$, $z^i_4 = t + 3$. Periods are disjoint and the ordering of periods is assumed to be compatible with that of T, that is, if $i < j$ then $z^i_4 < z^j_1$. Moreover, we assume that the first period begins at instant 1: $z^1_1 = 1$.

(4) A set A of primitive actions,[6] $A \subseteq Po(S) \times Po(S)$.

(5) A set J of at least two individuals.

(6) A set $\mathbf{G} \subseteq Po(J)$ of *sets of individuals*. The sets in $\mathbf{G}$ can be interpreted as groups but we will not impose and use any structure on those sets. Although the model is general in this respect, we will below consider only one set of individuals I and its complement or the "rest," R, that is, the other individuals not in I so that $J = I \cup R$.

(7) A set ATT of *attitude kinds*. ATT contains at least belief (*bel*) and intention (*int*).

(8) A frame contains a *state description*, function

$$x: \mathbf{G} \times T \rightarrow Po(S)$$

For set $I \varepsilon \mathbf{G}$ and time t, x(I,t) is the set of sentences describing the state of I at t. In general, $\cup_{I \varepsilon \mathbf{G}} x(I,t)$ may be logically inconsistent, but weaker forms of consistency, like paraconsistency, might still usefully be applied.

(9) There is a relation *caus* that we regard formally as a partial function of the following type *caus*: $T \times Po(S) \times T \rightarrow Po(S)$

Cause and effect are both described by sets of sentences. We interpret *caus*(t,X,t') = Y as "the (partial) state X being present at t causes a state Y at t'." Here causality can be regarded as an irreducible basic notion.[7] Because Po(S) will contain many inconsistent sets that do not describe any kind of state whatsoever, *caus* must be partial.

(10) A frame contains an action representation in the form of a relation

$$act \subseteq T \times \mathbf{G} \times Po(S) \times Po(S)$$

where *act*(t,I,C,E) is read "the action (C,E) is performed by I at t." In general, I is a set of individuals, and the action is a collective or possibly even a joint action. For $I = \{i\}$ we obtain individual actions as a special case.

The following items are specific for the characterization of social practices.

(11) Functions describing conditions that trigger the realization of attitudes and actions. Usually, a collective attitude is built up only under special conditions. For instance, the members of an orchestra can have the joint intention of giving a concert tonight, but if the concert hall had burnt down in the morning, this intention would not have been rationally possible to have. Similarly, the actual performance of an action requires that the "right" conditions obtain. Part of the right conditions for going, say, to the Saturday morning market, is trivially that it be Saturday morning. Such conditions we represent by the functions

$$trigatt\colon \mathbf{G} \times \mathrm{ATT} \times \mathrm{S} \times \mathrm{T} \to \mathrm{Po(S)}$$

and

$$trigact\colon \mathbf{G} \times \mathrm{ATT} \times \mathrm{S} \times \mathrm{T} \to \mathrm{Po(S)}.$$

Here $trigatt(I,att,p,t)$ is a description of the sufficient conditions that will trigger the collective attitude of kind *att* with content p in set I at time t, while $trigact(I,att,p,t)$ is a description of the trigger conditions for a collective action aiming at p. The function *trigact* is needed and used here only for (collective) actions that belong to a corresponding (collective) attitude in the sense that the action is suited to reach the goal inherent in p. Thus $trigact(I,att,p,t)$ is precisely interpreted as a description of the trigger conditions for actions (C,E) "belonging to" the collective attitude of the kind *att* with content p: $catt(I,att,p,t)$ (this explains the arguments for *trigact*).

(12) Finally, a frame contains two functions dealing with the "success" and longevity of social practices. First, we have a real-valued *success* function

$$suc\colon \mathbf{G} \times \mathrm{ATT} \times \mathrm{S} \times \mathrm{P} \to \mathbf{R}$$

where $\mathbf{R}$ denotes the set of real numbers. Secondly, there is a *threshold* function

$$thr\colon \mathbf{G} \times \mathrm{ATT} \times \mathrm{S} \to \mathbf{R}$$

$suc(I,att,p,z^i)$ denotes the level of success that the collective attitude of kind *att* and content p has in set of individuals I in period z^i. Success can formally be measured simply by the number of successful actions in the past, where an action is successful if its result fits with its causal effect (see section 7.5). The success value is the same for all the instants in a period z^i and is updated only at the end of the period. Periods are used as a technical device to disentangle those causal changes pertinent to a social practice from other changes that may occur at each arbitrary point of time. $thr(I,att,p)$ denotes the threshold for an attitude of the kind *att* and content p in set of individuals I. If the level of success in I for attitude (att,p) in z^i falls below the threshold (viz., $suc(I,att,p,z^i) \leq thr(I,att,p)$) then that attitude will no longer be built up, that is during period z^{i+1} there will be no collective attitude $catt(I,att,p,t)$. Such thresholds are frequently used in psychological theories (e.g. Westermann, 2000). These two functions are broad theoretical terms, which, in special applications, may be specified and replaced by actual conditions pertaining to the practice in question. The threshold could be made dependent on time and on macro parameters of the system, like the number of participants at a given time.

In summary, a frame takes the form

$$(S,T,P,A,J,\mathbf{G},ATT,x, \textit{caus, act, trigatt, trigact, suc, thr})$$

and it is required to satisfy the following axioms for all $t,t' \; \varepsilon \; T, C, E \subseteq S, I \subseteq J$, and all $z, z^i \; \varepsilon \; P, z = (z_1,...,z_4), z^i = (z_1^i,...,z_4^i)$:

(A1) if $catt(I,att,p,z_2) \; \varepsilon \; x(I, z_2)$ then $trigact(I,att,p,z_2) \subseteq x(I,z_2)$ if and only if there exist $C',E' \subseteq S$ such that ($p \; \varepsilon \; E'$ and $act(z_3,I,C',E') \; \varepsilon \; caus(z_2,\{catt(I,att,p,z_2)\},z_3)$).

(A2) $[trigatt(I,att,p,z_1) \subseteq x(I,z_1)$ and $thr(I,att,p) \leq suc(I,att,p,z)]$ if and only if $catt(I,att,p,z_2) \; \varepsilon \; caus(z_1,x(I,z_1),z_2) \cap x(I,z_2)$.

(A3) For all $C,E,C',E' \subseteq S$ and all $z' = (z_1',...,z_4') \; \varepsilon \; P$: if $act(z_3,I,C,E) \; \varepsilon \; caus(z_2,\{catt(I,att,p,z_2)\},z_3)$ and $act(z_3',I,C',E') \; \varepsilon \; caus(z_2',\{catt(I,att,p,z_2')\},z_3')$ then $(C,E) = (C',E')$.

(A4) For all $z^{i+1} \; \varepsilon \; P$ and all C,E such that

$$act(z_3^i,I,C,E) \; \varepsilon \; caus(z_2^i, \{catt(I, att, p, z_2^i)\},z_3^i):$$
$$suc(I, att, p,z^{i+1}) > suc(I, att, p,z^i), \text{ in case}$$
$$p \; \varepsilon \; caus(z_4^i, C \cap \{act(z_3^i,I,C,E)\},z_4^i) \cap x(I,z_4^i), \text{ and}$$
$$suc(I,att,p, z^{i+1}) < suc(I,att,p,z^i) \text{ in all other cases.}$$

(A5) For all $X,Y \subseteq S$: $caus(t,X \cup Y,t') = caus(t,X,t') \cup caus(t,Y,t')$.

(A6) For all $X \subseteq S$: if X is consistent, then so is $caus(t,X,t')$.

(A7) If $X \subseteq Y \subseteq S$ then $caus(t,X,t') \subseteq caus(t,Y,t')$.

(A1) says that the collective attitude *catt* plus the attitude trigger conditions *trigatt* together are necessary and sufficient to cause at least one action that successfully realizes the attitude's content. According to our simplifying assumption (A2), the presence of the trigger conditions for the attitude plus a sufficiently high success level are necessary and sufficient for the attitude being caused (built up). The principle (A2) seems to contradict the principle that when acting intentionally an agent could (at least in a metaphysical if not in a practical sense of "could") have willed otherwise. This principle expresses freedom of the will that an intentionally acting agent is assumed to have. We wish to note here that our present approach, using (A2), can accept that from a first-person point of view there is freedom of will, because the agent may well think that he could have formed the intention to do something else without falsifying (A2). (Even so, in a finer analysis a liberalized principle should be used to replace (A2) to represent our view that metaphysical determinism seems not to be a true doctrine. A more realistic mathematical treatment would introduce some indeterminacy in the sufficiency condition. The use of either point-valued or interval-valued probabilities would be one way of doing it.)

(A3) says that the action (C,E) which is caused by a collective attitude $catt(I,att,p,\cdot)$ is uniquely determined in terms of att and p. (This is a simplifying assumption.)

(A4) updates the success values. In a period z^i an action (C,E) under consideration is caused by the collective attitude (att,p). If p is among the causal consequences of C and the action $act(z^i_3,I,C,E)$, then the action (C,E) was successful, and the success function is increased, otherwise it is decreased. Thus success means that the attitude content p is causally realized (or realized in the right manner, depending on precisely what the criteria of success on each occasion are taken to be). Note that we distinguish as *unintended* consequences of an action those causal consequences that are not members of E.

A fuller treatment of success would require a detailed discussion of the criteria of "goodness" or "satisfaction" of a performance. We will not here say more about the matter.

7.5 SOCIAL PRACTICES MATHEMATICALLY ANALYZED

A social practice in the core sense is a recurrent pattern of action performed because of a collective attitude, viz., a shared we-attitude. In each period, the pattern is realized once by the changes of state occurring in that period.

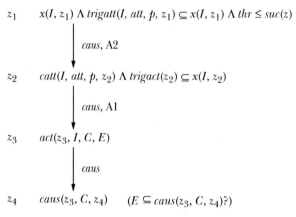

z_1 $x(I, z_1) \wedge trigatt(I, att, p, z_1) \subseteq x(I, z_1) \wedge thr \leq suc(z)$

         caus, A2

z_2 $catt(I, att, p, z_2) \wedge trigact(z_2) \subseteq x(I, z_2)$

         caus, A1

z_3 $act(z_3, I, C, E)$

         caus

z_4 $caus(z_3, C, z_4)$ $(E \subseteq caus(z_3, C, z_4)?)$

Fig. 2 Pattern of a social practice

DEF. 1: y is a *pattern with att,p,C,E for I* if and only if there is some z ε P, z $= (z_1,...,z_4)$ such that y $= (z,att,p,C,E)$ and

(1) p ε E

(2) $catt(I,att,p,z_2)$ ε $caus(z_1,x(I,z_2),z_2) \cap x(I,z_2)$

(3) $act(z_3,I,C,E)$ ε $caus(z_2, \{catt(I,att,p,z_2)\},z_3)$.

Figure 2 shows the essentials of a pattern. At the first instant z_1 of the pattern the set of individuals is in state $x(I,z_1)$. If in that state the trigger conditions for the attitude (att,p) are satisfied and the attitude had been sufficiently successful, this will causally lead to the presence of the attitude $catt(I,att,p,z_2)$ at the next instant z_2 (this is part of the content of (A2)). If at z_2 the trigger conditions for action corresponding to (att,p) are satisfied this will causally lead to the performance of such an action $act(z_3,I,C,E)$ in the next period z_3 (this is part of the content of (A1)). A third causal transition then produces the result $caus(z_3,C,z_4)$ of that action, which may be different from the intended effect E of (C,E).

A pattern basically comprises the build-up or activation of a collective attitude plus a collective action that is performed as the effect of this attitude as well as the causal result of that action.[8]

The two crucial causal steps are covered by conditions (2) and (3) of clause definition 1. (2) states that the attitude is caused by the previous state of the set of individuals, and (3) says that this attitude in turn causes a corresponding action. It is not ruled out that causal transitions of the kind captured in (2) and (3) also occur at other instants in a period. This does not matter; they simply are ignored. What matters are those transitions occurring at the "right" instances, and this is technically captured by the use of periods.

We say that a pattern (z,att,p,C,E) for I is *successful* if and only if $p \, \varepsilon$ $caus(z_3, C \cap act(z_3, I, C, E), z_4) \cap x(I, z_4)$, otherwise we say that the pattern is a *failure*. By axiom (A4) at the end of a successful pattern the participants' success level with respect to the attitude in question is increased, whereas in the case of a failure it is decreased.[9]

DEF. 2: x is a *social practice (of duration n) given att,p,C,E for I* if and only if

(1) $n \, \varepsilon \, \mathbf{N}, n > 1$

(2) $x = (z^i, att, p, C, E), i = 1,...,n$

(3) for all $i \leq n$, (z^i, att, p, C, E) is a pattern with att, p, C, E for I.

A social practice thus comprises a sufficiently large initial segment of the sequence of periods $P = (z^1, z^2,...)$. In each period the pattern is realized once and the collective attitude (shared we-attitude) is built up, causing collective action and thus the effect of this action.

Two important special cases obtain when the trigger conditions for action are fully caused by those for the attitude, and when the trigger conditions recur periodically. In the first case the trigger conditions for action are automatically satisfied whenever the attitude trigger conditions are satisfied, and thus need not be considered. For instance, actions in which the agents control themselves to the extent that they are independent of environmental disturbances are endogenous actions and can form endogenous social practices. Social practices with these properties we call endogenous. An endogenous social practice cannot be disturbed by effects that are consistent with the attitude trigger conditions. The second special case is provided by routines. They are regularly performed actions that the agents can (easily) perform, and they form our second special case. Accordingly, the case where the trigger conditions recur periodically can in our approach be called a *routine*. In this case the requirements for a social practice follow from those stating the periodicity of the system (plus certain initial conditions). (For a proof and discussion of the results concerning exogenous practices and routines, see Balzer and Tuomela, 2001.)

7.6 TOWARDS A SOCIAL DYNAMICS

In this section we will study some dynamic aspects of social practices (the developments below will enrich the previous mathematical treatment given in Tuomela, 1995, chapter 10). By this kind of dynamics we mean the maintenance and change of social practices in time when they are recurrently performed and get feedback both directly from their performance ("internal" feedback) and from the surrounding social and physical environment ("external" feedback). The issue of dynamics is obviously a complex and difficult one. Furthermore, it mostly depends on contingent causal happenings in the world and therefore such study, having an a posteriori character, must be mainly the task of a sociologist. However, also a philosopher can do something: He can try to sketch the general features of change in view of a certain conceptual framework used for the study of social practices and thus possibly find a priori constraints and perhaps also suggest some heuristics for the empirical study of the dynamics of social practices. Before discussing the broader features of social change, let us start by considering the maintenance of social practices from the point of view of the framework created above.

We can formulate two necessary and jointly sufficient conditions for the maintenance of a social practice in our core sense. The basis of each practice is given by a collective attitude (att,p) and a collective action (C,E) resulting from that attitude. The first condition requires that the trigger conditions for the attitude (att,p) as well as for the action (C,E) recur (conditions (1) and (2) of the theorem below). This condition is clearly necessary because when the trigger conditions stop holding then the causal flow is likely to stop, too. The second condition simply says that the success level of the attitude for the set of individuals must always stay above the threshold (condition (3) in the theorem). This roughly means that the rate of successful actions to satisfy the attitude is always ahead of the rate at which these actions fail.

Let $x = (z^i,att,p,C,E)$, $i = 1,...,n$, be a social practice of duration n for I. We say that x is *maintained into period* z^{n+1} if and only if (z^{n+1},att,p,C,E) is a pattern with att,p,C,E for I. The following result can now be proved:

THEOREM: Let $x = (y_i)$, $i = 1,...,n$, with $y_i = (z^i,att,p,C,E)$, be a social practice of duration n for I, and let z^{n+1} be the next element of $P = (z^1,...,z^n,z^{n+1},...)$. Then x is maintained into period z^{n+1} if and only if

(1) $trigatt(I,att,p,z_1^{n+1}) \subseteq x(I, z_1^{n+1})$

(2) $trigact(I,att,p,z_2^{n+1}) \subseteq x(I, z_2^{n+1})$

(3) $thr(I,att,p) < suc(I,att,p,z^n)$ or $[thr(I,att,p) = suc(I,att,p,z^n)$ and y_n is successful].

The reader is referred to Balzer and Tuomela (2001) for a proof of this theorem.

The conditions for maintenance in this theorem refer to the trigger conditions, the success function, and the threshold. The theorem thus shows that these items can capture everything needed to guarantee the maintenance and stability of a social practice. Put differently, in applications the question of whether a social practice can be maintained reduces to a specification of these items such that the conditions of the theorem are satisfied.

As a first step towards a more comprehensive model of social dynamics let us consider a simple scheme from systems theory.[10] Focusing on one set of individuals I in **G**, all other individuals in the system are lumped together to form the "society" R external to I so that $\mathbf{G} = \{I,R\}$. Of course, "the system" need not comprise all of society. Thus R can have various interpretations. Referring to R also as a set of individuals, we assume that both sets' states can be partitioned as follows. The state of each set of individuals X in **G**, $x(X,t)$ is divided into an "internal" part $x^{int}(X,t)$, which is in part the causal result of X's own collective action, and an "external" part $x^{ext}(X,t)$ resulting from the actions of the other set of individuals. In the case of I, we may also put the effects of "nature" into $x^{ext}(I,t)$, so that R is really society plus nature. The states of both sets are coupled in the sense that they influence each other causally. However, it is often possible to separate these influences so that a set of individuals' internal states is only affected by causal effects produced by that very set. Using functions $f^{X,int}$ and $f^{X \to Y}$: $Po(S) \to Po(S)$, which map the causal effects of X's actions into X's and Y's internal states, respectively, we obtain the picture shown in figure 3.[11]

Figure 3 is to be read as a flowchart diagram. At time t, R is in state $x(R,t)$ that causally leads to $caus(t,x(R,t),t+1)$ at $t+1$. This result is taken as input by $f^{R,int}$ that produces the value $x^{int}(R,t+1)$: $f^{R,int}(caus(t,x(R,t), t+1)) = x^{int}(R,t+1)$. This is now inserted as the new value (for $t+1$) in the upper-left box, replacing $x^{int}(R,t)$. The other loops are interpreted analogously. For instance, starting from the top-right box function $f^{R \to I}$ will produce $f^{R \to I}(caus(t,x(R,t),t+1)) = x^{ext}(I,t+1)$, which replaces the value $x^{ext}(I,t)$ in the third box on the left.

Adjusting to our frame we may somewhat coarsen this picture and take one transition of the scheme to cover one period $z^i = (z^i_1,...,z^i_4)$ in P.

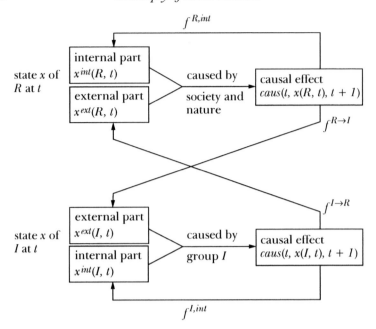

Fig. 3 Flowchart of social dynamics

The states on the left-hand side are then assigned to time z_1^i and those on the right to time z_4^i, and in the next period z_1^{i+1} the states on the left are replaced by those obtaining at z_1^{i+1}. In a minimal version we can even restrict the states on the right to contain only elements of S that explicitly occur in a social practice (z^i, att, p, C, E), $i = 1,...,n$. A minimal scheme corresponding to such a social practice thus takes the form shown in Fig. 4.

On the upper level society and nature reproduce the trigger conditions for the next period which by $f^{R \to I}$ are mapped into $x^{ext}(I, z_1^{i+1})$. On the lower level I's state at z_1^i, in which the trigger conditions are satisfied, initiates the pattern (z^i, att, p, C, E) that leads to $caus(z_3^i, C, z_4^i)$ at time z_4^i. The effects of I's action(s) both influence society, via $f^{G \to R}$, and the next state of I at z_1^{i+1} by means of updating the success function according to whether the action was (taken to be) a failure or a success.[12] In order to make the scheme work, we have to require that, for all z in P: $trigact(I, att, p, z_1) = trigact(I, att, p, z_2)$ because in a pattern the *trigact* condition need not hold at z_2.[13]

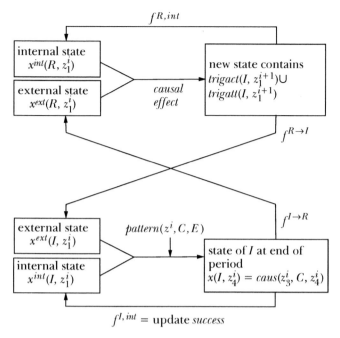

$f^{R,int}$

internal state
$x^{int}(R, z_1^i)$

external state
$x^{ext}(R, z_1^i)$

causal effect

new state contains
$trigact(I, z_1^{i+1}) \cup$
$trigatt(I, z_1^{i+1})$

$f^{R \rightarrow I}$

$f^{I \rightarrow R}$

external state
$x^{ext}(I, z_1^i)$

internal state
$x^{int}(I, z_1^i)$

pattern(z^i, C, E)

state of I at end of period
$x(I, z_4^i) = caus(z_3^i, C, z_4^i)$

$f^{I, int}$ = update *success*

Fig. 4 Developed flowchart of social dynamics

The total state x(I,t) can be further divided into components representing different kinds of attitudes and causing different kinds of actions. Thus, there is the collective attitude – conceptualized in the participants' conceptual framework for action – which accounts for collective action of various kinds. There is standard *causal action* such as is involved in jointly building a house or going to have a swim together. But there is also symbolically creative collective *acceptance action*, which functions in analogy with linguistic performatives. As can be recalled especially from chapters 5 and 6, the participants may collectively come to accept that some physical goods (squirrel fur or pieces of gold) qualify as money, thus creating new symbolic and social status for those entities and often giving the participants relevant deontic powers concerning the institutionalized items (cf. chapter 6 and Searle, 1995).

As we have shown, our mathematical approach can take into account both the intended and unintended consequences of collective action and is thus compatible with the occurrence of both. However, there are other important distinctions related to the knowledge or beliefs about the situation that the agents may have which we have not taken up in our present account. One such distinction is that between foreseen and unforeseen consequences, while another one is the question about known and unknown initial conditions. Our model allows for the possibility of "invisible hand" processes, which not only lead to some unintended results but are such that these unintended results (as a kind of goals), via feeding back information from those results, really repetitively affect the agents' collective attitudes and hence their relevant activities.[14] Thus the feedback can occur without the agents being aware of it, and we can have functional, self-reinforcing invisible hand processes in the strong sense Adam Smith seems to have conceived of them: "[the individual] generally, indeed, neither intends to promote the publick interest, nor knows how much he is promoting it . . . he intends only his own security . . . and he is led . . . by an invisible hand to promote an end which was not part of his intention" (Smith, 1776/1982, IV, ii, 9).[15]

7.7 THE INDIVIDUAL LEVEL

Integration of the individual level requires substantial steps that cannot routinely be performed on the basis of the logical systems presently available. The main difficulty lies in our global functions describing state change and causal effects. Functions of this specific type are not used in other formalisms, there is no widely accepted "causal logic," and a global state transition function for social systems will remain a *desideratum* for a very long time. The best that can be done at the moment is to incorporate the "rest" of the model, that is, all the items except the causal and the transition function, into a possible worlds system. As this system becomes rather complex, we will only sketch the essentials.

First, the states of a set of individuals, I, are decomposed into states of the set's members. We assume that all individuals who at some time belong to set I are given by a finite or infinite sequence $(i_1,...,i_n,...)$ and we use a predicate $exists(t,i_j)$ to express that at time t, individual i_j is an active participant, or belongs to the set of individuals. Considering state functions $x(\{i_j\},t)$ such that $x(\{i_j\},t) = \phi$ in case i_j does not *exist* at t, we require that $x(I,t) = \cup \{x(\{i_j\},t) \mathbin{/} i_j \; \varepsilon \; I\}$.

Second, the notion of action covered by *act* that was previously applied invariantly at the collective and individual level is refined so that proper collective action is constituted by properly individual actions. We use a set of primitive individual actions, which are combined to yield more complex and collective actions in the way of dynamic logic (cf. Harel,

1984). For any two actions a,b, we consider their being performed in parallel, (a ∥ b) and one after the other (a; b), and a collective action is taken to be a sequence of such concatenations governed by an explicit plan in the sense of Balzer and Tuomela (1997a). The state transition given by any action is then described by a transition function on possible worlds in the way of dynamic logic.

Third, all actions, beliefs, and intentions are ordered in time. The easiest way to do this is simply to use numerals in the way of Cohen and Levesque (1990). This means that in applications the ordering of events in the plans must be checked against the overall timescale of the model. A general constraint here is that the actor performing an action at time t must exist at that time.

Last, but not least, collective attitudes are tied to individual ones.[16] For example, on the usual, iterative approach, the formula for joint intention *jint*(I,p,t) among members of I with content p at a given time t is characterized in terms of the corresponding individual intentions *int*(i_j,I,p,t) of the members i_j, and their individual beliefs *bel*(t, i_j, ·) in the I-mode case, with no part structure, as follows (the formula is restricted to the case of a two-member set I = {i,j} and one instant t):

$$jint(I,p,t) \leftrightarrow int(i,I,p,t) \;\&\; int(j,I,p,t) \;\&$$

$$bel(t,i,int(j,I,p,t)) \;\&\; bel(t,j,int(i,I,p,t)) \;\&$$

$$bel(t,i,bel(t,j,int(i,I,p,t))) \;\&$$

$$bel(t,j,bel(t,i,int(j,I,p,t))) \;\&\;\ldots$$

Belief is denoted by *bel* and the conjunction is extended over all combinations of actors. (We recall that in the we-mode case an actor can only intend to do his part of p).[17]

At the individual level we may also consider how a practice is transmitted, or spreads, from individual to individual. Such spreading may range from simple imitation to various forms of learning. In general, we can work with an asymmetric relation stating that an action (or the contents of a corresponding goal) has been adopted by a "new" individual who thus gets involved in the practice for the first time. We call this relation the *imitation* relation and assume that it will cover any learning involving information transmission. In principle, the success of an instance of imitation of the collective action involved in a social practice must be judged on the basis of the whole social practice, whereas the process of learning or imitating an individual action may function more locally. In the special case where the collective action involved in a social practice is represented by a plan, it is basically this plan that makes up the content of the collective attitude governing the practice. In this case the imitation relation can be relativized to such a plan, thus taking the form $imit(t,i,j,a,b,p)$ ("at time t, actor i's action a is imitated by j's action b in the context of plan p"). This opens the way for substantive assumptions on the imitation relation, binding together the "isolated" individual action and the larger context of the social practice in which imitation is meaningful or useful. On the cognitive level, one might accordingly take the content of the collective attitude as the *meme* that is spread. Of course, the general constraint on existence applies here too.

7.8 AN EXAMPLE OF A SOCIAL PRACTICE

Let us look at a real-life example of a social practice – regular sauna bathing on Saturdays. Suppose i and j acquired the habit of going for a sauna together each Saturday afternoon at 3 p.m., $I = \{i,j\}$. The kind of attitude on which this practice is based is intention (*att = int*) and its contents may be expressed by p = "We will have a sauna together next Saturday." Let us focus on an action description (C,E) for which C contains "i and j go from their homes to the sauna, meet there, get ready, and enter," and E contains "i and j bathe and cool down together," and so forth. Each period comprises one week and contains four instants salient for the practice. The instants $z_1,...,z_4$ may be as follows. $z_1 =$ Saturday morning, $z_2 =$ Saturday 1 p.m., $z_3 =$ Saturday 2 p.m., $z_4 =$ Saturday 3 p.m., and so on until the end of the event. At z_1 the trigger conditions for the attitude must be satisfied, and the success level must be above the threshold. $trigatt(I,int,p,z_1)$ contains sentences like "i and j are both healthy, have no other extraordinary obligations for next Saturday afternoon, and believe that this is also so for the other individual." The success level is initially above the threshold because in earlier rounds the action's expected, positive effect was realized.

On Saturday morning (z_1) the trigger conditions for the intentions are presumably satisfied and the success level is above the threshold. Under these conditions both individuals form the collective attitude (a shared we-intention in this case) to go to the sauna together at 3 p.m. (See Balzer and Tuomela, 1997b, for considerations of how this might happen in detail.) At 1 p.m. (z_2) the joint intention is present, and if the trigger conditions for the actions obtain, the actions will be performed, beginning at 2 p.m. (z_3). The trigger conditions for the actions could be something like "mutual belief that the sauna is heated and that there are no exceptional obstacles to getting there." From 3 p.m. to, say, 5 p.m. the effect E caused by previous events, bathing together takes place. This means success and the success level will be increased, so that in this respect the ground is prepared for the following week. Failure could occur, for instance, when the car in which i drives to the sauna breaks down or when the electricity is shut off shortly after 3 p.m., or when the sauna is public and overcrowded, so that they are not let in. None of these events is mentioned in the action conditions C.

7.9 SOCIAL NORMS, TASK-RIGHT SYSTEMS, AND SOCIAL INSTITUTIONS

In this section the treatment begun in section 6.5 concerning social institutions in the organization sense will be elaborated in mathematical terms. Especially, we wish to indicate how that view of organizational social institutions as collectives with a task-right system and relevant social practices to go with it can be fitted in the mathematical framework of the present chapter.

Social norms have a more objective status than attitudes, both in an epistemic sense and in the ontic sense that they are "groupjective" as opposed to subjective (recall chapter 5). Attitudes are held by individuals, that is, they are properties of individuals. By contrast, the usual syntax for norms is to say that a norm is in force in a group, system, or institution. So social norms are not attached to individuals but to the group, system, or institution as a whole. Ordinary language provides a special vocabulary to talk about norms: deontic operators and forms. In theory it seems sufficient to deal with just two deontic forms, obligations and rights, with the understanding that other deontic forms concerning action can be conceptually reduced to these two.[18] Earlier in this book two types of social norms were distinguished, viz., authority-based norms and proper social norms (see section 6.2). In the present chapter we will not explicitly use this central distinction.

We will below deal almost solely with action obligations (thus ought-to-do norms) and rights (thus may-do norms). Each obligation and each right can be taken to have its specific context, which can be described by a local state, that is by a set of sentences in our logico-mathematical framework. If a person is in the context specific to an obligation, she will get sanctioned for *not* doing the thing she is obliged to do in that context, and if she is in the context specific for a right, any other person who does something conflicting with the things circumscribed by that right will be sanctioned. Sanctions may be spontaneous or well organized, and many institutions have developed their own apparatus and staff to do the sanctioning. In our modern, highly organized societies, the mere presence of such an apparatus and the resulting threat of sanctions is sufficient to uphold the normative system.

In our logical system we use the predicate *sanc* to express sanctions. This predicate is used to express that an action b is a sanction for another action a. We distinguish between sanctions of the form $(+,a,b)$ representing a sanction b following the performance of action a, and sanctions of the form $(-,a,b)$ in which b is a sanction for action a not having been performed. We say that *i's action a at t is sanctioned* if and only if there exist b, j, t' ($t < t'$ & $(+,a,b)$ ε *sanc* & $act(t,i,a)$ & $act(t',j,b)$). Similarly *i's not doing a at t is sanctioned* if and only if not $act(t,i,a)$ and there are b, j and $t' > t$ such that $(-,a,b)$ ε *sanc* and $act(t',j,b)$. For simplicity's sake, sanctions are here always understood in the negative sense.

For logical purposes, action obligations and rights can be described as sets of action types. Our account of actions as represented by two sets of sentences (for the action's conceptually and factually presupposed conditions and result) also applies to action types. An action type may be described by two sets of formulas, one for the conditions and one for the result. Considering a single obligation to perform a single action (of a certain type) in a specified situation, the description of this situation can be taken to be part of the conditions for the action type. In general, an obligation may comprise several actions conditioned on different contexts. The same applies to rights.

In general, we take an *obligation ob* to consist of a set of action types

$$ob = \{(C_1,E_1),...,(C_n,E_n)\}$$

such that each set of sentences C_i specifies some conditions or context in which the obligation requires action, and each E_i spells out the result of that action. According to our account of action, the conditions C_i at the same time also are the necessary conditions for the actions of the type under consideration. If an actor has an obligation of this form, he is obliged to perform any of the actions whenever the conditions pertinent to it obtain.

Analogously, a *right ri* is a set of action types

$$ri = \{(C'_1,E'_1),...,(C'_n,E'_n)\}.$$

An actor who has this right may perform any of the right's action types whenever the conditions for that type are satisfied. Each C_i' specifies a context and states necessary conditions for action, and each E_i' describes the result of the action, which an actor has the right to perform.

Norms come in clusters, they form a system (or systems). As we use only action obligations and rights, a system of action-governing norms will consist of a system of obligations (thus ought-to-do norms) and rights (may-do norms). The organization's basic goals can be stated in terms of ought-to-be norms (recall chapter 6). But we will not incorporate them into our analysis below, nor will we take into account the metanorms governing the system that a fuller analysis might need. As seen in chapter 6, social institutions in the organization sense can be structured in terms of positions. Each member of the institution holds one or more positions, which are relatively stable over time and which are defined in terms of obligations and rights that are assigned to the holder of the position – whoever that is. A (social) position in a given social system will be understood here basically as a set of obligations and rights (cf. section 6.5). When a person comes to occupy the position she must fulfil the obligations, and she acquires the rights pertaining to the position.

We represent a system of norms by a set of positions, and we represent each *position pos* as a set of obligations ($OB = \{ob_1,...,ob_n\}$) and rights ($RI = \{ri_1,...,ri_m\}$):

$$pos = (\{ob_1,...,ob_n\},\{ri_1,...,ri_m\}).$$

In principle, social norms functionally play a role similar to that of shared we-attitudes (thus collective attitudes in general): they interlock and bind together the actions of several individuals so that these form a larger unit. The difference between the two is that norms are more objective (viz., "groupjective," as seen in chapter 5). In comparison with collective attitudes, they are detached both from the actors "holding" them, and from actors submitted to them. No particular individuals are specified that uphold a system of norms, the norms simply "exist" in a system. Furthermore, no particular individual is specified to which a system of norms applies.

Although normative stabilization by a system of obligations and rights is certainly an important feature, also the social practices component of a social institution is central. Both parts are necessary for our understanding of an institution. A normative system without actions is empty, whereas a mere system of social practices cannot account for the complexity and stability of institutions.

The conceptual connection between obligations and rights (viz., social norms) and social practices within a social institution can be easily described by means of our framework. Social practices as types of activities consist of recurrently performed collective social actions. The latter include actions that can consistently be performed by individuals and actions that can be performed by several individuals collectively. In these cases there will be some individual position-related actions (component actions of the collective social action or part actions in the case of joint action). The individual actions, in general, will have to be performed at least in part because of a we-attitude that is shared by the individuals. The we-attitude is or must include a we-belief with the content that such and such a norm obtains or is in force in the group in question (cf. note 5 of chapter 6). In the case at hand the norm has been technically built into the action(s), so to speak (recall *ob* and *n̄*). (These actions can occur in Boolean and possibly other, e.g. modally conditioned, temporally and spatially differently related, combinations.)

As seen, then, the individual part or component actions, conceived of as action types, are the central content of obligations and rights. We say that a normative system is *anchored* in a system of social practices (a collection of social practices capable of consistently taking place in the organization at stake) if and only if each action type occurring in the obligations and rights of the normative system can be obtained in this way, that is, as an individual part of some kind of action belonging to a social practice in the system of social practices. (This relation may also be expressed by saying that the system of social practices *underlies* the normative system and that the latter is *in force* in the group relative to those social practices.) In some cases the anchoring may be incomplete in that some normative action types are not found in the underlying practices. This means that the establishment of the norms was at least partly induced by external forces.

Besides the conceptual connection just discussed, the normative system (viz., the task-right system) and the system of social practices are related in more subtle ways, which are best seen from a dynamical perspective. Over time, each part clearly exerts influence on the other. More efficient enforcement of the norms may lead to more compliance and thus to changes of some practices. The same can happen when the norms are changed by powerful groups in order to induce corresponding change in the practices. Conversely, change in the social practices may lead to change in norms. New social practices may emerge in some group (in the institution) requiring new norms, and established practices may die out, thus making certain norms obsolete. For instance, in the light of unfair obligations, people may change their practices in such a way as to avoid subsumption under these obligations, which in turn may lead to a change in the formulation of the obligations so as to include the new, evasive types of behavior.

In technical terms, we go about as follows. Using the format (C,E) for action types, with condition C and result E, and the state function x and the performance relation *act* described earlier, this representation of rights and obligations may easily be connected with actions. Consider some person i in position *pos*, and some action type $ob = (C,E)$ obligatory for *pos*, that is, *ob* ε OB in *pos*. If i is in a state $x(t,i)$ in which the conditions for *ob* are satisfied $(C[t,i] \subseteq x(i,t))$ then i should perform the obligated action *ob*. To get at the nonnormative level we hypothesize that "i should perform *ob*" corresponds to "if i does not perform *ob* then i will be sanctioned": (not $act(t,i,C,E)$) $\rightarrow$ there exist j, t',b $(t < t'$ & $act(t',j,b)$ & $sanc(-,ob,b))$. In the case of rights the connection is a bit more complicated. If $ri = (C,E)$ is covered by a right ri belonging to RI in *pos* such that $holds(t,i,pos)$ – where *holds* simply is a predicate expressing holding a position – and i is in a state in which she could perform the permitted action ri $(C[t,i] \subseteq x(i,t))$, then no other person j should perform any action b interfering with ri. That is, we hypothesize that for any other person j and action $b = (C',E')$ which j could perform at time t $(C'[t,j] \subseteq x(j,t))$, and which is incompatible with ri $(incom(ri[t,i],b[t,j]))$, j should not perform b. (Here the *incom* is a predicate expressing incompatibility such as logical incompatibility or incompatibility concerning the considered satisfiability of one's goals, both possibilities hypothesized to reflect deontic incompatibility at the nonnormative level.)

Again, "j should not perform b" at the nonnormative level corresponds to "if j would perform b then j would be sanctioned: $act(t,j,b)$ $\rightarrow$ there exist k,t',c $(t < t'$ & $act(t',k,c)$ & $sanc(+,b,c))$."

On our way to an account of social institutions in the organization sense, we next have to give an exact characterization of the notion of a task-right system, *tr*. As a task-right system is going to depend on the notion of a system of social practices, let us first give a characterization of it. In order to define a system of several different social practices we use a set SP of names for social practices, and a function f which to each (name of a) social practice assigns a value $(g,att,(C,E))$ specifying the group g (corresponding to the earlier I), the kind of attitude *att* and the action type (C,E) specific to that practice (its *core*).

DEF. 3: s is a *system of social practices* if and only if s $= (J,T,ATT,P,O,$
$SP,G,<,S,A,x,caus,act,catt,incom,exists,sanc,f)$ and

(1) $y=(J,T,ATT,P,O,\mathbf{G},<,S,A,x,caus,act,catt,incom,exists,sanc)$ is a frame
    extended by a set O of objects (and functions defined earlier)

(2) SP is a finite, nonempty set (of labels of social practices)

(3) f: $SP \rightarrow \mathbf{G} \times ATT \times CA$ and $\cup \{\pi_1(f(sp))\,/sp\ \varepsilon\ SP\} = J$

(4) for all sp in SP and all g,att,a, if $f(sp) = (g,att,a)$ then in y there
    exists a social practice with core (g,att,a).

The practices in a system of practices need not be compatible, although
this assumption makes good sense in most institutions, and in particular
in organizations whose task-right system is officially specified.

Let us write $part((C,E),i,(C_i,E_i))$ to express that (C_i,E_i) is an individual
action (type) which forms person i's part of the collective many-person
action (type) (C,E). A part (C_i,E_i) need not be unique; a person i may
have several parts to perform in the collective action (C,E). As before,
we use the predicate *holds* for a person holding a specific position. By IA
we denote the set of all individual action types in the system, and by CA
the set of all collective (= many-person) action types. In the following
definition $ex(t,j)$ means that at t, individual j exists as an active member.
For each $g\ \varepsilon\ \mathbf{G}$ and each t, we denote by g_t the set of members of g
existing at t, $g_t = \{i\ \varepsilon\ J\,/\,ex(t,i)\}$. We assume that for each $j\ \varepsilon\ J$ there exist
t_j^l, t_j^u such that $t_j^l < t_j^u$ and for all t with $t_j^l \leq t \leq t_j^u$, $ex(t,j)$, and t_j^l and t_j^u are
the "smallest" and "largest" such instants.

DEF. 4: tr is a *task-right system* for the system of social practices s $=$
$(J,T,ATT,P,O,SP,\mathbf{G},<,S,A,x,caus,act,catt,incom,exists,sanc,f)$ if and only if
there exist POS, *part* and *holds* such that $tr = (POS,part,holds)$ and

(1) for all *pos*, *pos* ε POS if and only if there exist $ob_1,...,ob_n$, $ri_1,...,ri_m$
    such that $pos = (OB_{pos}, RI_{pos})$, where $OB_{pos} = \{ob_1,...,ob_n\} \subseteq$ IA
    and $RI_{pos} = \{ri_1,...,ri_m\} \subseteq$ IA

(2) *part* $\subseteq$ CA $\times$ J $\times$ IA

(3) *holds* $\subseteq$ T $\times$ J $\times$ POS

(4) for all *pos,t,i*, if *holds*(t,i,*pos*) then *exists*(t,i)

(5) for all *pos* $= (OB_{pos}, RI_{pos})\ \varepsilon$ POS, all $(C,E)\ \varepsilon\ OB_{pos} \cup RI_{pos}$, all
    $i\ \varepsilon$ J and all $t\ \varepsilon$ T, if *holds*(t,i,*pos*) then there exist $(C^*,E^*) \in$ A,

g ∈ **G**, *att* ∈ ATT, sp ε SP such that

(5.1) f(sp) = (g,*att*,(C*,E*))

(5.2) *part*((C*,E*),i,(C,E)).

The action types (C,E) in OB$_{pos}$ are those which holders of position *pos* are obliged to perform (under the right conditions). Whenever the conditions C are satisfied for a person i holding position *pos* (i.e. C ⊆ x(i,t)), then i is obliged to perform an action of type (C,E). Action types a in RI$_{pos}$ specify the rights of persons holding position *pos*. Person i has the right to perform actions of type a (within the frame considered) if and only if every other person j is obliged to refrain from performing any potential action b that is incompatible with an action a* of type a (*incom*(a*,b)). (Also rights can depend on some conditions and can be conditional.)

Using a weak negation of action ("it is not the case that i performs a"), inflating the number of obligations, and assuming some kind of consistency of the task-right system, we can express the usual connection between rights and obligations as follows. If a ε RI$_{pos}$ and *holds*(t,i,*pos*), then for all a* of type a, all b and all j: if *incom*(a*,b) and *holds*(t,j,*pos'*) then among the obligations of *pos'* there is one obliging j not to perform b ("if i has the right to do a then every j ought to refrain from actions incompatible with a"). Conversely, if a ε OB$_{pos}$ then there is no right (in the system) of performing an action incompatible with a.

Our above account of obligations and rights actually has to be extended in two directions to cover the full range of real phenomena. The first extension is needed to incorporate the cases of obligations and rights that cannot be described by *individual* action types. Clearly, there exist obligations and rights that apply to groups of individuals. For instance, there are laws regulating business companies. This leads to more general notions of obligations and rights. Obligations and rights in the general sense, then, must include actions performed by collective actors (groups). This extension requires a corresponding change in the way norms are anchored in systems of practices.[19] We are now ready to give our technical analysis of a social institution in the organization sense. The core notion of such a social institution consists of a system of social practices and a task-right system for it. The system of tasks and rights on the one hand normatively mirrors certain combinations of collective action as found in the system of social practices. On the other hand, the normative task-right system by its obligations and rights provides external reasons of institutional action. Our analysis will contain the core notion and will add to it some assumptions so that we get hold of a notion that might be termed *functional social institution in the organization sense*, where functionality primarily means that there is a sanctioning system in place in the organization. The collective attitudes in our model are assumed to be compatible with the Collective Acceptance account so that the CAT formula can be taken to be satisfied by the social institutions in question – recall chapter 6.

In our account we present three basic assumptions. The first one, D5-4, is a central, analytic condition serving to define the mentioned core notion. It states that among the members of an institution there is a mutual or common belief (here symbolized by *mubel*); recall chapter 2. The mutual belief has the content that everybody behaves according to the obligations and rights attached to his position. The other two assumptions concern the functional successfulness of the institutional practices. These assumptions are of a contingent, empirical nature, and aim at explaining the role of the normative system. D5-5 and 6 say that people "usually" perform the actions they are obliged to perform, and "usually" refrain from actions conflicting with the rights of other members. "Usually" has to be understood in a statistical way, referring to the numbers of performances and the weights of the different actions and types.[20]

In order to formulate these regularities, let us define, for a = (C,E) ε A, and *pos* ε POS, the numbers

> *exopp*(a,*pos*), the number of execution opportunities of a in *pos*, as the number of (t,i) ε T $\times$ J such that *holds*(t,i,*pos*) & C[t,i] $\subseteq$ x(i,t)

> *exec*(a,*pos*), the number of executions of a in *pos* as the number of (t,i) ε T $\times$ J such that *holds*(t,i,*pos*) and C[t,i] $\subseteq$ x(i,t) & *act*(t,i,(C,E))

> *freq*(a,*pos*), the frequency of executions of a in *pos*, by *exec*(a,*pos*)/ *exopp*(a,*pos*)

> *vio*(a/*pos*), the number of actions conflicting with a in *pos* as the number of (t,i,j,b) in T $\times$ J $\times$ J $\times$ A such that *holds*(t,i,*pos*) and *incom*(a[t,i],b[t,j]) and *act*(t,i,a[t,i]) and *act*(t,j,b[t,j]).

Note that, as in *exopp*, C[t,i] $\subseteq$ x(i,t) need not lead to action, the trigger conditions also must occur. It will be assumed below that, following common ways of speaking of institutions that do not allow business companies to be institutions, an institution must be constituted to serve the collective (a community) in question and serve some of its basic goals (and, more generally, its "ethos"). This entails that the task-right system

for the institution under discussion must be compatible with a goal, say
P (which might be a conjunctive goal), which is constituted to serve the
basic goals and interests or the collective, g, and its members. We may call
P the constitutive goal of the institution. It corresponds to the demand
expressed in chapter 6 by *(FSI)* for the general case that a functional
institution succeed in solving a relevant collective action dilemma, and
serves to give the organization a special conceptual and social status.

DEF. 5: x is a *functional social institution in the organization sense* if and only if
there exist y, *tr*, and such that x = (y,*tr*,P) and

(1) P is the constitutive goal of x

(2) y is a system of social practices

(3) *tr* is a task-right system for y compatible with the constitutive goal P
of x

(4) for all t ε T: *mubel*(t,J,p) where p = (p$_1$ and p$_2$) is the following sentence

p$_1$ $\leftrightarrow$ for all j ε J for all *pos* in POS, for all t ε T, for all (C,E) ε A

if *pos* ε POS & (C,E) ε OB$_{pos}$ & C[t,j] $\subseteq$ x(j,t) & *holds*(t,j,*pos*) then
act(t,j,C,E), and

p$_2$ $\leftrightarrow$ for all i,j ε J, for all *pos* ε POS, for all (C,E) ε RI$_{pos}$, for all
t ε T, for all (C*,E*) ε A,

if *holds*(t,j,*pos*) & C[t,j] $\subseteq$ x(j,t) & C*[t,i] $\subseteq$ x(i,t) & *act*(t,i,(C*,E*)) &

incom((C[t,j],E[t,j]),(C*[t,i],E*[t,i])) then i gets sanctioned (see the
above definition)

(5) for all *pos* = (OB$_{pos}$,RI$_{pos}$) ε POS and all a ε OB$_{pos}$, *freq*(a,*pos*) is close
to 1

(6) for all *pos* = (OB$_{pos}$,RI$_{pos}$) ε POS and all a ε RI$_{pos}$, *vio*(a/*pos*) is close
to 0.

Sentence p expresses that all members behave (in the social practices)
according to their positions (tasks and rights). p$_1$ says that whenever the
conditions of an action type to which i is obliged in her position obtain,
then i will perform an action of that type. p$_2$ expresses that all persons can
act according to their rights. If another person i performs some action
incompatible with j's potential action (C[t,j],E[t,j]) to which j is entitled
((C,E) ε RI$_{pos}$ & *holds*(t,j,*pos*)), then i gets sanctioned. These are, of course,
the ideal versions of proxy formulations.

The hypotheses D5-5 and 6 may be read as criteria indicating the
extent to which people behave according to the normative frame, and

recall that the notion of incompatibility used here is a hypothesized factual, nonnormative notion meant to reflect the notion of *deontic* incompatibility that the normative system in question involves.

We will end with a summary of the notion of a social institution that is meant especially for those readers who have preferred to read the mathematical treatment only cursorily. A social institution in the organization sense consists of a system of social practices and a normative system. Each social practice can be characterized in the present framework by stating a subgroup, a type of attitude, and the collective social action type or types, instances of which are repeatedly performed within the group according to the patterns described above. A normative system is a set of positions, each position consisting of obligations and rights (either in the authority-based or in the proper social norm sense). Obligations and rights in turn are represented by sets of personal position-related action types (or in an extended version, also group action types). The normative system is anchored in the system of social practices in the sense that each normative action type is identical with, or is obtained as, an individual part of the action type of a social practice. Figures 5 and 6 give a simple sketch of the conceptual situation in graphical terms.

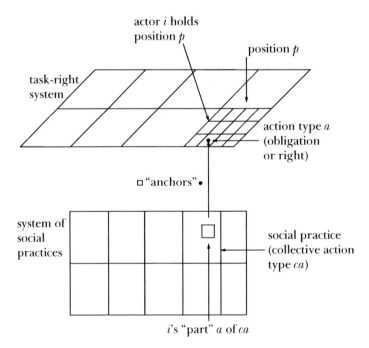

Fig. 5 Social institution model

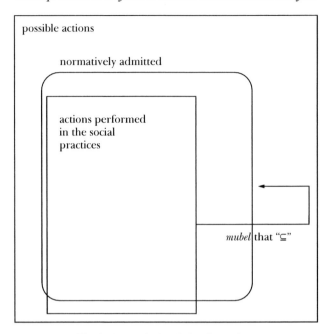

Fig. 6 Normatively admitted practices

D5-4 can be spelled out by reference to an individual's belief that everybody in the system acts in accordance with the norms, and by putting people's beliefs together to form a mutual belief in the manner of modal logic. The content of this belief "everybody acts in accordance with the norms," may be made precise as follows. Every actor in the system believes two things: (a) whenever any actor i holding a position p is in a context described by the condition of an action type from one of the obligations of that position, then, if the actor does not perform an action of that type, he will be sanctioned; and (b) whenever any actor i holding a position p is in a context described by the condition of an action type τ of one of the rights of that position, then, if any *other* actor j performs an action incompatible with actions of type τ, j gets sanctioned. Some further comments can be made on this. First, the mutual belief must obtain at every point in time at which the institution exists, but at such a point in time it has to obtain only among the members which exist at that time. Second, there are two different ways of sanctioning. An actor can be sanctioned for having performed a particular action, but he can also be sanctioned for *not* having performed a particular action. The first kind of sanction applies in the context of rights. If an actor i has a right, say, to perform action types $a_1,...,a_n$ and another actor j performs some action b that is incompatible with, say, the actions of type a_i, then j has interfered with, or violated, i's right. Consequently j will get sanctioned for having performed b. The second kind of sanction is needed to uphold obligations. If an actor in a position has an obligation consisting of action types $a_1,...,a_n$, and the conditions of, say, a_i obtain at time t, then the actor is obliged to perform an action of type a_i. If he does *not* fulfil his obligation he will be sanctioned. That is, he gets sanctioned for not performing an action. That an actor i gets sanctioned simply means that there is some other actor who performs a sanctioning action. The sanctioning actor may be one who is immediately affected by the "positive" or "negative" performance of some action, but in general it can be any other individual in the institution. If there are official staff for sanctioning, then the sanctioning actor usually will come from there.

Third, it is clear that in large institutions this complicated belief will not be present in all details, but only with some degree of approximation. Fourth, an individual even may believe that there are some exceptions, some norm violators. Fifth, if among the actors there are corporate actors, the notion of mutual belief has to be emended to include these. This can be done in terms of operative members representing the corporate actor (see Tuomela, 1995, chapter 5).

As argued in chapter 6, it is only organizations that are constituted for the group that are proper social institutions in the "standard" sense. Accordingly, it has been assumed in this chapter that the organizations under discussion satisfy the CAT formula and are social institutions in the "standard" sense of chapter 6. Given this, the present account shows what kinds of details the Collective Acceptance model of social institutions (SI) (and (SI^*)) involves when it applies to organizations.

7.10 CONCLUSION

In this chapter core social practices (which cover also institutional, norm-governed practices) have been mathematically analyzed and a dynamical schema for representing their maintenance has been proposed. Such social practices tie together collective attitudes (mainly shared we-intentions and we-beliefs) with collective action. They are stable patterns of repeated collective social action. Their maintenance is modeled by means of trigger conditions and a success function. The recurrent presence of trigger conditions and the overall success of the actions within a social practice point to a favorable environment.

Social practices can be understood as efficient means for maintaining collective goals and views. Once a social practice has been established among some actors, the collective attitude (with a goal or view content) inherent in the practice tends to become routine, so that it can be handled by mere reference to a fixed set of trigger conditions.

The present analysis shows why and how certain long-term collective goals and views are maintained. They are maintained ultimately because reaching or maintaining them is satisfactory for all participants. They are maintained as "parts" of a recurrent pattern in which they are bound together with a type of collective action and favorable external conditions. The formation of the collective goal or view can either be repeated each time the goal has been achieved or the view has been rehearsed, or the social content can be assumed to be conditionally present.

This account provides a basis for studying the spreading of social practices by learning mechanisms involving imitation as a typical element. Such mechanisms could be useful as a means to improve coordination (thus, e.g., coordination research in AI). In order to give substance to the well-known general picture of things (fashions, types of behavior, *memes*) spreading by imitation (recall chapter 4; also cf., e.g., Blackmore, 1999; Aunger, 2000), some structure is needed for the entities that carry our liberal imitation relation. In view of the present analysis the content of collective attitudes might be a good candidate for these entities.

Towards the end of this chapter social institutions in the organization sense were discussed in somewhat informal terms. Our basic account of social practices was extended to include social practices that rely on a normative and institutional background. This was done by relating them to an institutional structure, specifically a task-right system (cf. chapter 6 above). Briefly, a task-right system specifies a complex of obligations and permissions related to various positions in a normatively structured collective such as an organization.

Epilogue

To round up this book, I will briefly summarize its most important accomplishments and new results in a concise, almost telegram-like style.

1. The *Collective Acceptance (CA) model* was formulated in a precise logical way to represent performative conceptual construction in the social case. To my knowledge, this is the first attempt at precision, even if there is much discussion about social construction and constructivism both in philosophy and in social science.

   The versions of social constructivism (the "*wide*" and the "*narrow*" version) defended in this book is compatible with (scientific) realism concerning the physical world, and it does not claim that all of the social world is collectively constructed, because there are naturally social phenomena.

2. *Collective intentionality*, especially in the form of *shared weak we-attitudes*, has been argued to be centrally involved in the account of social practices and institutions (this the core of narrow constructivism) and also in the collective artificial construction of central parts of the social world such as institutions (this is the core of wide constructivism).

   In spite of the strong role of collective intentionality in this book, it is shown that there still is plenty of room for unintended action, unintended and unforeseen consequences of action, and spontaneously created social structures to play a role in the ontology of the social world.

3. The *we-mode–I-mode* distinction, applicable to (propositional) attitudes and actions, has been taken as central in the account created. Collective acceptance in the we-mode – in contrast to the I-mode – involves that the acceptance is *for the use* of the group in question, where the group is, furthermore, *collectively committed* to the collectively accepted items.

4. The notion of social practice is very often used in philosophical and social science literature but it is hard to find any analyses at all of the

notion. In this book I have given a novel account of *social practices* in terms of *shared we-attitudes*, thus collective intentionality. My theory isolates a central notion of social practice, called *core social practice*, and discusses it from various angles and shows its importance. Shared we-attitudes play a twofold role. Firstly, all core social practices require shared we-attitudes as their reason basis. Secondly, collective acceptance amounts to the group members' collectively holding relevant we-attitudes, and here the Collective Acceptance account requires that the CAT formula – expressing self-referentiality in a group context – must be satisfied and that the we-attitudes thus are in the we-mode. This does not require two layers of we-attitudes; the point is rather that in the case of mere social practices I-mode we-attitudes suffice, whereas in stronger cases, such as in the case of institutional social practices, we-mode we-attitudes are required.

5. The book advances three basic types of *arguments for the centrality of social practices* and discusses these arguments in detail. First, the deepest sense in which social practices can be argued to be primary is that they are conceptually the basis of thinking and other conceptual activities, viz., thinking and acting on the basis of concepts. Secondly, social life centrally contains recurrent social activities. Social practices thus are, and must be, part of the domain of investigation of social studies, insofar as it attempts to capture even approximately the important aspects of the social world. Thirdly, social practices have been argued to be both conceptually and factually central for the creation, maintenance, and renewal of social systems and structures.

6. The notion of core social practice helps to understand *social customs* and *traditions* better than before.

7. Social routines are discussed in the book in terms of "presuppositional" social reasons (we-attitudes). In the account of routines and routine-like practices the notion of *collective pattern-governed behavior*, which is also central for accounting for the conceptual primacy of social practices, is given a central role.

8. The book gives an analysis of *social institutions* and a classification of different kinds of institutions. The "concept sense" of institutions appears not to have been analytically treated in the literature before. The account given is more refined than other accounts that I have seen, for example that by Searle (1995), and it leads to the following classification of social institutions: (a) institution as norm-governed social practice; (b) institution as conferring a new conceptual and social status to some entity (e.g., person, object, or activity);

(c) institution as conferring a new deontic status (and status functions to go with it) to the members of the collective in question (Searlean institution); (d) institution as an organization involving social positions and a task-right system.

9. It is frequently claimed in the literature that the notion of institution is a *reflexive* notion. The present book also claims this and for the first time gives a detailed logical account of the reflexivity in question.

10. The last chapter of the book gives a precise *mathematical analysis* of the central aspects of social practices and institutions (especially of organizations as institutions) and, what is more, sketches a *dynamical account* of some conceptually central aspects of the development and maintenance of social practices and institutions. This formal analysis will interest researchers in the fields of (distributed) artificial intelligence (DAI) and computer simulation of social systems.

Notes

1 COLLECTIVE INTENTIONALITY AND THE CONSTRUCTION OF THE SOCIAL WORLD

1 The central idea of the social world as a human artifact is old. We find in Vico (1744/1970) the following statement, which emphasizes the superiority of a collectively created social world over what individuals by themselves could have achieved (p. 333):

> It is true that men have themselves made this world of nations, although not in full cognizance of the outcomes of their activities, for this world without doubt has issued from a mind often diverse, at times quite contrary, and always superior to the particular ends that men had proposed to themselves... That which did all this was mind, for men did it with intelligence; it was not fate, for they did it by choice; not chance, for the results of their always so acting are perpetually the same.

Karl Marx famously said that human beings "make their own history, but not in circumstances of their own choosing" (1867/1967, p. 15).

Karl Popper even regarded the study of unintended consequences of (intentional) human action to be the main concern of the social sciences. This topic undeniably is central. This is in part because people make a lot of errors and have only limited knowledge of the surroundings in which they act. Thus many unintended and unforeseen consequences occur. (Cf. Popper, 1945/1962, p. 93, and chapter 7 below for unintended consequences and invisible hand accounts.)

2 COLLECTIVE INTENTIONALITY

1 The notion of a social representation as used by social psychologists is a general and rather vaguely used notion, but at least it can be said that it involves sharedness and thus some kind of collective intentionality. Of the notions discussed in the present book, shared we-attitudes, normative group beliefs and goals, as well as, thirdly, concept institutions (in the sense of chapter 6) are central kinds of social representations. (For discussion see, e.g., Wagner, 1996; Bar-Tal, 2000. I disagree with many of the views in this literature, but cannot here discuss the matter.)

2 Joint and collective intentions in their basic sense apply to a number of agents. Thus a collective intention can be expressed by an $(m + 1)$-place predicate $CI(x_1,..., x_m, X)$ standing for "the agents $x_1,..., x_m$ jointly intend to perform the action X jointly." By analogy the same can be said of joint intentions. I will also speak, in a distributive sense, of a single agent personally having a collective intention. This is the case when the agent is one to which the predicate CI applies, and this entails also that the agent in question endorses or accepts the collective intention in a commitment generating sense (to be commented on later). As to my technical notions, the notion of we-intention is a social intention that an individual has: $WI(x_i, X)$ standing for "agent x_i we-intends to do X." A group, g, can have an intention to perform something: $I(g, Y)$ standing for "group g intends to perform group action Y" (Y could be "invading the town" or "painting the house"). See Tuomela, 1995, chapter 3, and section 2.3 below for a discussion of these notions.

3 My account in this book is compatible with various philosophical views of single-agent action. In Tuomela (1977) I developed the "purposive-causal" theory of action, according to which prior intentions can be taken to cause actions in a "purposive" sense in part by causing the behavior in the action "under its action description" as intended. (Today I would prefer to say that the fact-like event having as its central element an agent acting on his prior intention purposively causes the event of the intended action to come about.) Every action contains and indeed consists of a "trying" (or "willing," or to use Searle's terminology, "intention-in-action") and a bodily behavior component that the trying causes (cf. Tuomela, 1977, chapter 6 and 1995, chapter 2). The trying may be the result of a causal process initiated by a prior intention, but it need not be so created (viz. when no prior intention exists). The notion of purposive causation seems to be more or less equivalent to Searle's notion of "intentional causation" that he originally developed in his 1983 book (see Searle, 2001, for a short summary).

4 See section 2.5 of this chapter for the notion of mutual belief.

5 The present characterization of a we-attitude – when generalized to concern all group members – is called the *direct* characterization in Balzer and Tuomela (1997b). It is also possible to give a *fixed point* characterization, which is reflexive (self-referential) in the sense of referring to all the group members being believed by every member to have the we-attitude in question. These two characterizations are proved to be equivalent in Balzer and Tuomela (1997b). Cf. section 2.5 below.

6 My account of the notion of the intention to act together is modeled on the analysis of acting together given in Tuomela and Bonnevier-Tuomela (1997). The account that follows is meant to cover also the most general, "rudimentary" notion of acting together (for the case of a dyad).

(*AT*) You and I *intentionally act together* in performing X if and only if

(1) X is a collective action type (in the sense of an "achievement-whole" divided into your and my parts)

(2a) I intend that we perform X together, and I perform my part of X (or participate in the performance of X) in accordance with and (partly) because of this intention

(2b) you intend that we perform X together, and you perform your part of X (or participate in the performance of X) in accordance with and (partly) because of this intention

(3a) I believe that you will do your part of X (or participate in the performance of X)

(3b) you believe that I will do my part of X (or participate in the performance of X)

(4) (2a) in part because of (3a), and (2b) in part because of (3b).

In some nonstandard cases the intentions here are only in the I-mode (cf. the appendix), but when they are in the we-mode we can write the second clause as:

(2*a) we intend to perform X together, and I perform my part of X (or participate in the performance of X) in accordance with and (partly) because of this intention

(2*b) we intend to perform X together, and you perform your part of X (or participate in the performance of X) in accordance with and (partly) because of this intention

Clause (2*) is taken to entail (2), but the converse holds only in we-mode contexts (cf. Tuomela, 1995, chapter 3, for we-intention).

The notion of a shared intention to act together has a counterpart in the case of collective goals (cf. the notion of an intended collective goal in Tuomela, 1998a and 2000a).

7 To highlight some of the most central issues related to collective goals, let us consider the following dichotomous factors relevant to having a goal or intention: (1) content of goal: single-agent (S) versus collective (C); (2) holder: single-agent (P) versus collective agent or several agents (G); (3) mode: I-mode (I) versus we-mode (W).

The following combinations are logically possible: (a) SPI; (b) SPW; (c) SGI; (d) SGW; (e) CPI; (f) CPW; (g) CGI; (h) CGW. Combinations (b) and (f) are inadmissible, if collective goals are taken to require at least two holders and thus to be objectively shared. Consider the combination of the we-mode with single-agent content. We can collectively accept that John will buy food for our group. This is in a sense a single-agent content but in another sense it is not. Let us distinguish between collective action realizing the collective commitment in question, viz., an action by which the participants try to see to it that the goal comes about (or is maintained, as the case may be). Call this a c-action, and distinguish it clearly from the actual concrete means-action (m-action), which serves, normally causally, to bring about the goal-state. Then we can say that (b) and (d) are inadmissible combinations if both c-actions and m-actions are involved. Nevertheless, if only m-actions are taken into account in the content variable, then these cases are admissible. My suggestion is to treat c-action as belonging to underlying presuppositions rather than to content.

The following claims, stated in the present shorthand notation, are true: (i) W entails G; (ii) W entails c-action; (iii) W is compatible with m-action with noncollective content; (iv) W entails non-I in the sense that if a sentence token attributes a we-mode content then it cannot also attribute an I-mode content (cf. (*WM*)); (v) nevertheless, a person can have an attitude (e.g., a goal) in the we-mode but also in the I-mode at the same time.

Proper intended collective goals in the "objective sharedness" sense of this chapter are covered by (h), when c-actions are regarded as part of the content of the goal. Cases (b), (d), and (f) are weaker and represent collective goals only if the discussed qualifications are taken to hold. We recall that plan-based joint goals form a subclass of (h) (or, if c-actions are left out of consideration, of (d)). Collective goals as shared we-attitudes belong to (c) or (g) when in the I-mode, otherwise they are classified as intended collective goals or we-mode wants (not explicitly dealt with in this chapter). Mere aggregated goals are usually of the kind (c), but might also belong to (g). (a) and (e) represent typical noncollective I-mode goals.

3 CONCEPTUAL ACTIVITY, RULE FOLLOWING, AND SOCIAL PRACTICES

1 The word "meaningful" is ambiguous and vague. Basically, if an item of behavior or human activity is meaningful it must be representational or intentional in the "aboutness" sense and thus have conceptual content (thus a nonlogical predicate, with an established use, of a natural language must correctly apply it). However, its having conceptual content can be either objective or only intersubjective and dependent on people's conventional use of language. In this chapter I am interested in the objective grounding of meaningfulness, and that has to do with the functionality or teleology of the activity in question. This entails that there must be goals that the activity serves, and at least at the end of the chain of activities and goals there must be some objective elements such as the basic needs and interests of the organism that give the ultimate objective justification of the kind of meaningfulness in question. See sections 3.4–3.6 for relevant elucidation.

2 A functionalist program of the Sellarsian kind must satisfy two central demands:

(1) It requires that a form of linguistic behaviour be describable which, though rich enough to serve as a basis for the explicit introduction of the framework of conceptual episodes, does not, as thus described, presuppose any reference, however implicit, to such episodes. In other words, it must be possible to have a conception pertaining to linguistic behaviour which, though adapted to the above purpose, is genuinely independent of concepts pertaining to mental acts, as we actually can conceive of physical objects in a way which is genuinely free of reference to microphysical particles. Otherwise the supposed "introduction" of the framework would be a sham.
(2) It requires an account of how a framework adopted as an explanatory hypothesis could come to serve as the vehicle of direct or non-inferential self knowledge (apperception). (Sellars, 1968, pp. 71–72)

I will below be concerned only with the first topic (cf. Tuomela, 1977, chapter 3, for a discussion of the second).

3 Note, however, that for Sellars the concept of reference is intralinguistic, e.g., "The predicate 'cat' refers to cats" but still, on factual "psycho-social-historical" grounds the predicate "cat" can be correctly applied to cats much in the way, e.g., causal theories of reference have it.

4 The following quotation from Sellars on pattern-governed behavior is worth consideration:

> Essential to any language are three types of pattern-governed linguistic behavior
>   1. Language Entry Transition: the speaker responds to objects in perceptual situations, and to certain states of himself, with appropriate linguistic conceptual episodes.
>   2. Intra-linguistic Moves: the speaker's linguistic conceptual episodes tend to occur in patterns of valid inference (theoretical and practical), and tend not to occur in patterns which violate logical principles.
>   3. Language Departure Transitions: the speaker responds to such linguistic conceptual episodes as "I will now raise my hand" with an upward motion of the hand, etc.
>
> It is essential to note that not only are the abilities to engage in these types of linguistic conceptual activity *acquired as* pattern governed activity, but they *remain* pattern governed activity. The linguistic conceptual activities, which are perceptual takings, inferences and volitions *never* become *obeyings* of *ought-to-do* rules. (Sellars, 1973b, p. 490)

Note that Sellars need not claim that novices such as children, to which the language is being taught – in a sense satisfying the relevant ought-to-be rules – need themselves have available the concept of a rule in any clear sense. Although beliefs like this can perhaps be required of full-blown language users, novices can act conceptually and be in conceptual mental states in a weaker sense. Sellars, too, says this explicitly in his writings.

It is obvious that the above processes or transitions 1–3 correspond respectively to world–language, language–language, and language–world linguistic rules. (As will be seen, pattern-governed behaviors of course cannot be actions obeying ought-to-do rules, but they can obey ought-to-be rules in the sense to be defined later.)

5 A technical construal of concepts as rules would be the possible world's characterization of them. Concepts (predicates) can thus be understood as rules (viz., functions) mapping objects into suitable sets (cf. chapter 6). Informally explicated, e.g. the predicate "red" can be taken as a function mapping objects (in suitable circumstances) into either the set of red objects or the set of nonred objects. Similarly "love" maps couples x,y into the set of persons loving the relatum person and the set of persons who do not love the relatum person. In view of this characterization, it is easy to see how normativity can be included in concept use. For instance, one ought to use "red" so that all red objects fall under "red" while no nonred object falls under it.

Note that "rule" in this chapter is more general than "rule-norm" in later chapters. A rule-norm is a social norm based on authority, but this need not apply to rules in the present, highly general sense.

6 One can also argue in more general, non-Sellarsian terms that rules of language *as such* do not presuppose the existence of inner mental episodes, but only the conceptuality of psychological episodes, be they inner or overt. Thus the concept of a rule of language would as such only presuppose suitable kinds of psychological concepts and sentences and leave open whether the psychological truth-makers are ontically construed as inner or overt. Ontology would be an additional and separate issue.

7 The following quotation indicates that Sellars is committed to a kind of conceptual dependence relevant to Marras' second argument:

> One isn't a full-fledged member of the linguistic community until one not only *conforms* to linguistic ought-to-be's (and may-be's) by exhibiting the required uniformities, but grasps these ought-to-be's and may-be's themselves (i.e., knows the rules of language). One must, therefore, have the concept of oneself as an agent, as not only the *subject-matter* subject of ought-to-be's but the *agent*-subject of ought-to-do's. Thus, even though conceptual activity rests on a foundation of *conforming* to ought-to-be's of *uniformities* in linguistic behavior, these uniformities exist in an ambience of action, epistemic or otherwise. To be a language user is to conceive of oneself as an agent subject to rules. My point has been that one can grant this without holding that all meaningful linguistic episodes are actions in the conduct sense, and all linguistic rules, rules for doing. (Sellars, 1974, p. 101)

8 Here is a quotation from Sellars, which I basically agree with and which shows how wide his account can be made.

> A state which refers to a perceptual object and characterizes it as F, and which, therefore, can be classified functionally as a ·This is F· state, is the very paradigm of a propositional state, and while the sortal in terms of which we classify it is built from an expression in our background language, it must be remembered that such functional sortals apply not only to *expressions* in any *language* which play in that language a *relevantly similar* role to that played in our language by the dot-quoted expression, but, as we can now put it, to representational states in any RS [representational system, here an organism] which play in that RS the relevantly similar role in question. (Sellars, 1981, p. 340)

9 Sellars says this:

> Thus, at the primary level, instead of classifying the intentionality or aboutness of verbal behavior in terms of its expressing or being used to express classically conceived thoughts or beliefs, we should recognize that this verbal behavior is *already thinking in its own right*, and its intentionality or aboutness is simply the appropriateness of classifying it in terms which relate to the linguistic behavior of the group to which one belongs. (Sellars, 1974, pp. 116–117)

10 As to Pettit's (1993) ethocentric approach, we also arrive at the basic response dispositions in his sense. These basic practices and dispositions exemplify correctness but their coming about is not given a philosophical justification. Only an account of the factual truth conditions is given. The story is typically social but need not be in principle.

11 The above version of the Collective Acceptance account based on negotiation works well for social customs and social norms. In the case of, e.g., mathematical rules (cf. Kripke's well-known examples), more must be required. Rationality requirements concerning the participants may have to be added.

12 See Brandom (1994, 2000) for a more detailed discussion much on the same lines as my above brief treatment.

4 AN ACCOUNT OF SOCIAL PRACTICES

1 Conceptually, Giddens (1984) does not have much of philosophical interest to offer concerning social practices, in part because in his theory "jointness" notions such as joint intention and action do not play a role. Bourdieu (1977) does not either regard jointness notions and thus collective intentionality as central – see my discussion of his views in section 4.6.

2 Schatzki's (1996) book is written in a Wittgensteinian spirit and, accordingly, does not contain much detailed analysis and theory-building. However, the book is rich in examples and is well informed about German theorizing concerning social practices in the past century. According to Schatzki (and using his language and terminology), a practice is a temporally unfolding and spatially interspersed nexus of doings and sayings (p. 89). Three major avenues of linkage are involved. The individual actions in a social practice can be linked (1) through understandings, for example, of what to say and do, (2) through explicit rules, principles, precepts, and instructions, and (3) through what are called teleoaffective structures – embracing ends, projects, tasks, purposes, beliefs, emotions, and moods. Social practices are divided into dispersed and integrative ones. Dispersed practices contain, so to speak, small-scale practices like describing, ordering, following rules, explaining, questioning, reporting, and imagining. These are language games in a wide sense. The constituent actions in dispersed practices are held together mostly by understanding. In contrast, integrative practices are the more complex practices found in and constitutive of particular domains of social life. Examples are farming, business, teaching, cooking, and religious practices. Here all three kinds of linkage come into play. These principles form the organization of the practice. The entirety of a practice's organization is normative (p. 101). By normativity is meant "oughtness" or "rightness" in the first place and secondarily it means acceptability.

In general, integrative practices are doings and sayings linked by understandings, explicit rules, and teleoaffective structures. Through participating in a practice a person *eo ipso* "coexists" with others, not merely those individuals with whom she interacts, but also in a wider setting including the collection of all those party to the practice. All integrative and dispersed practices are social, above all because participating in them entails immersion in an extensive tissue of coexistence with indefinitely many other people.

The theory presented in this chapter basically takes into account the rather vaguely stated central elements that Schatzki mentions, viz., (a) understanding, (b) rules and norms, and (c) teleoaffective structures. Of these (a) and (c) are – at least to some extent – already built into my central notion of a shared we-attitude, and norms will be introduced separately in the theses on social practices to be discussed below and used in chapter 6.

3 Social practices have evolutionary histories, which I will here comment on. In ethology the word "cultural" is commonly used in the place of "social." Accordingly, cultural evolution of behaviors (practices) involving cultural variation are spoken of. Cultural variation has been defined as differences between individuals that exist due to some kind of social learning and are not due to genes or to the nonsocial environment (cf. Boyd and Richerson, 1996; Byrne, 1997). Cultural variation in this sense seems common in nature (e.g. among birds and apes). Typically this cultural variation comes about because of individual learning of the "local enhancement" type which has been made possible or more likely by the learning that has taken place in previous generations. Individuals here learn on their own without the direct help of others, but this can still lead to cultural variation and change. In contrast, "cumulative cultural evolution" seems rare (Boyd and Richerson, 1996). Such cultural evolution leads to behaviors that no single individual is likely to invent on his own. It seems to require special capacities, "adaptations," that only higher animals – like chimpanzees and humans and possibly some birds – have. The ability to acquire new kinds of behaviors by observation, or *imitation*, has been argued to be essential for cumulative cultural change (Boyd and Richerson, 1996).

Ethologists have mentioned song dialects of some birds and foraging behaviors (practices) in apes as examples depending on imitation-based social learning. Thus, chimpanzees engage in social practices which are "cultural" phenomena in the sense of being independent of ecological factors and genes. Boesch (1996) argues that chimpanzees have cultural social practices. He found socially transmitted, but not necessarily imitation-based, behaviors in chimpanzees which, furthermore, are (in some cases suboptimal) solutions to tasks which can be solved in more than one way and where individual, nonsocial learning typically leads to different results. Special kinds of leaf-clipping, leaf-grooming, and knuckle-knocking seem to be social practices exhibiting cultural variation: different chimpanzee communities differ from each other with respect to their specific techniques, and some of these techniques are instrumentally better than others.

In the case of hominids, not only learning as local enhancement but also observational teaching and learning come into the picture (e.g. in the case of making stone tools). Culturally preservable skills will emerge. Then we can speak of social practices and their cumulative cultural evolution. Thus pupils learn from masters by observation, and this applies not only to teaching children but also to teaching special skills to adults. Pupils may improve on their master's work. Accumulation of knowledge and skills thus often takes place. (In the case of stone tools, this started happening and led to different cultural styles – see Mithen, 1996.) Recalling Isaac Newton's dictum about standing on the shoulders of giants, we can say that human cultures accumulate changes over many generations, resulting in culturally transmitted behaviors that probably no single individual could invent on his own.

Observational learning (at least genuine imitation) can take place via special communicative psychological mechanisms involving (functional equivalents of) social belief of the kind "I believe that you believe that p" and in fuller cases also social loop beliefs of the kind "I believe that you believe that I believe that (or will do) p." This may suggest that the psychological mechanisms that enable humans to learn by observation are adaptations that have been shaped by natural selection because culture is beneficial. The reason for this would be that these mechanisms are too complex to be mere by-products of evolution. However, it seems that imitation can take place on the basis of simpler mechanisms. Suppose thus that I believe that you are doing something p and that doing p solves your problem q. Now, if I also have the problem q and come to notice that your solution to it is p, I may imitate your action and do p irrespective of whether I believe that you believe that p solves q. Here the *meme*, viz., what is imitated, can be regarded as the thought that p solves q or it can just be regarded as a skill without a clear propositional content. (On the other hand, imitation may be too simple a mechanism to account for, e.g., learning of language.)

4 The diagram uses the notions of a *coaction* and *acting together*. For analyses and discussion, see Tuomela and Bonnevier-Tuomela (1997) and Tuomela (2000a), chapters 1, 3. The notion of acting together (AT) was summarized in note 6 of chapter 2 above. Here is a summary of the notion of coaction (CO).

(*CO*) Agents A_1 and A_2 *coact* compatibly in a situation S relative to their I-mode goals G_1 and G_2 if and only if

   (1) their respective primary goals (viz., action-goals) in S, i.e. types of states or actions, G_1 and G_2, which relate to the same field of action dependence in S, are compatible in the sense of being satisfiable without making it impossible for the other agent to satisfy her goal

   (2a) A_1 intends to achieve G_1 without means-actions conflicting with A_2's attempts to satisfy his goal and believing that he can achieve it at least with some probability in that context, although his relevant G_1-related actions are dependent on A_2's relevant G_2-related actions, and he acts successfully so as to achieve G_1

   (2b) analogously for A_2:

   (3a) A_1 believes that (1) and (2), and

   (3b) analogously for A_2.

(A more rudimentary version of coaction need not even satisfy clause (3).)

5 A *primary* reason is taken to be motivationally more important ("stronger") than a secondary one (possibly a strategic reason could qualify as a secondary

one here). It is not easy to clearly define the notion of a primary reason. If a motivating reason is both necessary and sufficient for action, then it is a primary one. Furthermore, if a reason is the only necessary reason in the case in question, it is a primary reason. Other cases analyzed in terms of necessary and sufficient conditions are trickier. I will not discuss them here.

Over and above being a primary reason, the we-attitude reason at least ideally is an *exclusive* and *conclusive* (viz., overriding) reason, which thus overrides and, indeed, psychologically excludes strategic thinking in the situation. This involves that the agent in the first place acts on his having internalized the we-attitude reason (typically a we-belief), and thus need not explicitly think about it, but nevertheless acts on it rather than on his strategic thinking ("rather than" here having the force of exclusion).

One could extend this view to problematic cases like the (iterated) Prisoner's Dilemma. Thus, while the strategic case, based on a suitable strategy like the tit-for-tat beginning with the cooperative alternative (C), does lead to mutual cooperation in the maximization of expected utility sense, mutual cooperation can alternatively be based on the conformative reason given by a shared we-belief without strategic considerations playing at least a primary role. The we-belief would be simply that the others also believe that everyone recurrently chooses C and that this is mutually believed. This we-belief, in turn, might be based on a nonstrategic reason such as group solidarity or custom or convention. (Whether conformism can be based on a higher-level strategic reason is a moot point, but I will not comment on it here.)

6 Here is a simple formulation for the generalized version of (CC): (GCC) It is true on quasiconceptual grounds that the participants' shared we-attitude content forming their reason for performing a social practice is satisfied for a member A_i of g if and only if it is satisfied for every member of g.

The other conditions of collectivity in chapter 2, viz. (CC*), (WM), and (WM*) can be generalized analogously.

7 I wish to thank Sergio Benvenuto and Maj Tuomela for points related to the notions of fashion, custom, and tradition.

8 The we-attitudes in a routine can be in the we-mode, but to capture this it seems best to employ a slightly weaker notion of we-modeness than in chapter 2. I suggest in Tuomela (2002a) the following account of a rudimentary we-mode relationship that I call *experiential we-modeness*. In the simple dyadic case, with the members A and B, we have:

A and B function in a *we-mode relation* and form a "*we*" (however temporarily) if and only if there is an ATT and a content p such that they actively share ATT towards the same content p and are collectively ATT-committed to p, and they are in addition disposed to express their attitudes in effect by ".We share WATT(p)." (viz., by something having the dot-quoted role), e.g., when asked about the matter.

Here active sharing of WATT(p) entails that both agents have ATT(p) and focus attentively to their having it, and believe in an active, occurrent way that the other one has ATT(p) and also that they both mutually believe that. (This kind of weak we-modeness seems pertinent to a face-to-face relationship.)

As to the logic of routines, Krister Segerberg (1985) gives a logical analysis of single-agent routines on the level of action, without using social attitudes. It remains a future project to analyze social practices in the core sense in a precise logical way, but some tools for that task are to be found in Sandu and Tuomela (1996).

9 Gilbert (1989), p. 404 presents the following analysis of the notion of custom:

> Population P has the *custom* that one does action A in circumstances C if and only if the members of P jointly accept that they are to do A in C, for the simple reason that that is what members of P (regularly) do.

As compared with my view of customs, this analysis is far too strong, because it makes it an obligation for the members of P to participate in the custom (or at least to do A in C). This follows from Gilbert's analysis of joint acceptance in terms of joint commitment and her analysis of joint commitment as entailing obligation to participate. (To wit, in Gilbert, 2000, p. 84, she says that "members of a population P *jointly accept a requirement* if and only if they are jointly committed to accept that requirement as a body," which also makes P a "plural subject," and on p. 83 we learn that "one who is a party of joint commitment has an *obligation* to perform the relevant act or acts.") Customs do not, however, always involve obligations. For instance, in at least some part of Finland it is a custom to eat ham at Christmas, but there is no obligation involved here, and we have a counterexample here. Furthermore, Finns (or the Finns living in such and such an area) do not form a "plural subject" (a collective actor).

10 Consider yet another example of a custom, viz., the case of the QWERTY keyboard (cf. Schlicht, 1998, pp. 65–67). The layout of this keyboard was developed to prevent the jamming of keys in an old-fashioned typewriter. However, this keyboard design, which according to many commentators today is not optimal, still persists and is customarily built into modern computer keyboards. There are more optimal keyboard designs available but the pressure of custom, maintained by users' typing skills, has retained the QWERTY keyboard as the prevalent one. One can say that even if it perhaps is not globally or overall optimal, it still is locally optimal today, given the history of keyboards.

11 Consider this example about the rise of a social practice based on a strategic situation in which two farmers are selling their goods at the same marketplace (cf. Bromley, 1989, chapter 4). Let us call these farmers Veggie and Meat. Veggie sells fresh vegetables and Meat sells meat. (Both Veggie and Meat could be sets of farmers as well.) They can go to the market on Wednesdays (W) or on Saturdays (S) or on both days (B). Buyers prefer vegetables twice a week but do not need meat more often than once a week. On the whole,

on Saturdays there tend to be more buyers at the marketplace than on Wednesdays. The following matrix might illustrate the case:

		Meat		
		W	S	B
	W	1,7	2,3	3,4
Veggie	S	4,1	6,9	5,5
	B	7,2	8,8	9,6

We can see that BS (Veggie going both on Wednesdays and Saturdays and Meat going only on Saturdays) is an *equilibrium* point. However, Veggie would prefer the joint outcome BB to be materialized while the best joint outcome for Meat is SS. I am not assuming even interval scale utilities here, nor am I assuming interpersonal comparability of utilities. But I am assuming interpersonal comparability of rankings. Thus, e.g., Veggie is taken to understand and know that for Meat the SS combination is better than the BS combination.

Things being as they are, the rational, equilibrium-based choice for a market practice would be that Veggie goes on Wednesdays and Saturdays but Meat only on Saturdays. There would of course be relevant shared we-knowledge. Thus a social practice based on this kind of shared we-knowledge could arise so that we would be dealing with a core social practice here. The present example shows that customs can in a *historical* sense be based on strategic thinking. Such customs can be optimal in that they result in equilibrium states.

12 In recent literature in philosophy and the social sciences there are some attempts to discuss social practices in a *dynamic* setting. See chapter 7 for my account.

5 A COLLECTIVE ACCEPTANCE ACCOUNT OF COLLECTIVE-SOCIAL NOTIONS

1 It is not always clear in these texts whether "things" in this connection mean concepts, or referents of concepts, or both.

2 To apply the "conditions of satisfaction" terminology used by Searle (1995, 2001) to the present context, the collective creation of an institutional fact is seen to involve this: by collectively accepting something p, expressing a new institutional fact to-be-created (e.g. p = Tom will be our leader or p = squirrel fur is money) to be true or correctly assertable for them, the members of a community create new conditions of satisfaction upon conditions of satisfaction. The following is involved here, assuming collective acceptance to be intentional and based on the collective intention to produce the sentence p: "We intend to make it the case that Tom is our leader." This collective intention involves among other things the condition of satisfaction that we utter or are disposed to utter the sentence "Tom is our leader" (or a

variant of this sentence). Secondly, it also involves creating a condition of satisfaction for "Tom is our leader" which involves that he is to be given the new status of being a leader and to be treated by us as our leader. (Here it is presupposed that "leader" is a meaningful notion. If it is not, the conditions of satisfaction for it also have to be collectively created by collective acceptance.)

3 It can be noted that in my framework any talk about "ideas," "thoughts," "views," "contents," "concepts," "properties," "facts," etc. will in the last analysis be handled basically in terms of the mentioned linguistic and metalinguistic apparatus, its resources, and analogical extensions to nonlinguistic items (cf. Tuomela, 1985, and chapter 3 for this, primarily Sellarsian view). As pointed out in chapter 3, actually we can also in principle get along with propositional representational systems involving the use of logic, but as I will concentrate on human beings in this book, language use can of course be assumed.

Strictly speaking it need not be required here that all the group members accept the same sentence. They may actually accept intensionally different sentences as long as an external observer can speak of the group's acceptance of s. Thus, in our example, while the group members need to share a rudimentary idea of money, they need not possess the concept in a full sense and may each accept one of a class of sentences equivalent in the sense of all suitably expressing that squirrel fur is money. We could here also speak of the group members accepting a sentence "to the effect that" squirrel fur is money.

4 I wish to point out that there are cases of collective acceptance for the group involving only I-mode or private commitments. Suppose thus that it is mutually believed – in a private, tacit sense – by the Finns that they are the toughest people in the world. This kind of collective acceptance based on mutual private belief only entails private commitments but it could still be for the group and even be a reason for collective social action. There is also collective acceptance which is not for the group. For instance, the group members might all accept to go picking mushrooms and accept it as true that everybody will go, without accepting all this for the group. There might be mutual knowledge about this in the group, but the group members would compete for the mushrooms. This can be collective acceptance in the I-mode without collective commitment to the accepted activity.

5 I assume that normally all the participants participate in acceptance. This assumption can be relaxed. The individuals might share a we-belief and be collectively committed to the believed proposition, but (as in the case of e.g. "Americans believe in democracy") exceptions can be tolerated, and here sharing can be less than full sharing without claims of this kind being falsified. Another possibility for having disagreement is that there is the kind of power structure in the collective that one individual or a clique of individuals is able to determine the collective's view, being suitably authorized by the others. In this latter case we are dealing with binding group-level acceptance or "group belief" (where the belief is an acceptance belief). I have analyzed

this kind of group belief as applicable to groups that can act (see chapter 4) in the following way ("accepts" is used in the analysandum instead of "believes").

Group g *accepts* ("believes") that p in a normative, group-binding sense in the social and normative circumstances C if and only if in C there are operative members $x_1,..., x_m$ of g in respective positions $P_1,..., P_m$ such that

(a) the agents $x_1,..., x_m$, when they are performing their (we-mode) tasks in their positions $P_1,..., P_m$ and due to their exercising the relevant authority system of g, (intentionally) jointly accept p and because of this exercise of the authority system they ought to continue to accept and positionally believe it

(b) there is a mutual knowledge among the operative members $x_1,..., x_m$ to the effect that (a)

(c) because of (a), the (full-fledged and adequately informed) nonoperative members of g tend to tacitly accept – or at least ought to accept – p, as members of g

(d) there is a mutual knowledge in g to the effect that (c)

Here the authority system means the group's system of joint intention formation, which also authorizes the operative members to act for the group. Joint acceptance in this context requires explicit or implicit agreement making, which entails a group-binding obligation. For instance, the members of a board may vote or otherwise jointly decide or agree on a certain view p for g.

Groups can also have beliefs in weaker group-binding senses which, however, all require collective commitment to the accepted item (see Tuomela, 2002e). In general, joint acceptance – a special case of collective acceptance – amounts to coming to hold and holding a relevant we-attitude. It can be a we-mode we-intention, or a we-mode we-belief, or both.

The present kind of "positional" account applies also to group action and group attitudes (see Tuomela, 1995, chapters 5–7, and, for belief versus acceptance, Tuomela, 2000c).

Note that while full normative, group-binding group acceptance in the above sense is too strong to be used generally in this book, group acceptance in a suitable weaker sense – in the sense used in this book – can be logically analyzed to be a case of the notion ACT^{joint} as defined on p. 342 of Sandu and Tuomela (1996). (In contrast, group-binding acceptance can logically be regarded as a case of $Stit^{joint}$ of the aforementioned paper.)

6 The assumption here, more accurately, is that $\rightarrow$ stands for a conceptually *necessary* implication deriving its necessity from the concept of collective acceptance (CA). As the collective acceptance is for the group, also the converse implication $\leftarrow$ in this context is necessary, necessity concerning all specific group contexts, viz., all the "possible worlds" belonging to the group's "intentional horizon" in which the members act qua group members (cf. section 5.3). (Cf. the treatment in Tuomela and Balzer [1999], where

the equivalence is a standard extensional one to begin with.) My present suggestion means in formal terms that the analysans of (CAT^*) can be formulated as:

$$FG (CA(g, s) \& N((CA(g, s) \rightarrow s) \& (s \rightarrow CA(g, s))))$$

where N stands for the conceptual necessity in question. The latter implication here is an ordinary implication, but one which occurs within the scope of the intentional operator "FG". A logic with semantics is sketched in Tuomela and Balzer (1999) for the present system.

(CAT) is explicitly concerned only with sentences, the structure of which is not laid bare. Thomasson (2002) investigates a principle somewhat resembling (CAT) and makes a distinction between sentences with universal form and sentences with existential or singular form. However, crucially, her formula does not include any feature corresponding to the central Forgroup-operator.

7 Collective acceptance in its full sense involves the thought that what is accepted is accepted for the group and hence is shared, with collective commitment, by the group members qua group members. The collectivity in the formation of the attitude is meant to carry over to whatever is collectively brought about or comes about in reliance on its acceptance.

8 One can actually formulate Sellarsian "semantical" (in his broad sense) rules of the world-to-language, language-to-language, and language-to-world (or more broadly, world-to-mind, mind-to-mind, and mind-to-world) kinds to account for inferences such as those below. (Actually, the first example is a language-to-language rule and the second and the third could be reformulated so as to be instances of mind-to-world rules.)

9 Compare Barnes (1983), Kusch (1997), Searle (1995), and Bloor (1997) for discussion. Here I just wish to make two points.

(a) As noted, group members generally need not be concerned with any circularities (such as money is not money unless collectively accepted to be money), as they are not required to possess the full concept of money that our Collective Acceptance account yields. Even in a context where they have – and are required to have such as in the case of, say, the notion of a cocktail party – the full circular concept in their minds, there is in principle nothing vicious about this circularity, for the account of collective attitudes given in Balzer and Tuomela (1997b) removes the viciousness. This is because we prove that one can in principle (and under idealized conditions) always give up the circular, fixed point account in favor of a noncircular, "direct" account.

(b) Searle's basic formula for collective acceptance in the context of social institutions is "We accept that S has power (S does A)" (Searle, 1995, pp. 104, 111). In the present account the central acceptance sentence is "We collectively accept s" (or CA(g,s)), and what is explicitly accepted here is the dot-quoted sentence s, e.g. s = .squirrel fur is money., and not underlying powers, rights, and duties, possibly concerning the possessors of squirrel furs and other members of the group (see below section 6.4).

10 Let us systematically consider how collective acceptance (CA), forgroupness (FG), and collective commitment (CoCom) can be combined. We consider the domain of all things that are in a group's concern, something the group actually or dispositionally is concerned with. Let us call this domain of items (sentences) the group's intentional horizon (IH). Within IH we may now consider the following contents:

$$(+-)CA(g, s) \& (+-)FG(g, s) \& (+-)CoCom(g, s)$$

Here the $+$ and $-$ signs obviously mean, respectively, inclusion and exclusion relating to the sets in question. Next consider the subclasses of IH in obvious shorthand notation: (1) CA & FG & CoCom; (2) CA & FG & $-$CoCom; (3) CA & $-$FG & CoCom; (4) CA & $-$FG & $-$CoCom; (5) $-$CA & FG & CoCom; (6) $-$CA & FG & $-$CoCom; (7) $-$CA & $-$FG & CoCom; (8) $-$CA & $-$FG & $-$CoCom.

Our discussion in section 5.2 has shown that collective acceptance in the fullest sense must be of kind (1), viz., it must be collective acceptance for the group and it must – at least in the case of the creation as opposed to the maintenance of a social item – involve a substantial amount of collective commitment (cf. below section 6.3 for further discussion). Keeping in mind that we-mode thinking and acting means in its core sense thinking and acting as a group member, I now propose the explicative thesis that the strongest kind of we-modeness (WM) (cf. (a1) of chapter 2) is truth-equivalent to collective acceptance with collective commitment for the group, viz.,

(i) $WM(g, s) \leftrightarrow CA(g, s) \& FG(g, s) \& CoCom(g, s)$

The second conjunct could also have been $CA(FG(g, s))$, but in the present context the latter entails the former and conversely. Recall that in the present context s may be one of the following: $s =$ We will do X together (expresses a joint intention to perform X); $s = Y$ is F (expresses the group's view or acceptance belief that something Y is F); $s =$ One ought to do Z in C (expresses a norm to perform Z in circumstances C for the members of g).

I discuss the rational possibility of cases (1)–(8) in Tuomela (2003) and will not present any arguments here. The upshot of my investigation is that of the combinatory possibilities (1)–(8) only CA & $-$FG & CoCom (case 3), $-$CA & FG & CoCom (case 5), and $-$CA & $-$FG & CoCom (case 7) are not "conceptual-rationally" possible, if we take collective acceptance (CA) to be a disposition to collective social action or directly collective social action.

11 To bring some more precision into the picture, I will here define some commitment notions for the case where x and y are supposed to commit

themselves to perform a collective (viz. many-person) action X. Here social commitment (SCom) is taken as a general logical notion concerned with x being committed to y to do something Y, and denotes a collective (e.g. joint) action or "project" (which could also be an institution).

$SCom(x, y, Y) =$ agent x is socially committed to y to perform action Y

$Com(x, X^x) =$ x is committed to performing X^x as his part of X

$CoCom(\{x, y\}, X) =$ x and y are collectively committed to performing X together

$SCom(x, y, X^x) =$ agent x is socially committed to y to do his part X^x of X as his part of it

$SCoCom(\{x, y\}, X) =$ agents x and y are collectively and socially committed to performing X together $= CoCom(\{x, y\}, X)$ & $SCom(x, y, X^x)$ & $SCom(y, x, X^y)$

According to the last definition, x and y are socially and collectively committed to performing X together if and only if both are collectively committed to performing it and are also socially committed to each other to perform their parts of this many-person action. Note that obviously Co-$Com(\{x, y\}, X)$ entails the conjunction $Com(x, X^x)$ & $Com(y, X^y)$. The notion SCoCom of full-blown commitment in a sense also involves for the participants to be committed also to intending to perform their parts in the sense that they cannot without criticism unilaterally give up their participation intention.

As I have argued elsewhere (see Tuomela, 2003) the following claims are warranted: (i) CoCom entails forgroupness; (ii) CoCom entails functioning qua a member of the group, but not conversely; (iii) functioning qua a member of the group entails forgroupness.

12 The case of a person, x, insulting another person, y, does involve much conceptual construction and is culture-dependent. Let us say that x's insulting y involves his intending to hurt y and that y accordingly becomes hurt having found out what x intended (and did). Even in a case like this, clearly there is something "construction-independent" happening in the world which in part constitutes the present action token of insulting.

13 The Collective Acceptance model resembles Scanlon's (1998) contractualism to some extent. Its basic idea is that all principles that people can justify to others so that those others cannot reasonably reject them are collectively acceptable. I see this as a process that tends towards a reflective equilibrium among rational persons. This kind of theory is closely related to my Collective Acceptance account, as I briefly argue in Tuomela (2003).

14 A referee of this book made the point that if the members of the group performatively made squirrel fur money by accepting for themselves the

sentence "Squirrel fur is money," then, if squirrel fur was in fact "hyper-abundant," my account would not work. This is because I have claimed that it is entirely up to the group members to make up an institution, such as the institution of money. My rebuttal is the following. We must distinguish between rational and irrational (and "silly") collective acceptance. Surely, in the critic's example it would be very silly to accept squirrel fur as money (or, to have an even crazier example, to accept that sand is money). So, the referee's purported counterexample does not work.

6 SOCIAL INSTITUTIONS

1 Here is a typical statement of this kind of view (by Turner, 1997, p. 6): "With the above considerations in mind, a social institution can be defined as a complex of positions, roles, norms, and values lodged in particular types of social structures and organizing relatively stable patterns of human activity with respect to fundamental problems in reproducing life-sustaining resources, in reproducing individuals, and in sustaining viable societal structures within a given environment." Scott (1995), p. 33 gives the following definition: "Institutions consist of cognitive, normative, and regulative structures that provide stability and meaning to social behavior. Institutions are transported by various carriers – cultures, structures, and routines – and they operate at multiple levels of jurisdiction." However, this definition seems not to be restricted only to organizations, but can also be taken to characterize institutions in the first, general sense.

There is new, interesting literature in the social sciences relating to "neo-institutionalism," which emphasizes the social embeddedness of social institutions often in a holistic way. We have neo-institutionalism in economics, sociology, and political science, especially. The reader can be referred to such texts as Powell and DiMaggio (1991), Smelser and Swedberg (1994), Brinton and Nee (1998), Martin and Simmons (2001), Mantzavinos (2001), and Walsh (2002). (Walsh applies the theory of positional group beliefs developed in Tuomela, 1992 and 1995; cf. note 5 to chapter 5 above.)

2 Schotter (1981) advocates the economic, equilibrium-based account of social institutions. His basic definition, based mainly but not completely on Lewis' (1969) account of convention, is as follows (p. 11):

A regularity R in the behavior of members of a population P when they are agents in a recurrent situation S is an *institution* if and only if it is true that and is common knowledge in P that (1) everyone conforms to R; (2) everyone expects everyone else to conform to R; and (3) either everyone prefers to conform to R on the condition that the others do, if S is a coordination problem, in which case uniform conformity to R is a coordination equilibrium; or (4) if anyone ever deviates from R it is known that some or all of the others will also deviate and the payoffs associated with the recurrent play of S using these deviating strategies are worse for all agents than the payoff associated with R.

There are many things to criticize in the analysis. Let me mention some problems in it.

(i) Institutions are intimately related to social norms, "oughts" and "mays" of either the "rule-kind" or of the kind termed "proper social norms." The crucial normative aspect of social institutions is missing in the above analysis – at least it is not explicitly there.

(ii) It seems obvious that at least some members should operate on the basis of relevant normative thoughts when they conform to and obey R (see section 6.3). In general, they or at least some of them should conform in part because they think they ought to (or are permitted to, depending on the case) act in a way entailing conformance to R, but there are no normative requirements of this kind in the above account either.

(iii) The analysis seems not to apply to what I call rule-norms and institutions. This is because rule-norms are not based on expectations related to others' behavior, but get their character as norms from the authority that created the norm (usually with the power that may be necessary for enforcing it).

(iv) We should distinguish between cases in which an institution is "self-enforcing" (in the game-theoretical best-reply sense) and thus is in force without sanctions such as disapproval or punishments in a stricter sense, and cases in which the norm's being in force essentially depends on sanctions. In the latter kind of situation, we may have a case where for most members of P the institutional behaviors are in equilibrium but are so partly because of external sanctions (be they s-sanctions or r-sanctions, in my terminology).

(v) As to the problem of social order, regularities in behavior which are in Nash equilibrium (or a stronger kind of equilibrium, such as subgame perfect equilibrium) obviously generate more order and stability in P than behavioral regularities that are not in equilibrium. However, an institution may be in force in a collective without its being stable in any game-theoretical equilibrium sense. Social institutions that are in force largely due to sanctions qualify as examples here, assuming that the game-theoretic analysis relies on the self-enforcement requirement. This also indicates that the game-theoretical notion is meant for a community of more rational beings than human beings are.

(vi) The equilibrium requirement is not informative concerning people's reasons for action, as already seen in (ii) and (iv). Considering cases of disobedience, the agents' *given* (viz., antecedent) preferences may relevantly differ from each other's. Some people may find themselves in a collective action dilemma while others do not. Thus, also the *final* or truly motivating preferences of people differ, and thus people differ in their behavior related to the institution in question. Some obey without (external and social) sanctions, while others obey only because of sanctions and yet others violate the norms of the institution.

   (vii) The agents may lack the information they need for obeying the normative contents of an institution and for equilibrium behavior.

  (viii) There may be multiple equilibria in a situation, and the resulting selection problem may be hard to solve. More specifically, there might be both *local* and *global* equilibria in the situation. Some actors might go for the local ones, while others would go for the global ones.

   (ix) There may be no equilibrium in the situation.

To say something in favor of the equilibrium view, I would like to suggest that the equilibrium idea be regarded as a kind of "ought-to-be" desideratum for designers of a society (viz., legislators and the like) for creating order especially by selecting equilibria which are as "natural" as possible. By natural I mean that they should be based on "normal" desires and beliefs rather than on sanction-generated ones. To take a trivial example, traffic rules for citizens should not require people to walk more than absolutely necessary for maintaining order (and fulfilling whatever other desiderata there may be), otherwise people start finding short-cuts and disobey the rules – unless strongly sanctioned. (See Tuomela, 2000a, for further discussion related to equilibria and joint equilibria.)

3 Bloor (1997) sums up his analysis of social institutions by saying this: "We can treat them like giant performative utterances, produced by the social collective" (p. 32). "We now have a simple answer to our question: what is an institution? It is a collective pattern of self-referring activity" (p. 33).

4 My noncontingently true (but stylized) analysis of simple social ought-to-do authority-based norms, summarizing the central aspects, is as follows (cf. the more extensive analysis and discussion in Tuomela, 1995, chapter 1, also cf. Tuomela, 2000a, chapter 6).

    (*RN*) A norm N of the form "Everyone in g ought to perform task T when in situation S" is a *social ought-to-do rule in the authority-based sense* (or is an ought-to-do *r-norm*) motivationally in force in social collective g if and only if

   (1i) N (or at least a prescription whose logical or conceptual consequence N is) has been acceptably issued by an authority (either an authority external to the group g or by an authoritative body of members of g)

  (1ii) the members of g can acquire the mutual belief that they ought to perform T in situation S from linguistic (typically verbal) information made available by the aforementioned authority to the members of g

  (2i) many members of g perform T in S (or at least are so disposed)

  (2ii) at least some of them sometimes perform T because of their believing, in part due to the factors specified in clauses (1) and (3), that they ought to perform T in S

   (3) there is in g some pressure – mutually believed by at least those members referred to in clause (2ii) – which is at least in part due to rule-sanctions, against deviating from performing T in S (and this may in part account for both (2i) and (2ii))

My analysis of proper social ought-to-do norms (conventions and group-specific norms) is this.

(*SN*) A norm N of the form "Everyone in g ought to perform task T when in situation S" is a *proper social ought-to-do norm* (or an ought-to-do *s-norm*) motivationally in force in social collective g if and only if

(1) there is a mutual belief in g to the effect that the members of g ought to perform T in situation S

(2i) many members of g perform T when in S (or at least are so disposed)

(2ii) at least some of them sometimes perform T at least in part because of their believing that they ought to perform T in S, and also in part because they are, in accordance with (1), expected by other members of g to perform T in S

(2iii) there is a mutual belief approximately to the effect that (2i) and (2ii) in g

(3) there is in g some pressure, at least in part due to social sanctions, against deviating from performing T in S; and there is a mutual belief to this effect in g (and this mutually recognized pressure may in part account for both (2i) and (2ii))

Some aspects of the distinction between what I call r-norms and s-norms, and more generally r-concepts and s-concepts, have been noted earlier in the literature (cf. e.g. Tönnies' celebrated *Gesellschaft–Gemeinschaft* distinction). As far as I know, analytical precision to this distinction has been effected for the first time in Tuomela and Bonnevier-Tuomela (1992) and Tuomela (1995).

5 Consider a concept institution like the Sunday Match case. Before the Sunday Match became a we-mode concept for the group members, it did not figure in their thoughts as anything like "our Sunday match." It could just have been an I-mode notion, such that different group members could have conceptualized the situation differently, for example "I will play soccer on Sunday afternoons as there will then be other players available for a good match." Furthermore, a social norm might develop to the effect that young people ought to come to the village lawn to play soccer on Sunday afternoons. The existence of a social practice that is governed by such a norm is certainly a conceptual possibility. As long as it is based on I-mode thinking, no group concept concerning the match which involves collective commitment to participation and to the use of the Sunday Match concept will arise. (Notice that I am not making the linguistic point that the expression "Sunday Match" must be used; the concept in question can have different linguistic expressions.)

6 Let me indicate how (*SI*) should be modified to account for the case of structured collectives with specially authorized operative members. The matter is somewhat complicated and requires the kind of machinery (e.g. the specification of the "right social and normative circumstances" for collective acceptance and norm obedience) developed in Tuomela (1995), especially in chapter 5. Here is a simplified outline of this kind of an analysis.

(*SI**) A generic sentence s expresses a *social institution* (in the "standard" sense) in a structured collective g if and only if

(1a) the operative members of g, say $x_1,...,x_m$, when performing their (we-mode) tasks in their respective positions $P_1,...,P_m$ and due to their exercising the relevant authority system ("joint – decision-making" system) of g, collectively accept s, and because of this exercise of the authority system they ought to continue to "positionally" accept it

(1b) here it is assumed that collective acceptance for the group entails and is entailed by the correct assertability of s

(2) there is a mutual belief among the operative members $x_1,...,x_m$ to the effect that (1a)

(3) s expresses or entails the existence of a social practice (or a system of interconnected social practices) and a norm (or a system of interconnected norms, including a constitutive norm) for g, such that the social practice generally is performed at least in part because of the norm

(4) because of (1), the (full-fledged and adequately informed) nonoperative members of g tend to tacitly accept – or at least ought to accept – to obey the normative content of s, as members of g

(5) there is generally a mutual belief in g to the effect that (4)

In this summary outline, (4) allows for the possibility that the nonoperative members disagree at least in their thoughts with what s expresses and it also allows for some amount of coercion organized by the group concerning the norms entailed by s.

7 Yet another partial argument relates to collective commitment and we-modeness. Suppose the institutional state to be created and maintained is something described by a proposition p. Then assume counterfactually that people are not collectively committed to p but that, quite the contrary, they are collectively committed to −p. This counterfactual possibility is not rationally actualizable, given the institutional status of p. So, minimally, the participants are required not to be collectively committed to −p. But this kind of passive state is not satisfactory for maintaining p. Collective commitment to p at least in the case of rational, well-informed group members would seem to be the ideal requirement to make here. This argument of course does not suffice to guarantee we-modeness.

Kaarlo Miller has claimed that collective commitment is too strong a requirement in general – possibly even for the creation of social institutions. A case in point is repressive institutions opposed by possibly even the majority of group members. These members can be taken to be collectively committed to −p (and not to p), and the rest of the members might not either be collectively committed to p but perhaps neutral (viz., they lack collective commitment to p and to −p). I take all this to be possible and to create a conflict between acting according to what one personally thinks is right and what is right for the subgroup in question, on the one hand, and, on the other hand, what is right thinking and acting qua a member of the repression-involving group governed by a dictator, perhaps. (The groups here might be extensionally the same but differ intensionally.)

Finally I would like to mention that Mäkelä and Ylikoski (2002) argue against the view of social institutions that is found in Tuomela and Balzer (1999). Their basic thesis is that social institutions do not require the presence of shared we-attitudes *in the we-mode*. The present chapter provides several counterarguments to their critical point, even if I allow I-mode institutional acting and especially "pro-group" I-mode institutional acting (see Tuomela, 2002a, for the latter notion, and Tuomela, 2002e, for my response to the aforementioned critics).

8 Searle discusses the question of whether the reflexivity or self-referentiality of the concept of money leads it into a circularity of infinite regress. He claims that it does not.

> But the resolution of the paradox is quite simple. The word "money" marks one node in a whole network of practices, the practices of owning, buying, selling, earning, paying for services, paying of debts, etc. As long as the object is regarded as having that role in the practices, we do not actually need the word "money" in the definition of money, so there is no circularity or infinite regress. The word "money" functions as a placeholder for the linguistic articulation of all these practices. To believe that something is money, one does not actually need the word "money." It is sufficient that one believes that the entities in question are media of exchange, repositories of value, payment for debts, salaries for services rendered, etc. (Searle, 1995, p. 52)

However, I think that this response will not do. The central point is that the use of money in all the mentioned practices requires precisely that money in effect be thought of as money (this is a conceptual-rational requirement; money can, of course, be used in actual exchange practice without this much). Even if we know that, for instance, certain pieces of metal do the job in a shop (e.g. get one the newspaper), this presupposes that these pieces of metal be money and be thought of as money. There is no theoretical way of getting rid of this circularity. It is not of much interest to a philosopher to be told that in practice money can be made to work as it should even if the concept of money is circular. A better solution to the circularity problem is the solution which says that the use of money must be learned as a skill (much in Wittgenstein's "blind action" sense), as discussed in chapter 3.

My point above has been in part that Searle seems to confuse the reflexivity of a concept with the pragmatics of its use. A related remark can be made concerning what he says about types and tokens in the context of reflexive notions such as money (p. 33): "About particular tokens it is possible for people to be systematically mistaken. But where the *type* of thing is concerned, the belief that the type is a type of money is constitutive of its being money." There are two factors relevant here. First, as my account in the appendix shows, contrary to Searle, the reflexivity aspect concerns all tokens and not only some: every token of money must in principle be collectively accepted as money. The second thing is that one can perhaps successfully use money without having the belief that any token of the money is money. This fact in no way speaks against my Collective Acceptance account. Searle does not sufficiently emphasize the distinction between the theoretical situation (e.g. that money is a reflexive notion) and the down-to-earth functioning of a social institution (that one can live one's life without having theoretical knowledge about money or without having a very adequate concept of money).

9 Searle's constitutive rule "X counts as Y" is supposed to govern activities in a more basic account, but he does not give a detailed general account of how this can be done, and gives only one detailed example. This example and the accompanying discussion are only concerned with powers assigned to persons mentioned inside the content expressed by p (e.g., p = S has the power (S does A)). Searle's example – "X, this piece of paper, counts as Y, a five dollar bill" – would according to S be in part "We accept (S, the bearer of X, is enabled (S buys with X up to the value of five dollars))."

10 As seen above in chapter 2, there is a variety of we-intentions ranging from what was called weak we-intentions to strong agreement-based we-intentions.

Searle (1990) presents a criticism to the analysis of we-intentions given by Tuomela and Miller (1988), the analysis of which is, with some minor amendments, essentially the same as the one given in Tuomela (1984), chapter 2. I have responded to Searle's criticism in my book Tuomela (1995), pp. 427–428. Searle gives an example in which a person (one of a group of businessmen influenced by Adam Smith's theory of the invisible hand) is assumed to intend to help humanity by pursuing his own selfish interests. This person correctly forms the intention to pursue his own interests and believes it to be his part in their helping humanity. Searle claims that this example is a counterexample to our analysis (WI) (summarized above in section 2.4). However, Searle's alleged counterexample fails because it is in the I-mode, whereas our analysis takes we-intentions to be in the we-mode, based on the agents' acceptance of suitable we-intention expressions (such as "We will do X") and inferences from them to their personal (but nonprivate) group-mode intentions (expressible by, e.g., "I will do my part of the joint action X"). A we-intention of the kind "Agent A we-intends to perform X" is in our summary analysis (WI) taken to entail and be entailed by "A intends to perform his part of X (qua his part of X)" (together with some presupposition beliefs). This is all very clearly stated in the paper, and Searle's counterexample does not even get off the ground. In it X is not a joint action and the businessmen do not intend to perform their parts of any joint action; or at least Searle assumes that collectively helping humanity is not a joint action.

11 Seumas Miller has recently criticized Searle's account (see Miller, 2001a; 2001b, chapter 6). Miller's first central point is that deontic powers and functionality do not go together in Searle's account. According to this criticism, it is compatible with Searle's account that there are deontic powers without functionality: a certified surgeon has the right to perform an operation on

anybody who grants his permission, but he might be completely incompetent in actual practice. However, my response is that we must distinguish between successful functionality and intended functionality. Only the latter need be required, and the matter does not affect my theory.

Miller's second point is that it is compatible with Searle's account that there is a system of exchange that is functional but that lacks deontology (powers) in the Searlean sense. Thus, a set of individuals might use a certain sort of relatively rare shell as a medium of exchange, and do so notwithstanding the fact that no one had any desire to possess these shells independent of the fact that they should be used as a medium of exchange. My response is that we are not dealing with an institution here at all, neither in Searle's nor in my sense. Miller's example is a case of a nonnormative social practice, and I prefer not to count such cases among institutions.

Miller also claims that collective acceptance (collective intentionality) is not necessary for the creation and upholding of social institutions. Thus, in the case of language use, hearers have the right to expect that the speakers will aim at the truth. But, Miller argues, hearers have this moral right quite independently of whether the community we-intends that this be the case, or accepts that it is. However, I claim that one need not accept Miller's view of rights. Briefly, rights are basically man-made, collectively accepted things, no matter how strong other kinds of constraints on collective acceptance may be.

Furthermore, Miller claims that collective acceptance must collapse into functionality. Consider the case of leaders. According to Miller, for someone to have the functional properties of a leader is in part for the latter to be collectively accepted in the sense of having his directives obeyed. My response here again is that this does not need *successful* functionality. Secondly, acceptance is a dispositional mental state (a conative or doxastic state) and that it thus can exist without leading to successful action. Thirdly, concerning specifically *collective* acceptance, for someone to be a group's leader he must be collectively accepted as the group's leader. Thus, it is not enough that the members separately and independently obey the leader's directives believing that they ought to do so and (perhaps) mutually believing that the other members also do so. Collective acceptance involves at least ideally that the members are collectively committed to somebody's being a leader and to obeying his directives and accordingly the we-belief that the participants ought to obey the leader, and such a we-mode belief also disposes the members to obey the directives and to see to it that the others obey. (Cf. my arguments in section 6.3.)

While Miller's critical points do have some bite against Searle's account, my account of social institutions can provide an adequate reply to them.

12 To give the flavor of some recent discussion within neo-institutionalism, consider the following hypotheses by Nee and Ingram (1998), concerning the relationship between "formal" and "informal" norms, in their terminology. (1) Individuals jointly produce and uphold norms to capture the gains from

cooperation. (2) The more frequent the interactions between the members of a group, the more effective the monitoring of its norms. (3a) The successful attainment of values by members of a group provides effective reinforcement for the joint production and maintenance of informal norms. The more frequently ego's compliance (noncompliance) to a norm is rewarded (met by disapproval) by alter, the more likely ego will uphold the norm. (3b) Competitive striving for social approval results in a self-reinforcing mechanism rewarding individuals for second-order contributions in upholding the norms of a group. (4) The close coupling between informal norms and formal organizational rules results in high organizational performance. (5) When formal rules are at variance with the preferences and interests of subgroups in organizations, a decoupling of the informal rules and the formal rules of the organization will occur. (6) When the organizational leadership and formal norms are perceived to be at odds with the interests and preferences of actors in subgroups, informal norms opposing formal rules will emerge to "bend the bars of the iron cage" of the formal organizational rules.

(While the considerations in Tuomela and Bonnevier-Tuomela, 1998, rather favor the general idea that r-norms tend to override s-norms, there still is not strict incompatibility with the present hypotheses.)

7 SOCIAL PRACTICES IN A DYNAMIC CONTEXT: A MATHEMATICAL ANALYSIS

* The technical developments in this chapter are based on my joint work with Wolfgang Balzer. Indeed, the technical formulations, using symbolism different from above, are primarily due to him. I am grateful for his permission to use this material here. Below, I will speak in terms of "we" as the plural author of this chapter, which draws on an earlier coauthored version and on our joint papers (especially Balzer and Tuomela, 2000 and 2001).

1 This does not mean any downgrading of individual notions. Our model simply works without making the micro–macro connection precise, as it simply speaks only of macro-level things. However, in section 7.8 and in our examples we will connect the two levels. Introducing the full, logical apparatus necessary for the individual level would mean substantial additional complexity. Compare, e.g., Cohen and Levesque (1990), Dignum and van Linder (1996), Rao *et al.* (1992) as well as Wooldridge and Jennings (1999) for action formalisms.

Joint actions have been discussed in philosophical literature on a technical logical level by, e.g., Sandu and Tuomela (1996) and in the AI literature, e.g., by Cohen and Levesque (1990) and Wooldridge and Jennings (1997, 1999). As far as we know, social practices have not been previously properly modeled in logical and mathematical terms.

2 The importance of social practices for multiagent research in AI lies in the fact that their structure can serve as a template for programing recurrent, or routine cooperative behavior. One main ingredient of multiagent systems

must be the build-up and maintenance of "social" goals, i.e. goals which can be satisfied only by coordinated or planned common action. (Conte and Castelfranchi, 1995 use a much broader concept of social goal, according to which influencing and aggression can be social goals.) For relevant discussion of coordination in AI, see, e.g., Prietula *et al.* (1998) and Weiss (1999). Also cf. Moses and Tennenholtz (1995), who consider "social laws," i.e. action constraints that help to "socially" coordinate action when conflicts are possible.

3 Sociologist Giddens' (1984) structuration theory is concerned with the maintenance aspect, but on a nontechnical level. We are not aware of mathematical accounts except that developed in Tuomela (1995), chapter 10.

4 See, e.g., Tuomela (1977), chapter 7, (1984), chapter 5, where the terminology "logical action and joint action opportunities" is used for the preconditions of action. Searle (1995), chapter 6, speaks of the "Background."

5 Compare, e.g., Balzer and Tuomela (1997b) and section 7.

6 Throughout this chapter "action" is used synonymously with "action type."

7 See, for instance Suppes (1970), Mackie (1974), and Koons (2000).

8 The actions to be covered here may be actions performed by groups (involving joint action by at least some group members in the sense of Tuomela, 1995, chapter 5) as well as collective social actions (CSAs) in a more liberal sense (actions performed for a reason shared by some agents in the sense of chapter 4). Note that in the case of CSA (which is our broadest class of social action here and which includes joint action in the full sense) a distinction should be made between "causal" action (e.g. building a house together) and acceptance action (e.g. collectively accepting that squirrel fur is money).

9 As noted, the evaluation of success may also concern the manners and ways of performing the action in question as viewed by the agents and to their normative standards. If such cases are to be covered by the present formalism the language S (section 7.3) must be extended to contain the required vocabulary. This can easily be done.

10 Compare Tuomela (1995), chapter 10, where a somewhat similar systems-theoretic approach to social action is developed.

11 We rely on Tuomela (1995), p. 394 here. Note that this kind of separation is not only a conceptual, but also an ontic possibility.

12 Though the success function is not explicitly included as a component of the states, this could be done easily, for instance, by requiring that sentences expressing mutual belief in the value of the success function are also elements of S and occur in the states of sets of individuals. Under such a construal $f^{int,I}$ would simply be the identity, as would $f^{R \to I}$.

13 Our model serves to make precise and also to improve on the central aspects of Giddens' structuration theory. In Tuomela (1995) the previous accounts, especially Giddens', are criticized for ignoring the "*jointness*" level, viz., joint actions and joint attitudes. The present model is an obvious improvement in the sense that it takes into account the joint attitudes and actions that the participants have. This is accomplished primarily through the central

notion of a shared we-attitude, taken to be partially definitory of core social practices.

Some aspects of the present mathematical account of social practices have been codified into a simulation program – see Hofmann (2002), and Hofmann *et al.* (2002).

14 In a recent paper Castelfranchi (2001) discusses unintended ends and functions. In his rich discussion many important distinctions are made, but these cannot be discussed here.

15 Some aspects of the dynamics of social practices have been discussed by Giddens (1984) in his structuration theory (cf. note 13), Castelfranchi (2001; cf. above note 14), and by Bhaskar (1989). In all these accounts collective actions (practices) are taken to feed back on themselves, so to speak, and either reinforce or weaken the practices in question (cf. also the systems-theoretic account given in Tuomela, 1995, chapter 10).

Bhaskar has discussed social dynamics under the label "the transformational model of social activity" (see, e.g., Bhaskar, 1989). He emphasizes factors such as (a) acknowledged versus unacknowledged conditions of action, (b) intended versus unintended consequences of action, (c) explicit versus tacit skills in the maintenance and change of social practices. Here is a quotation from his text.

Society is both the ever-present *condition* (material cause) and the continually reproduced *outcome* of human agency. And praxis is both work, that is, conscious *production*, and (normally unconscious) *reproduction* of the conditions of production, that is society. One could refer to the former as the *duality of structure* and the latter as the *duality of praxis*. (Bhaskar, 1989, pp. 34–35)

According to Bhaskar's rather imprecise account, the agents reproduce, *non-teleologically and recursively*, in their substantive motivated productions, the unmotivated conditions necessary for – as means of – those productions; and society is both the medium and result of this activity.

Collier nicely exemplifies Bhaskar's model (cf. the above quotation) in the case of language as follows.

We must have learnt a pre-existing language to be able to talk at all (structure as condition). We talk not as a rule to reproduce or transform the language but for personal ends of which we are conscious (practice as productions). But our language only continues to exist because we talk, for it has no existence apart from people talking (structure as outcome). So our acts of talking do reproduce and transform the language, without our for the most part intending it to do so. For example, our children pick up the language to a large extent without its being taught (reproduction); and the language they learn is different from the one we learnt, since our usage differs (mostly without our noticing it) from the usage we learnt, with the latter in each case supplanting the former (transformation). (Collier, 1994, p. 146)

In this account of social practices, society as the condition of action and society as its outcome both belong to the subject matter of social science. But in the personal case, it is action as production that is central. The duality of practice is on the whole a duality between social and personal aspects of practice. The account of this chapter does not explicitly deal with all the above features, but it can in principle be extended to cover them, it seems.

16 See above chapter 2 for joint intentions, and for their formal treatment Wooldridge and Jennings (1999) and Balzer and Tuomela (1997a); see Fagin *et al.* (1995) for mutual belief (and knowledge), and Balzer and Tuomela (1997b) for a fixed-point approach applying to arbitrary attitudes.

17 When individual attitudes are available, the repeated build-up of a collective attitude can be treated in a computationally more economic way by using the notion of a *permanent-conditional attitude*. See Balzer and Tuomela (2001) for discussion.

18 See e.g. the papers in Hilpinen (1971) for standard views in deontic logic.

19 See Tuomela (1995), chapter 5 for an analysis of such group actions in terms of the group's operative members' position-related joint and other actions.

20 In order to avoid the mutual beliefs in D5-4 becoming irrational, given the probabilistic formulations of D5-5 and 6, we should rather use an approximate version of D5-4, too. However, as this would involve substantial additional formalism, we prefer to stick to the simpler, somewhat problematic formulation.

References

Asch, S., 1987, *Social Psychology*, Oxford University Press, Oxford.

Audi, R., 1994, "Dispositional Beliefs and Dispositions to Believe," *Noûs* 28, 419–434.

Aunger, R. (ed.), 2000, *Darwinizing Culture: The Status of Memetics as a Science*, Oxford University Press, Oxford.

Balzer, W. and Tuomela, R., 1997a, "The Structure and Verification of Plan-Based Joint Intentions," *International Journal of Cooperative Information Systems* 6, 3–26.

Balzer, W. and Tuomela, R., 1997b, "A Fixed Point Approach to Collective Attitudes," in G. Holmström-Hintikka and R. Tuomela (eds.), *Contemporary Action Theory* 2, Kluwer Academic Publishers, Dordrecht, pp. 115–142.

Balzer, W. and Tuomela, R., 2000, "Social Institutions, Norms, and Practices," in R. Conte and C. Dellarocas (eds.), *Social Order in Multiagent Systems*, Kluwer Academic Publishers, Dordrecht, forthcoming.

Balzer, W. and Tuomela, R., 2001, "Social Practices and Collective Attitudes," *Autonomous Agents and Multi-Agent Systems*, forthcoming.

Bar-Tal, D., 2000, *Shared Beliefs in a Society*, Sage Publications, Thousand Oaks, London, and New Delhi.

Barnes, B., 1983, "Social Life as Bootstrapped Induction," *Sociology* 17, 524–545.

Bhaskar, R., 1989, *Reclaiming Reality: A Critical Introduction to Contemporary Philosophy*, Verso, London.

Blackmore, S., 1999, *The Meme Machine*, Oxford University Press, Oxford.

Bloor, D., 1997, *Wittgenstein, Rules and Institutions*, Routledge, London and New York.

Boesch, C., 1996, "The Emergence of Cultures Among Wild Chimpanzees," in Runciman, *et al.*, 1996, pp. 251–268.

Bourdieu, P., 1977, *Outline of a Theory of Practice*, Cambridge University Press, Cambridge.

Bourdieu, P., 1980, *The Logic of Practice*, Cambridge University Press, Cambridge.

Bourdieu, P. and Wacquant, L., 1992, *An Invitation to Reflexive Sociology*, University of Chicago Press, Chicago.

Boyd, R. and Richerson, P., 1996, "Why Cultural Evolution is Rare," in Runciman, *et al.*, 1996, pp. 77–93.

266

Brandom, R., 1994, *Making it Explicit*, Harvard University Press, Cambridge, Mass.

Brandom, R., 2000, *Articulating Reasons: An Introduction to Inferentialism*, Harvard University Press, Cambridge, Mass.

Brinton, M. and Nee, V., 1998, *The New Institutionalism in Sociology*, Stanford University Press, Stanford (original hardcover edn published by Russell Sage Foundation).

Bromley, D., 1989, *Economic Interests and Institutions*, Blackwell, Oxford.

Byrne, R., 1997, *The Thinking Ape: Evolutionary Origins of Intelligence*, Oxford University Press, Oxford.

Castelfranchi, C., 2001, "The Theory of Social Functions: Challenges for Computational Social Science and Multi-Agent Learning," *Cognitive Systems Research* 2, 5–38.

Cohen, J., 1992, *An Essay on Belief and Acceptance*, Oxford University Press, Oxford.

Cohen, P. and Levesque, H., 1990, "Intention is Choice with Commitment," *Artificial Intelligence* 42, 213–261.

Collier, A., 1994, *Critical Realism*, Verso, London.

Conte, R. and Castelfranchi, C., 1995, *Cognitive and Social Action*, University College London Press, London.

Dignum, F. and van Linder, B., 1996, "Modelling Social Agents: Communication as Action," in J. P. Mueller, *et al.* (eds.), *Intelligent Agents* 3, Springer, Berlin, pp. 205–218.

Fagin, R., Halpern, J. Y., Moses, Y., and Vardi, M. Y., 1995, *Reasoning About Knowledge*, MIT Press, Cambridge, Mass.

Giddens, A., 1984, *The Constitution of Society*, Polity Press, Cambridge.

Gilbert, M., 1989, *On Social Facts*, Routledge, London.

Gilbert, M., 2000, *Sociality and Responsibility*, Rowman and Littlefield, Lanham.

Grice, P., 1989, *Studies in the Ways of Words*, Harvard University Press, Cambridge, Mass.

Halpern, J. and Moses, Y., 1992, "A Guide to Completeness and Complexity for Modal Logics of Knowledge and Belief," *Artificial Intelligence* 54, 319–379.

Harel, D., 1984, "Dynamic Logic," in D. Gabbay and F. Guenthner (eds.), *Handbook of Philosophical Logic*, vol. II, Reidel, Dordrecht, pp. 497–604.

Heidegger, M., 1993 (1927), *Sein und Zeit*, Max Niemayer Verlag, Tübingen.

Hilpinen, R., 1971, *Deontic Logic: Introductory and Systematic Readings*, Reidel, Dordrecht.

Hofmann, S., 2002, "The Social Practice of a Women's Group: A First Simulation," *Grazer Philosophische Studien*, forthcoming.

Hofmann, S., Mäkelä, P., Pitz, T., and Chmura, T., 2002, "How Can We Avoid Traffic Jams? – Simulating the Social Practice of Joint Ride," in C. Urban (ed.), *Proceedings of the 3rd Workshop on Agent-Based Simulation*, 7–9 April, pp. 50–54.

Koons, R., 2000, *Realism Regained*, Oxford University Press, Oxford.

Kuhn, T., 1963, *The Structure of Scientific Revolutions*, University of Chicago Press, Chicago.

Kusch, M., 1997, "The Sociophilosophy of Folk Psychology," *Studies in History and Philosophy of Science* 28, 1–25.

Lagerspetz, E., 1995, *The Opposite Mirrors: An Essay on the Conventionalist Theory of Institutions*, Kluwer Academic Publishers, Dordrecht.

Lewis, D., 1969, *Convention: A Philosophical Study*, Harvard University Press, Cambridge, Mass.

MacIntyre, A., 1985, *After Virtue*, 2nd edn, Duckworth, London.

Mackie, J. L., 1974, *The Cement of the Universe*, Oxford University Press, Oxford.

Mäkelä, P. and Ylikoski, P., 2002, "We-Attitudes and Social Institutions," *Grazer Philosophische Studien*, forthcoming.

Mantzavinos, C., 2001, *Individuals, Institutions, and Markets*, Cambridge University Press, Cambridge.

Marras, A., 1973a, "Sellars on Thought and Language," *Noûs* 7, 152–163.

Marras, A., 1973b, "On Sellars' Linguistic Theory of Conceptual Activity," *Canadian Journal of Philosophy* 2, 471–483.

Marras, A., 1973c, "Reply to Sellars," *Canadian Journal of Philosophy* 2, 495–501.

Martin, L. and Simmons, B., 2001, *International Institutions: An International Organization Reader*, MIT Press, Cambridge, Mass.

Marx, K., 1967 (1867), *Capital: A Critique of Political Economy*, vol. I, International Publishers, New York.

Miller, K. and Tuomela, R., 2001, "What are Collective Goals?" in M. Kiikeri, and P. Ylikoski (eds.), *Explanatory Connections*, http://www.valt.helsinki.fi/kfil/matti/

Miller, S., 2001a, "Social Institutions," in M. Sintonen, *et al.* (eds.), *Realism in Action*, Kluwer Academic Publishers, Dordrecht, forthcoming.

Miller, S., 2001b, *Social Action: A Teleological Account*, Cambridge University Press, Cambridge.

Mithen, S., 1996, "The Early Prehistory of Human Social Behaviour: Issues of Archeological Inference and Cognitive Evolution," in Runciman *et al.*, 1996, pp. 145–177.

Moses, Y. and Tennenholtz, M., 1995, "Artificial Social Systems," *Computers and Artificial Intelligence* 14, 533–562.

Nee, V. and Ingram, P., 1998, "Embeddedness and Beyond: Institutions, Exchange, and Social Structure," in Brinton and Nee, 1998, pp. 19–45.

North, D. C., 1998, "Five Propositions about Institutional Change," in J. Knight and I. Sened (eds.), *Explaining Social Institutions*, University of Michigan Press, Ann Arbor, pp. 15–26.

Pettit, P., 1993, *The Common Mind*, Oxford University Press, Oxford.

Popper, K., 1962 (1945), *The Open Society and its Enemies* 2, Routledge and Kegan Paul, London.

Powell, W. and DiMaggio, P., 1991, *The New Institutionalism in Organizational Analysis*, University of Chicago Press, Chicago.

Prietula, M., Carley, M., and Gasser, L. (eds.), 1998, *Simulating Organizations: Computational Models of Institutions and Groups*, MIT Press, Cambridge, Mass.

Rao, A., Georgeff, M., and Sonenberg, E. (1992), "Social Plans: A Preliminary Report," in E. Werner and Y. Demazeau (eds.), *Decentralized A.I.* 3, North Holland Publishing Co., Amsterdam, pp. 57–76.

Ruben, D.-H., 1985, *The Metaphysics of the Social World*, Routledge, London.

Runciman, W. G., Maynard Smith, J., and Dunbar, R. I. M., 1996, *Evolution of Social Behaviour Patterns in Primates and Man*, Oxford University Press, Oxford.

Ryle, G., 1949, *The Concept of Mind*, Hutchinson, London.

Sandu, G. and Tuomela, R., 1996, "Joint Action and Group Action Made Precise," *Synthese* 105, 319–345.

Scanlon, T., 1998, *What We Owe to Each Other*, Harvard University Press, Cambridge, Mass.

Schatzki, T., 1996, *Social Practices: A Wittgensteinian Approach to Human Activity and the Social*, Cambridge University Press, Cambridge.

Scheff, R., 1967, "Toward a Sociological Model of Consensus," *American Sociological Review* 32, 32–46.

Schelling, R., 1960, *The Strategy of Conflict*, Harvard University Press, Cambridge, Mass.

Schiffer, S., 1972, *Meaning*, Oxford University Press, Oxford.

Schlicht, E., 1998, *On Custom in the Economy*, Oxford University Press, Oxford.

Schotter, A., 1981, *The Economic Theory of Institutions*, Cambridge University Press, Cambridge.

Scott, W. R., 1995, *Institutions and Organizations*, Sage Publications, Thousand Oaks, London, and New Delhi.

Searle, J., 1983, *Intentionality: An Essay on the Philosophy of Mind*, Cambridge University Press, Cambridge.

Searle, J., 1990, "Collective Intentions and Actions," in P. Cohen *et al.* (eds.), *Intentions in Communication*, MIT Press, Cambridge, Mass., pp. 401–415.

Searle, J., 1995, *The Construction of Social Reality*, Allen Lane, Penguin Press, London.

Searle, J., 2001, *Rationality in Action*, MIT Press, Cambridge, Mass.

Segerberg, K., 1985, "Routines," *Synthese* 65, 185–210.

Sellars, W., 1956, "Empiricism and the Philosophy of Mind," in H. Feigl and M. Scriven (eds.), *Minnesota Studies in the Philosophy of Science* 1, University of Minnesota Press, Minneapolis, pp. 253–329.

Sellars, W., 1963, *Science, Perception and Reality*, Routledge and Kegan Paul, London.

Sellars, W., 1967, *Philosophical Perspectives*, Charles C. Thomas, Springfield.

Sellars, W., 1968, *Science and Metaphysics*, Routledge and Kegan Paul, London.

Sellars, W., 1969, "Language as Thought and as Communication," in Sellars, 1974, pp. 93–117.

Sellars, W., 1973a, "Actions and Events," *Noûs* 7, 179–202.

Sellars, W., 1973b, "Reply to Marras," *Canadian Journal of Philosophy* 2, 485–493.

Sellars, W., 1974, *Essays in Philosophy and its History*, Reidel, Dordrecht.

Sellars, W., 1981, "Mental Events," *Philosophical Studies* 39, 325–345.

Simmel, G., 1971 (1904), "Fashion," in G. Simmel, *On Individuality and Social Forms*, ed. D. Levine, University of Chicago Press, Chicago, pp. 294–323.

Smelser, N. and Swedberg, R. (eds.), 1994, *The Handbook of Economic Sociology*, Princeton University Press, Princeton.

Smith, A., 1982 (1776), *An Inquiry into the Nature and Causes of the Wealth of Nations*, Penguin, Harmondsworth.

Suppes, P., 1970, *A Probabilistic Theory of Causality*, Acta Philosophica Fennica, North Holland Publishing Co., Amsterdam.

Thomasson, A., 2002, "Realism and Human Kinds," *Philosophy and Phenomenological Research*, forthcoming.

Tuomela, R., 1977, *Human Action and its Explanation*, Reidel, Dordrecht.

Tuomela, R., 1984, *A Theory of Social Action*, Synthese Library, Reidel, Dordrecht.

Tuomela, R., 1985, *Science, Action, and Reality*, Reidel, Dordrecht.

Tuomela, R., 1991, "Intentional Single and Joint Action," *Philosophical Studies* 62, 235–262.

Tuomela, R., 1992, "Group Beliefs," *Synthese* 91, 285–318.

Tuomela, R., 1995, *The Importance of Us: A Philosophical Study of Basic Social Notions*, Stanford University Press, Stanford.

Tuomela, R., 1997, "Searle on Social Institutions," *Philosophy and Phenomenological Research* 57, 435–441.

Tuomela, R., 1998a, "Collective Goals and Cooperation," in X. Arrazola, K. Korta, and F. Pelletier (eds.), *Discourse, Interaction, and Communication*, Kluwer Academic Publishers, Dordrecht, pp. 121–139.

Tuomela, R., 1998b, "A Defense of Mental Causation," *Philosophical Studies* 90, 1–34.

Tuomela, R., 1999, "Private Versus Collective Attitudes," in J. Nida-Ruemelin (ed.), *Analyomen* 3 (Perspektiven der Analytischen Philosophie), Walter de Gruyter, Berlin, pp. 317–321.

Tuomela, R., 2000a, "Belief Versus Acceptance," *Philosophical Explorations* 2, 122–137.

Tuomela, R., 2000b, *Cooperation: A Philosophical Study*, Philosophical Studies Series, Kluwer Academic Publishers, Dordrecht.

Tuomela, R., 2000c, "Reasons for Action," in B. Brogaard (ed.), *Rationality and Irrationality* (Contributions of the Austrian Ludwig Wittgenstein Society 8), Austrian L. Wittgenstein Society, Kirchberg, pp. 193–198.

Tuomela, R., 2001, "Shared Belief," in *International Elsevier Encyclopedia of the Social and Behavioral Sciences*, Elsevier, Oxford.

Tuomela, R., 2002a, "Collective Goals and Communicative Action," *Journal of Philosophical Research* 27, forthcoming.

Tuomela, R., 2002b, "Collective Intentionality and Social Institutions," in G. Grewendorf and G. Meggle (eds.), *Speech Acts, Mind, and Social Reality*, Kluwer Academic Publishers, Dordrecht, forthcoming.

Tuomela, R., 2002c, "Joint Intention and Commitment," *Grazer Philosophische Studien*, forthcoming.

Tuomela, R., 2002d, "We-Attitudes and Social Institutions: Response to Critics," *Grazer Philosophische Studien*, forthcoming.

Tuomela, R., 2002e, "The We-Mode and the I-Mode," in F. Schmitt (ed.), *Socializing Metaphysics: The Nature of Social Reality*, Rowman and Littlefield, Lanham, forthcoming.

Tuomela, R., 2003, "Collective Acceptance, Social Institutions, and Social Reality," *Journal of Economics and Sociology*, forthcoming (an early version entitled "Collective Acceptance and Social Reality" appeared in E. Lagerspetz *et al.* (eds.), 2001, *On the Nature of Social and Institutional Reality*, SoPhi, Jyväskylä, pp. 102–135, distributed by Drake International Services).

Tuomela, R. and Balzer, W., 1997, "Collectivity and Collective Attitudes," in U. Mäki (ed.), *Fact and Fiction in Economics*, Cambridge University Press, Cambridge, forthcoming.

Tuomela, R. and Balzer, W., 1999, "Collective Acceptance and Collective Social Notions," *Synthese* 117, 175–205.

Tuomela, R. and Bonnevier-Tuomela, M., 1992, *Social Norms, Tasks, and Roles*, Reports from the Department of Philosophy, University of Helsinki, 1, 46 pages.

Tuomela, R. and Bonnevier-Tuomela, M., 1997, "From Social Imitation to Teamwork," in G. Holmström-Hintikka and R. Tuomela (eds.), *Contemporary Action Theory* 2, Kluwer Academic Publishers, Dordrecht, pp. 1–47.

Tuomela, R. and Bonnevier-Tuomela, M., 1998, "Norms and Agreement," in E. Attwooll and P. Comanducci (eds.), *Sources of Law and Legislation*, Franz Steiner Verlag, Stuttgart, pp. 87–93.

Tuomela, R. and Miller, K. 1988, "We-Intentions," *Philosophical Studies* 53, 115–137.

Turner, J., 1997, *The Institutional Order: Economy, Kinship, Religion, Polity, Law, and Education in Evolutionary and Comparative Perspective*, Addison-Wesley, Harlow and London.

Vico, G., 1970, *The New Science of Giambattista Vico*, trans. Thomas G. Bergin and M. Fisch; abridged translation of the third edition (1744, *Principi di una scienza nuova*), Cornell University Press, Ithaca.

Wagner, W., 1996, "Queries about Social Representation and Construction," *Journal for the Theory of Social Behaviour* 26, 95–120.

Walsh, V., 2002, *Global Institutions and Social Knowledge*, forthcoming.

Weiss, G. (ed.), 1999, *Multiagent Systems*, MIT Press, Cambridge, Mass.

Westermann, R., 2000, "Festinger's Theory of Cognitive Dissonance: A Structuralist Theory Net," in W. Balzer, C. U. Moulines, and J. D. Sneed (eds.), *Structuralist Knowledge Representation: Paradigmatic Examples*, Rodopi, Amsterdam, pp. 189–217.

Wittgenstein, L., 1953, *Philosophical Investigations*, Blackwell, Oxford.

Wooldridge, M. and Jennings, N. R., 1997, "Formalizing the Cooperative Problem Solving Process," in G. Holmström-Hintikka and R. Tuomela (eds.), *Contemporary Action Theory* 2, Kluwer Academic Publishers, Dordrecht, pp. 143–161.

Wooldridge, M. and Jennings, N. R., 1999, "The Cooperative Problem-Solving Process," *Journal of Logic and Computation* 9, 563–592.

Index